Alien Legacies

Alien Legacies

The Evolution of the Franchise

Edited by

NATHAN ABRAMS
AND
GREGORY FRAME

OXFORD
UNIVERSITY PRESS

OXFORD
UNIVERSITY PRESS

Oxford University Press is a department of the University of Oxford. It furthers
the University's objective of excellence in research, scholarship, and education
by publishing worldwide. Oxford is a registered trade mark of Oxford University
Press in the UK and certain other countries.

Published in the United States of America by Oxford University Press
198 Madison Avenue, New York, NY 10016, United States of America.

Library of Congress Cataloging-in-Publication Data
Names: Abrams, Nathan, editor. | Frame, Gregory, 1985– editor.
Title: Alien legacies / [edited by] Nathan Abrams, Gregory Frame.
Description: New York : Oxford University Press, [2023] |
Includes bibliographical references and index.
Identifiers: LCCN 2022049826 (print) | LCCN 2022049827 (ebook) |
ISBN 9780197556030 (paperback) | ISBN 9780197556023 (hardcover) |
ISBN 9780197556054 (epub) | ISBN 9780197556061
Subjects: LCSH: Alien films—History and criticism. | Science fiction films—History and criticism. |
Horror films—History and criticism. | Women heroes in motion pictures. |
Extraterrestrial beings in motion pictures. | Outer space in motion pictures.
Classification: LCC PN1995.9.A457 A445 2022 (print) | LCC PN1995.9.A457 (ebook) |
DDC 791.43/75—dc23/eng/20221221
LC record available at https://lccn.loc.gov/2022049826
LC ebook record available at https://lccn.loc.gov/2022049827

DOI: 10.1093/oso/9780197556023.001.0001

Paperback printed by Marquis, Canada
Hardback printed by Bridgeport National Bindery, Inc., United States of America

Contents

Foreword

Ridley Scott's *Alien* has all the trappings of science fiction movies we are used to seeing. It is set in the future, in outer space, on a spaceship far from Earth. The spaceship itself, in its carefully articulated exterior and interior, owes its design to the space vehicles in Stanley Kubrick's *2001: A Space Odyssey*, though with an important variation. The spaceship *Nostromo* is a towing vehicle for a mining corporation and as such is well-worn and something less than the streamlined, fluorescent bright ships that became the norm post-*2001*. And the *Nostromo* becomes more than a spaceship. With its alien visitor, it turns into an old archetype, an ancient place in the annals of horror films and horror literature, the old dark house.

This canny integration of science fiction and horror, along with the introduction of a strong female character, has made the film not only the source of horrified pleasure for viewers, but fodder for three sequels, two prequels, and a "mashup" with the *Predator* franchise. Scott's film has triggered something of a repetition compulsion in filmmakers and viewers alike, a "franchise" perhaps, but also the need to see that monster again and again to try and master its indestructible voraciousness, understand the woman who survives it, and, in *Alien: Covenant*, the robot who created it.

All of the *Alien* films are seeded with dread, which is a central part of their attraction: a dread that spreads throughout the inhabitants of the places where the monster reigns and, in the prequels, to the origins of life itself. Each of the directors—Scott, James Cameron, David Fincher, Jean-Pierre Jeunet—who have taken on the original and its sequels and prequels have reconsidered how dread is articulated. This in turn stimulates the study of the films in order to reveal varying perspectives, and varying ways in which dread is interpreted, created, and perpetuated. These are films of expanded vision; they want to make us see the possibilities of the imagination of the future and to consider the evolution of monsters and robots. They are spectacles made for the eye and the intellect, entertainments that also explore mysteries and horrors as only good science fiction can do. They also allow an understanding of the ways in which Hollywood exploits spectacle, because repetition only follows commercialization—in this case in comic books and video games.

The *Alien* collection is a trove for critical enquiry, pursuing as many or more perspectives as do the films themselves. The essays that follow wind their way through the spaces of the *Alien* films and spinoffs: their meanings, their creation, their reception, their exploitation. They interpret and honor these important and exciting entries into the science fiction genre.

Robert P. Kolker

Acknowledgments

We would like to thank Norm Hirschy at Oxford University Press for his support, inviting us to assemble the papers from our conference into a new contribution on the *Alien* franchise. With this in mind, we would also like to thank our authors for their patience through the whole process, delivering their chapters despite the challenges the pandemic has presented over the past three years. Their work makes an excellent contribution to our understanding of *Alien*, and its position within contemporary popular media.

We would also like to thank everyone who supported the initial conference commemorating the fortieth anniversary of Ridley Scott's original film: the British Association of Film, Television and Screen Studies which funded the travel and accommodation of our keynote speaker through their Event Grants scheme; Nerys Boggan, from the College of Arts, Humanities and Business, who provided invaluable support in the organization and execution of the event; and Emyr Williams, cinema coordinator at Pontio Arts and Innovation Centre, who secured a print of *Alien* on the opening night of the conference, which played to a packed audience. We would also like to thank the many volunteers from our postgraduate community who helped us make the event such a success.

List of Contributors

Nathan Abrams is professor in film at Bangor University, and the lead director for the Centre for Film, Television, and Screen Studies. He co-founded *Jewish Film and New Media: An International Journal*, and his most recent books are *New Wave, New Hollywood: Reassessment, Recovery, and Legacy* (with Greg Frame, Bloomsbury Academic, 2021), *The Bloomsbury Companion to Stanley Kubrick* (with I. Q. Hunter, Bloomsbury Academic, 2021), *Eyes Wide Shut: Stanley Kubrick and the Making of His Final Film* (with Robert Kolker, Oxford University Press, 2019), *Stanley Kubrick: New York Jewish Intellectual* (Rutgers University Press, 2018), *Hidden in Plain Sight: Jews and Jewishness in British Film, Television, and Popular Culture* (Northwestern University Press, 2016), and *The New Jew in Film: Exploring Jewishness and Judaism in Contemporary Cinema* (IB Tauris; Rutgers University Press, 2012). He is currently writing a biography of the legendary film director Stanley Kubrick with Robert Kolker to be published by Faber & Faber in 2023.

Carrie Lynn Evans is a PhD student in English literature at Université Laval in Quebec. Her master's thesis focused on gender, technology, and cyborg theory in Frank Herbert's *Dune*. Her dissertation work seeks a precedent for contemporary American astroculture, as expressed through fiction and the public imaginary, in ancient travel stories, including Homer's *Odyssey*. In addition to sci-fi, research interests include technology and culture, horror, and postmodern theory.

Gregory Frame is teaching associate in film and television studies at the University of Nottingham. His main area of interest and expertise is the politics of US film and television. He has published widely on these subjects in *Journal of American Studies*, *Journal of Popular Film and Television*, *New Review of Film and Television Studies*, and several high-profile edited collections. He is the co-editor (with Nathan Abrams) of *New Wave, New Hollywood: Reassessment, Recovery, and Legacy*, published in 2021. He is the author of *The American President in Film and Television: Myth, Politics and Representation*, which was runner-up for the Best Monograph Award at the British Association of Film, Television, and Screen Studies' annual conference in 2016.

Frances A. Kamm is a lecturer and course lead of film and media at the University of Kent, and co-organizer of the Gothic Feminism Research Project. She is co-editor of *Gothic Heroines on Screen: Representation, Interpretation and Feminist Enquiry*

(Routledge, 2019) in which she wrote a chapter on Ripley in *Aliens* (1986). In addition to theories of the Gothic, Frances is also interested in visual effects, the on-screen body, and film history. She is also an editor for *Devil's Advocates* (LUP).

Robert P. Kolker is professor emeritus at the University of Maryland. He is author of numerous books, including *The Extraordinary Image: Orson Welles, Alfred Hitchcock, Stanley Kubrick and the Reimagining of Cinema* and *Triumph Over Containment: American Film in the 1950s* (Rutgers University Press), *A Cinema of Loneliness* (OUP), *Film, Form, and Culture* (Routledge), and, with Nathan Abrams, *Eyes Wide Shut: Stanley Kubrick and the Making of his Final Film* (OUP) and *Stanley Kubrick: An Odyssey* (Faber & Faber).

Reuben Martens is an AMTD Waterloo Global Talent postdoctoral fellow at the University of Waterloo (2022–2024) and an affiliated researcher with the Literary Studies Research Unit at KU Leuven. His work is mainly situated within the fields of the energy humanities, ecocinema, postcolonial studies, contemporary North American literature, and critical infrastructure studies. He has published articles on energy and ontology in *The Matrix-trilogy* in *ISLE*, on petromelancholia in Indigenous Canadian fiction in *American Imago*, and on the dynamics of infrastructural prolepsis in contemporary American fiction in *Resilience.*

Bronwyn Miller is a PhD candidate with the School of Arts and Media at the University of New South Wales, whose research interests are centered around data and algorithmic justice, intersectional feminist praxis, and representation in media. They are a tutor in critical data studies, the co-lead of the Allens Hub Data Justice Research Network, and a member of the Media Futures Hub.

Christopher L. Robinson is assistant professor of English at the Institut Polytechnique de Paris, one of France's leading science and engineering schools. In addition to being co-author of *Alien, entre arts et sciences* (2019), and a contributor to *Dune: Exploration scientifique et culturelle d'une Planète-Univers* (2020), he has published articles in the United Kingdom, United States, and France on works of science fiction, horror and fantasy, including a comparative study of H. R. Giger and H. P. Lovecraft that appeared in *Lovecraft au prisme de l'image* (2017). He is the co-editor of *2001, l'odyssée de l'espace: au carrefour des arts et des sciences* (2021) and *The Legacies of Ursula K. Le Guin: Science, Fiction, Ethics* (2021).

Jonathan A. Rose is an assistant professor for English Cultural and Media Studies at the University of Passau, Germany. In his PhD dissertation, he examined transgender representation in fanfiction and its cultural contexts. Guided by an interest in all kinds of marginal(ized) figures like aliens, zombies, and fungi, his research lies at the intersections of literary, cultural, fan, media, and trans(gender) studies, with a focus on genders and sexualities, adaptation and related phenomena, as well as fandom and fanfiction. Recent publications include "'My Male Skin': (Self-)Narratives of Transmasculinity in Fanfiction" (*European Journal for the Study of English*, 2020) and

"The Last of Us: Fungi, EcoGothic Zombies and Posthuman Hybrids in *The Girl with All the Gifts*" (*Journal for the Study of British Cultures*, 2020).

Tonguç Ibrahim Sezen is a senior lecturer in transmedia production at Teesside University. He holds a PhD in communications from Istanbul University, School of Social Sciences. During his doctoral studies, he visited Georgia Institute of Technology, School of Literature, Media, and Communication as a Fulbright scholar. He has been an assistant professor and the founding department head of the Digital Game Design Department at Istanbul Bilgi University and a research fellow at Rheine Waal University of Applied Sciences. His research interests include cross-media narration, game design, interactive storytelling, and toy studies, and he has written chapters on these subjects in books published by Springer, Palgrave Macmillan, and Routledge. He is one of the editors of *Interactive Digital Narrative: History, Theory, and Practice* (2015) published by Routledge.

Kenneth Sloane is a graduate of the Institute of Communications Studies at the University of Leeds and works as a lecturer in film studies and audio-visual production in the School of Creative Arts at the Dundalk Institute of Technology, Ireland. His work focuses on film studies and production techniques, with research interests in Jungian archetypes and media effects. Kenneth cites the *Alien* franchise as the inspiration for his academic interest in the medium of film. An avid football fan, Kenneth is also the producer and host of "The Men Who Saved Football," a podcast dedicated to his hometown team Dundalk F.C.

Mario Slugan is senior lecturer in film studies, Queen Mary, University of London. He is the author of three monographs—*Montage as Perceptual Experience: Berlin Alexanderplatz from Döblin to Fassbinder* (Camden House, 2017), *Noël Carroll on Film: A Philosophy of Art and Popular Culture* (Bloomsbury, 2019), and *Fiction and Imagination in Early Cinema* (Bloomsbury, 2019).

Kim Walden is Senior Lecturer: Film and Television Cultures in the School of Creative Arts at the University of Hertfordshire. Her current research interests include media archaeology and transmedia film marketing and promotion. She is the author of "Nostalgia for the Future: How *Tron: Legacy*'s Paratextual Campaign Rebooted the Franchise" in *The Politics of Ephemeral Digital Media* edited by Sara Pesce and Paolo Noto (Routledge, 2016); "Archaeology of Mobile Film: Blink, Blue Vend, and the Pocket Shorts" *in Compact Cinematics: The Moving Image in the Age of Bit-Sized Media* edited by Pepita Hesselberth and Maria Poulaki (Bloomsbury, 2017); and "404: File Not Found: Web Archives and the Challenges of Preserving Film Promotion" published in *Historical Journal of Film Radio and Television* (2022). She is currently writing a book for the Transmedia series published by Amsterdam University Press.

Sara Louise Wheeler is a visiting research fellow in psychology at Glyndŵr University. She is an editorial board member for *Names: A Journal of Onomastics* and writes the

column *Synfyfyrion Llenyddol* (literary musings) for *Y Clawdd* community news-
paper. Her poetry, belles lettres, and artwork have been published by: *Tu Chwith,
Y Stamp, Meddwl.org, Gŵyl Y Ferch, Qualitative Inquiry, The Centre for Imaginative
Ethnography,* and *3am Magazine.* Sara currently has numerous intersecting projects
exploring themes of language, identity, and wellbeing, through a variety of creative
and scholarly mediums. She lives on the Wirral peninsula with her husband Peter
and their tortoise Kahless.

Zoé Wible is a PhD student in Film at the University of Kent. Her research interests
include science-fiction and cognitive film theory. Following her master's dissertation
on the reception of androids in contemporary television show *Westworld,* she is now
researching the relationship between imaginary creatures and spectator engagement
in visual narrative media. She also draws on recent developments in interactive media
and forms of engagement, including video games and online fandom spaces. The
provisional title for her thesis is: "Monster Schemas and the Space of Possible Minds:
A Cognitive Approach to Science Fiction Characters in Contemporary Cinema."

Florian Zitzelsberger is a PhD candidate in American Studies at the University of
Passau, Germany, where he studied English and German. His research is situated
at the nexus of queer theory and narratology, with a specific interest in narrative
metalepsis, performativity, and the American musical, and has appeared, among
others, in the *Iowa Journal of Cultural Studies, Humanities, and Comparative
American Studies.* He has additionally published chapters on environmentalist met-
afiction, representations of gender and sexuality in film, as well as the aesthetics of
the branded self on YouTube. More recently, his work has shifted toward questions of
(dis)embodiment as well as the discursive and material effects of virality in the confrontation of the COVID-19 pandemic and the memory of the HIV/AIDS crisis. This
shift also informs his latest collaboration, a research project examining posthuman
drag performance, on which he is currently co-editing a special issue.

1

Introduction

Alien: The Evolution of the Franchise

Nathan Abrams and Gregory Frame

On May 25, 1979, shocked audiences witnessed the birth of an alien lifeform, bursting from the chest of the bewildered, terrified Kane (John Hurt). Along with it, a new type of science fiction horror was born. The extra-terrestrial xenomorph that stalked and killed the crew of the Nostromo, as well as the hero that defeated it, Ellen Ripley (Sigourney Weaver), became icons of popular culture across multiple films and a variety of media forms in the subsequent twenty years. Almost exactly forty years later, across two days (May 23–24, 2019), academics, practitioners, and fans convened at Bangor University's Pontio Arts and Innovation Centre for a conference entitled *40 Years of Alien* to discuss and debate the meaning, significance and legacy of Ridley Scott's landmark film.

It was apparent from the passionate discussion and debate throughout the event that *Alien* still means a great deal to a lot of people: the papers were thoughtful and stimulating, encompassing everything from the audience responses to *Alien*, the film's religious and philosophical underpinnings, its attitudes towards artificial intelligence, the creature's evolutionary biology, and the fates of the franchise's pet animals. The screening of the original film was packed, both by academics and members of the public. We were privileged to welcome one of the film's prominent visual effects artists, Colin Arthur—designer of Ash's severed head, amongst other fantastic creations over a long and storied career—who talked about his experiences in the film industry. We were also delighted to be joined by Danielle Kummer and Lucy Harvey, the directors of *Alien on Stage*, a documentary about an amateur theatrical production of *Alien* by bus drivers from Dorset, which had its premiere in 2020 and has received critical praise at a number of international film festivals. Intellectually and affectively, *40 Years of Alien* proved that this film, and the broader franchise and universe which it birthed, still matters.

Nathan Abrams and Gregory Frame, *Introduction* In: *Alien Legacies*. Edited by: Nathan Abrams and Gregory Frame, Oxford University Press. © Oxford University Press 2023. DOI: 10.1093/oso/9780197556023.003.0001

There is also no doubt that the *Alien* franchise has had considerable cultural and scholarly significance. The original 1979 feature secured both commercial and critical success, while subsequent films developed the iconic figures of Ripley, her alien antagonist and fleeting alliances with other humans against a context of corporate corruption and future spaces redolent for contemporary audiences. It is certainly true that *Alien* and *Aliens* (James Cameron, 1986) have enjoyed considerable scrutiny by academics within film studies in a manner unsurprising given their cultural presence and resonance for debates concerning gender, otherness, technology and genetics. This analysis has tended toward the psychoanalytic feminist approach or consideration of the action heroine as an archetype, and whether Ellen Ripley can be considered a reflection of the gains and losses of the second- and third-wave feminist movements. What has received less focus is what *Alien* has become: a franchise that, even though it has not abandoned its roots in the medium of cinema, has proliferated, and mutated, across media. *Alien* and its progeny have left an indelible mark on popular culture, through its three direct sequels, two prequels, one "mashup" franchise, short films, series of comic books, graphic novels, novelizations, toys and games, and these aspects of the franchise have not yet received as much scholarly attention as one might otherwise have assumed. While transmedia storytelling is certainly prominent in contemporary scholarship, *Alien* has not been discussed in this context. It is also surprising that given *Alien*'s ubiquity there have, to date, been so few edited collections dealing with the franchise as a whole.

This collection seeks to correct this lack of attention, featuring chapters that provide fresh perspectives on the politics of the franchise, as well as interrogating the implications of its expansion across different media forms and styles. It sets out to explore the *Alien* franchise through interdisciplinary perspectives, considering its purchase not only within film studies but its development as a transmedia franchise encompassing video games and a variety of paratextual materials. It gives space to areas of the franchise much less talked about and a platform for scholars of transmediality and gaming, among other disciplines, to engage critically with the life of the series after *Alien Resurrection* (Jean-Pierre Jeunet, 1997). That *Alien: Covenant* (Ridley Scott, 2017), which underperformed at the box office and was poorly received by critics, receives substantive attention here is beneficial to our understanding of the series overall, and what position it holds in the contemporary media landscape. In this way, we hope that this collection will work to extend and broaden the scope of the critical discourse around the *Alien* franchise and highlight how we may understand it outside of merely cinematic terms more than four decades since it started. In this introduction, we will consider the legacy and impact of the *Alien* franchise, offer a broad summation of its position within scholarship, as well as demonstrate how contributions to this collection fit within this larger story.

Alien and the Canon

Roger Luckhurst has provided a fairly comprehensive account of the significance of *Alien*, the film that birthed the franchise. He argues that *Alien*'s conception during the interregnum between the post-war social and economic settlement and the neoliberal revolution renders the film "a symptom rather than a fully formulated political diagnosis of confused, transitional times."[1] These symptoms can be seen on the level of the film's gender relations. In the decisions and eventual fate of the Nostromo's captain, Dallas (Tom Skerritt), we see evidence of the decline of white, male authority and dominance precipitated by the disastrous failures of leadership in the war in Vietnam and the Watergate scandal, but also the achievements of the civil rights and feminist movements. As Luckhurst notes of Dallas's absence from the second half of the film, "we have forgotten that his simple disappearance, his non-return as the male saviour at the end, is truly remarkable for a Hollywood narrative at the time. There will be no restoration of male authority."[2]

The other social forces at work in *Alien* are seen in the emergence of Ripley, a new archetype of cinematic heroism, a woman determined initially to follow quarantine protocols mandated by the corporation, and then to resist both the corporation and the alien when their true intentions become clear. Using her ingenuity, nous and strength, Ripley is the only survivor of the ordeal. It is a well-worn observation, but Ripley represents a distinctive departure from the common theorization of women in mainstream cinema as submissive damsels in distress, and an inspiration for action heroines through the subsequent four decades. Luckhurst's wide-ranging analysis also takes in the film's Conradian pessimism about human nature through explicit and nonexplicit means, its potential to be read as a political allegory of social and economic disintegration, its allusions to World War II, fascism and the Holocaust, and its assessment of evolution as an interspecies death-match. His work reveals what a rich text *Alien* is, one that merits considerably more scholarly attention than it has hitherto been afforded, not least because

Alien—in many different forms—is still being revisited and reworked forty years since it was given frightening life. As Luckhurst notes in conclusion, "One is never done with this series because a myth, once effectively embedded, never stops being elaborated."[3]

Luckhurst is rather dismissive of these further elaborations, but the adaptation and reworking of *Alien* in myriad different forms will be the basis of the contributions on offer here. If *Alien* represents the beginning of a modern myth, then the fact that it has grown in size and scope—albeit in somewhat haphazard and occasionally clumsy ways—across the visual arts demands further investigation, rather than the derisory call Luckhurst's conclusion makes for it to be put out of its misery. Given that the book is published in the BFI Film Classics series it is hardly surprising that it would position *Alien* as the pinnacle of the series concerning what came after but, given that we are uninterested in such judgments of value, we consider it an important task to interrogate how the franchise has developed. In this, we find inspiration in David Thomson's treatment of the original "quartet" as he defined it, not by suggesting that everything produced under the auspices of *Alien* should be considered a masterwork or artistically accomplished but holds a cultural significance that demands further scrutiny nonetheless. Indeed, Thomson's desire, unfulfilled by the end of his exploration into the first four films in the series, is to figure out what the series means.[4] He first published *The Alien Quartet* in 1998, only a year after the critical and financial failure of *Alien Resurrection*. Considerably more has happened in the *Alien* universe since then, hence the need for fresh perspectives if we are to be able to answer the question Thomson posed.

Feminist Theory and Criticism

Given its subject matter, it is hardly surprising that *Alien* and its sequels have garnered significant attention from feminist theorists, critics and scholars. *Alien* proved amenable to the kind of psychoanalytically-informed feminist scrutiny pioneered by Laura Mulvey. Barbara Creed's analysis of *Alien* sees the film as underpinned by the Freudian concepts of the primal scene and the archaic mother, but that the two concepts are fused: "*Alien* presents various representations of the primal scene. Behind each of these lurks the figure of the archaic mother, that is, the image of the mother as the sole origin of all life."[5] However, far from being the nurturing figure we assume based on this description, when the archaic mother is translated through what Creed describes as the "patriarchal signifying practices" of the horror film she becomes an entirely negative presence. The "archaic mother" of the horror film devours everything in her path, or gives birth to horrifying offspring—these are accurate descriptions of the xenomorph queen. As Creed suggests, "it is the notion of the fecund mother-as-abyss that is central to *Alien*; it is the abyss, the cannibalizing black hole from which all life comes and to which all life returns that is represented in the film as a source of deepest terror."[6] In *Alien*, men are not "fathers," but hosts. In these terms, then, the "archaic mother" embodied by the xenomorph queen is, to borrow Julia Kristeva's term, abject: existing outside of the bounds of the patriarchal order, she poses an overwhelming threat to it. By contrast with the alien, Creed contends, Ripley is "pleasurable and reassuring to look at."[7]

This approach also informs Carol Clover's analysis of the film. Clover views Ripley as a "Final Girl," who in slasher films is the last remaining survivor of a horrific onslaught by a merciless killer whom she has managed to subdue largely by herself. In her intelligence, resourcefulness and active defiance of the killer, the "Final Girl," on the face of it, represents a rejection of the conventional portrayal of women in horror films as passive damsels in distress requiring male rescue. However, Clover argues that in her tomboyishness, the Final Girl is masculinized to reinforce conventional patterns of gender identification: any potential discomfort the assumed adolescent male audience may experience in their identification with the young woman as the hero is neutralized. As Clover suggests of the horror genre, "the discourse is wholly masculine, and females figure in it only insofar as they 'read' some aspect of male experience."[8] She critiques the reviews of *Aliens* that saw in Ripley a potentially "feminist development" as "a particularly grotesque expression of wishful thinking."[9]

Since the pioneering work of feminist theorists like Creed and Clover, there has been considerable resistance to this way of conceptualizing the *Alien* series and Ripley in particular. Elizabeth Hills argued that the entrenched binary thinking of much psychoanalytic feminist theory resulted in these kinds of reductive readings of Ripley and her fellow "Final Girls" as "pseudo-male," whereas they could (and should) be understood as genuinely transgressive, offering radical reimagination of gender roles on screen.[10] This more celebratory, affirmatory attitude is characteristic of later feminist analysis of the *Alien* series, and the growing volume of literature on the archetype of the action heroine, of which Yvonne Tasker argues Ripley has become the "reference point."[11] In particular, Christine Cornea suggests Ripley does not fit with either Creed or Clover's conceptualizations.[12] The reveal of Ripley's "reassuring" female form at the end of *Alien*, when she strips down to her underwear, is undermined by her final tangle with the alien, resulting in a form of punishment for the gaze of the viewer. Moreover, the complete absence of sex in *Alien* (a love scene between Ripley and Dallas did not make the final cut) means the puritanical punishment structure Clover identifies in the slasher film, in which any sexual activity results in death, and the virginity of the Final Girl enables her survival, does not apply. Ripley, Cornea contends, should be read as even more destabilizing and threatening to patriarchal norms than she has been previously, particularly as the character develops across the series, reaching excessive, even parodic, levels by *Alien Resurrection*. The cloned Ripley of the fourth film is a human/alien hybrid, and the film draws upon the nurturing side of Ripley's character most thoroughly explored in *Aliens* while also worrying at the threat to the patriarchal order she poses.

However, one should be careful in making too many grand claims about the impact of Ripley on gender roles in popular cinema: it is still considered worthy of mention and close attention when an active, dynamic heroine is presented in a mainstream film, and action heroines are more often than not discussed in these kinds of exceptionalist terms. The growing body of literature which examines this archetype demonstrates that, despite the efforts of media conglomerates to market the action heroine as the triumph of feminism, it is apparent that when these texts are subjected to greater scrutiny they often reinforce conservative notions of femininity and womanhood. As we will outline later in this introduction, the chapters that pertain to gender in this collection do not seek to rehearse the parameters of this debate, but aim to go beyond the discussions of the gender dynamics of *Alien* and *Aliens* to consider the wider gender politics of the transmedia franchise in relation particularly to the later films and videogames.

Transmedia

Alien was initially conceived as a cash-in on the popularity of science-fiction in the aftermath of *Star Wars* (George Lucas, 1977). The relationship between the films goes beyond this, however, as they have both developed into enormous transmedia franchises. As Sam Guynes and Dan Hassler-Forrest argue about *Star Wars*, "the franchise has pioneered ways of expanding storytelling that reach across media boundaries."[13] The chapters in their collection seek to comprehend the franchise not as a "unified and cohesive storyworld," but as an entity that is in constant flux due to changing creative, industrial, and reception practices. Therefore, as the current age of media conglomeration and consolidation continues to intensify, *Star Wars*' transmedia history can help us understand both the opportunities and the tensions that arise when commercial entertainment properties expand across multiple media platforms while engaging with different audiences. Guynes and Hassler-Forrest explain the development of *Star Wars* transmedia across time, through distinct phases in development, noting that the period following the production of the original trilogy, up until Disney purchased Lucasfilm in 2012, "not only solidified the fan culture surrounding the franchise, but also resulted in structured collaborative practices between media licensors, developers, and creative personnel that rendered a complicated landscape of *Star Wars* media."[14] Many of the essays in this collection look to address this very issue. They demonstrate the extent to which *Alien* transmedia speaks to the avid fan or the casual consumer, and what the relationship between these two groups (not rigidly demarcated or hermetically sealed, it must be said) is.

We can learn much about *Alien*'s transmedia proliferation and its future possibilities by looking at *Star Wars* not least because, with the purchase of 21st Century Fox in 2019, both franchises are now owned by the same multimedia conglomerate, the Walt Disney Company. Disney has exploited *Star Wars* relentlessly since purchasing Lucasfilm in 2012, with three sequels, two spin-off feature films, as well as television series, novels, comic books, and video games. Any planned sequel to *Covenant* is on hiatus following its relative financial failure, but there have been numerous speculations about what Disney will do with *Alien*. The obvious answer, given the company's reputation, would be to move in a more "family-friendly" direction, though even this would not be the distinct departure for the series many suppose, given that merchandise for *Alien* has been fairly consistently marketed at children and teenagers.[15] Furthermore, any such suggestion would depart from the strategy of diversification that Disney has adopted throughout the early 21st century in its acquisition practices. Indeed, the adult orientation of *Alien* would suit Disney's determination to expand its market share in streaming services. It is not out of the realm of possibility to imagine a proliferation of new *Alien*-related content designed to drive slightly different audience demographics to purchase Disney+ subscriptions.

It is also intriguing to speculate on its future when compared to *Star Wars*, given the frustration on the part of many fans with George Lucas's rigid control over the series. On the surface at least, *Alien*'s growth and expansion have appeared to be considerably more haphazard than *Star Wars*, which enjoyed (or endured?) Lucas was a unifying creative figure for considerably longer than *Alien* did of its original creators. The series went the route of hiring *auteur* directors with distinctive, idiosyncratic visions (even if these visions, as in the case of *Alien*³, ran up against the requirements of its corporate handlers), and its life story beyond the cinema has been fragmented, hybridized and rewritten more than once. If, as Thomson noted of the *Alien* series, "no one planned a quartet," it seems unlikely that anyone planned a transmedia franchise.[16] Disney's purchase of *Star Wars* seemed to free the franchise from what Henry Jenkins describes as "the increasingly embattled relationship between George Lucas—a cranky old white guy—and his more diverse fan base."[17] Given the apparently diminishing returns of the *Alien* series, the return of Ridley Scott to the helm of the prequels was considered by many to be a relief, though the general reception of both films suggests this may not remain the case for long. Indeed, his assertion of authorial control over the series included "retconning"—essentially erasing or rewriting—many of the narrative developments of the series after the original *Alien* in the two prequels, as well as becoming something of a spokesperson for the franchise. It appears Scott's determination to play this role over the past decade is designed to elide the complex, somewhat chaotic genesis of the original film, as well as the authorial battles that would ensue across subsequent instalments.

Indeed, one can compare the reception of *Prometheus* and *Covenant* with Lucas's return to the direction of the *Star Wars* prequels. The hostility levelled at Scott's desire to reinstate himself as the author of a series that had long since left him behind in its transmedial development and mutation is similar to that which greeted Lucas's attempts to do so. Just as Disney sought in *The Force Awakens* (J. J. Abrams, 2015) to produce what is now commonly termed a "requel"—bringing together the cast of the original films so beloved by fans and teaming them up with a younger, more diverse set of new characters in what is essentially a remake of the original film, *A New Hope* (George Lucas, 1977)—so, too, it may be tempted to do something similar with *Alien* after the supposed misfires of the recent prequels. While Sigourney Weaver's return to *Alien* remains primarily an internet rumor, it is easy to see how Disney might try to execute a similar resurrection of the series featuring Ripley as a "legacy" character alongside a younger cast. Such a strategy would suit the company's strategy to invest in intellectual property with a secure and reliable fanbase looking for a nostalgic return to a fictional world with which they have a strong affinity, while simultaneously making judicious tweaks to its constitution to appeal to a young, liberal demographic. Ripley's status as a popular feminist icon would further suit Disney's recent, rather obvious, attempts to recontextualize and cleanse the reactionary reputation of its back catalog. While such an approach is not always guaranteed to be successful—though *The Force Awakens* was a success, the new trilogy suffered from diminishing financial returns, and the plan to expand the universe rapidly through the release of a series of prequels, sequels and spinoffs culminated in the financial failure of *Solo: A Star Wars Story* (Ron Howard, 2018)—it would seem the most likely course the series would take based on Disney's wider strategies. Alternatively, the famously risk-averse corporation could just as easily exploit the existing *Alien* content and decline to invest further in a franchise that does not seem to capture the audience's imagination in the way that it once did.

Whether or not Disney seeks to revive *Alien by* employing the strategies outlined above might be an interesting question from the perspective of fans, but it does not address why transmedia franchises like *Alien* have grown in number and significance in the first two decades of the 21st century. *Star Wars* and the Marvel Cinematic Universe are just two of the most high-profile examples, with several others—from The Wachowskis' attempts to transform *The Matrix* from a standalone, groundbreaking film into a transmedia storyworld across multiple films, video games and anime, to the creation of the "Wizarding World" around the global phenomenon of Harry Potter, and DC Comics's somewhat unsuccessful "Extended Universe"— demonstrating the extent to which the conglomeratization of the media industry has been accompanied by the growth in this form of storytelling and fictional worldbuilding. Why this is the case might seem obvious from a financial perspective—the logic behind media mergers since the maturation of the internet has been to bottle up the most lucrative content and deliver it directly to consumers via streaming platforms—but what is less clear is why so many of these transmedia franchises exist in the realms of science fiction and fantasy. One is tempted to suggest that these all-encompassing fictional worlds are further evidence of the desire of audiences to escape the political, social, and environmental turbulence of our chaotic present in favor of realms where heroes and villains remain comfortingly distinct, and where it is still possible to slay dragons. Immersion in these worlds may not be as comprehensive as that envisioned by tech moguls who see in our futures the ability to withdraw completely from real life, but they provide something approximating this level of escape. As horrific and frightening as the *Alien* universe is, it can nevertheless be enjoyed from the safe, warm confines of a movie theatre or living room. These cosmic fantasies allow us to escape from horrors that are all too real.

Chapters

The chapters in this collection engage with the *Alien* series as a whole—the original films, prequels, video games, audiobooks, and online marketing campaigns—from a variety of perspectives, addressing gender, authorship and transmedia, among other concepts. The themes and concerns of the chapters have many overlaps with each other, but all contributions offer new perspectives and approaches to the series, whether that be in the application of new methods of analysis to the original films or the consideration and interrogation of underexplored aspects of the franchise.

The chapters demonstrate a profound fascination with the *Alien* universe that, in many instances, is an adoring one. But, as this collection seeks to give room to alternative perspectives on the franchise that have not hitherto been given an airing, we open with Sara Louise Wheeler's provocative and challenging take on the series. Wheeler suggests that her subjective revulsion towards the *Alien* series—which developed into a fully-formed phobia—has meant she has been left out of a significant popular cultural conversation and that greater attention should be paid to audiences that might be termed "anti-fans" or "non-fans": those who express discomfort with the style and themes of the series. Wheeler's argument, though personal (she describes it as an "auto-psychoanalysis"), is underpinned by Julia Kristeva's concept of the abject, as she seeks to understand her disgust concerning repressed personal experiences. While popular cultural studies more often than not demonstrate how close affinity to particular films, television programs and games can form part of one's identity, Wheeler's chapter shows that the reverse can also be true: her previous rejection of *Alien* was born of her own memories and experiences in a mutually reinforcing pattern. Such a perspective presents an important alternative to how *Alien* is commonly discussed and understood: While one of the popularly appreciated legacies of *Alien* is the legend it has acquired among fans much too young to see the film in its original run, and their desperate attempts to experience it through its novelization, or surreptitious, late-night viewing on television or VHS, it is important to acknowledge the potentially sizeable hinterland of consumers for whom *Alien* inspires not adoration or fascination, but fear and loathing. Wheeler's chapter represents an important initial corrective to *Alien's* fairly uncomplicated reputation in popular film appreciation and scholarship.

Carrie Lynn Evans reads the three films in the series directed by Ridley Scott (which she posits as a trilogy within the overall series) through the lens of chaos theory and, in particular, its fractal patterns. Evans suggests that Scott's trilogy challenges binary thinking in each of its instalments: from the distinction between male and female in *Alien*, the perceived opposition between religion and science in questions of creation in *Prometheus*, to the questioning of the motives and morals of creators, be they human, robot or deity. Evans suggests Scott's directorial contributions to the *Alien* series posits a bleak perspective of the universe as chaotic and amoral, though the pursuit of morality and order persists. Evans's contribution is beneficial to our understanding of the *Alien* series overall as it demonstrates, in contradistinction to the conventional critical treatment of many of the later films in the series, that it contains a complex, profound address of existential questions that is unusual in mainstream popular culture. Furthermore, it is beneficial to consider the extent to which we can read *Prometheus* and *Covenant* as a reassertion of authorial control and consistency over a series that became fragmented in its development across media.

Questions of authorship, creation and the disruption of binaries also underpin Christopher Robinson's chapter, which examines the role of artist H.R. Giger in the development of *Alien*, and his impact on science fiction and horror overall. Robinson provides a thorough account and detailed appreciation of the disturbing, disruptive influence of Giger's art to the thematic preoccupations of the original film, which questions binary thinking on divisions between body and machine, human and non-human, male and female, death and birth, beauty and terror. Robinson also demonstrates how the subsequent instalments in the series are gradually denuded of Giger's influence and, as a consequence, the films lapse into more conventional thinking on these subjects out of a desire on the part of these filmmakers to assert their own authorial visions. Robinson offers a welcome, detailed interrogation of Giger's art concerning the development of *Alien*, which has not been a subject tackled in substance or detail in studies of the film to date.

As has been noted, the *Alien* franchise has enjoyed (or, depending on your perspective, suffered) a multiplicity of authorial voices throughout its forty-year history, with idiosyncratic, often competing, visions of what the series could and should be resulting in its somewhat chaotic, fragmented development. Robinson's chapter makes a compelling case to return to the unsettling creations of the artist that inspired the original for answers.

*Alien*³'s tortured journey to the screen, and ultimate critical and commercial disappointment, is the stuff of legend. Multiple screenplays were written and rejected, a first-time feature filmmaker (David Fincher) was hired to direct an unfinished script and, ultimately, costly delays led to a drastic curtailing of the film by a nervous studio. Rather than merely rehearse this well-known (though, in film history, fairly typical) example of the clashing priorities of a multinational conglomerate and the artists working within this system, Kenneth Sloane provides an account of *why Alien*³ was doomed to fail through the prism of archetypal plot analysis. Specifically, concerning the *Alien* series, he considers the narrative structures around "Overcoming the Monster." Sloane argues that whereas *Alien* features a clear iteration of the archetypal plot structure, and *Aliens* repeats this with some clever innovations, the desire to recapture the formula that made its predecessors a success at the same time as providing an innovative and distinctive take on the story meant *Alien*³ abandoned many of the archetypal structures that were the essence of the first two instalments. He also considers the problematic legacy of *Aliens* in relation to the third film, arguing that in the determination on the part of its makers to abandon much of what James Cameron had done (which led to the questionable decision to kill off key surviving characters from *Aliens* before the action had even begun), *Alien*³ was bound to alienate fans of the hugely popular second instalment. Sloane's contribution is valuable because rather than simply rely upon received wisdom regarding the failures of *Alien*³, his chapter offers a theoretically and critically rigorous account of how and why the film has such a problematic place in the *Alien* series.

Kim Walden's chapter examines the innovative marketing campaigns for *Prometheus* and *Covenant*, where the promotion of these more recent instalments in the *Alien* series become an important part of the overall experience in the age of convergence. Walden demonstrates how these increasingly immersive experiences are blurring the lines between the marketing campaign and the film itself, as well as operating as crucial components of media corporations' attempts to obtain a competitive edge in a crowded marketplace. Certainly, the campaigns for *Prometheus* and *Covenant* played crucial roles in whetting the audience's appetite for new instalments in the *Alien* series, especially given the long period between the fourth and fifth films. What Walden also highlights, however, is how the frenzied fan activity that surrounds franchises like *Alien* is being increasingly co-opted by the corporate entities that own them. It would seem the consequences of this are (at least) twofold: an attempt on the part of multinational conglomerates to assert control over their properties in a fragmented media landscape, as well as injecting financially lucrative but artistically moribund franchises with fresh creative impetus. Walden's chapter offers an important analysis of the potential direction of travel for franchises that might have started life in the cinema, but are being forced to mutate across media boundaries to maintain market share.

Zoé Wible's chapter discusses the development of the *Alien* series across media with a specific focus on how the aliens themselves evolve and change depending on the demands of the medium in which they are presented. She shows how the film series itself developed different affective strategies, from suggestive horror in Scott's original to a more action-orientated spectacle in Cameron's sequel. Wible also shows how these differences can be attributed to developments in technology, where the alien becomes faster and the violence more graphic in subsequent, CGI-aided instalments. In particular, Wible considers the question of canonicity concerning the transmedia franchise and demonstrates the extent to which *Alien*'s rather haphazard, inconsistent development over the years has resulted in fevered debates about what should be included and excluded from consideration in establishing the overall narrative of the series universe. Wible demonstrates how this battle has played itself out across films, comic books and video games. Wible's chapter reveals a fictional species that has resisted categorization and consistency, in much the same way as the franchise as a whole. The chapter, therefore, offers important lessons as to how we might contend with transmedia franchises that have looser approaches to canonicity and seriality.

In keeping with Walden's and Wible's close attention to aspects of the *Alien* franchise that have not been otherwise afforded it, Tonguç Sezen looks at an almost entirely neglected aspect of the universe: the documents purporting to be "real" crew profiles, training manuals and diaries that expand upon and develop our knowledge and understanding of the fictional universe. Some of what Sezen describes as "epistolary paratexts" formed the basis for Cameron's original treatment for *Aliens*, but they have contributed significantly to the overall growth of the fictional universe despite being inaccessible to audiences, and now existing very much at the margins of the experience of the series as extras on Blu-Ray editions of the films. Ideas present in these marginalia have found their way into subsequent instalments of the franchise across media, picked up and explored by the many creative artists and writers who have worked in the *Alien* universe, be this in films or videogames. However, what Sezen also reveals, and which is consistent with other contributors to this volume, is how these previously marginal, some-times fan-produced ephemera have become increasingly important in the development of the franchise's storyworld, particularly as greater corporate control has been sought over the transmedia narrative of *Alien*. As Sezen notes in his conclusion, one can only speculate on how these developments might play themselves out now *Alien* finds itself the property of Disney, a company that has throughout its history shown itself willing and able to ex-ploit all aspects of its holdings if there is money to be made. The paratexts of the *Alien* universe, as Sezen notes, have the potential to form the basis of a whole host of new *Alien* stories across media.

Frances Kamm's chapter considers the original quartet of *Alien* films through the prism of the Female Gothic. She offers a clear and thoughtful reading of the series through the tropes and conventions of the Female Gothic, arguing that it is through this framework that we can see how it seeks to critique patriarchal structures and male threat and validate women's experiences within these situations. Kamm contextualizes this in relation to the broader revival of the Female Gothic in the 1970s, developments she considers as symptomatic of popular culture's broader engagements with the second wave feminist movement, through which Ripley has often been un-derstood. Crucially for the purposes of this collection, Kamm also considers how the *Alien* series can be understood in relation to transmedia, examining what she describes as the "transmedia afterlife" of the Female Gothic. The dis-parate, fragmented development of the series has already been noted in this introduction, and Kamm's work makes a compelling argument to consider the series as a coherent exploration of women's resistance to sexual threats and patriarchal domination, characteristics of the Gothic. In this, Kamm offers an intriguing perspective on what the series might "mean" (something with which this collection is itself preoccupied): *Alien* and its sequels are, in the Gothic tradition, about women who fight back when their lives are put in danger by patriarchal forces.

Kamm places some emphasis on motherhood in the *Alien* series, a the-matic concern that has preoccupied many of the feminist scholars who have explored it. Jonathan Rose and Florian Zitzelsberger offer a fresh take on the series' perspective of motherhood by considering the prequels in relation to the final two films of the original quartet, departing from the scholarly preoccupation with *Alien* and *Aliens*. The change in emphasis enables a move away from the conceptualization of motherhood as underpinned by Creed's concept of the "monstrous-feminine," to demonstrate the series' preoccupation with maternally coded kinship relations that resist the rather limited definitions of motherhood permitted by patriarchal norms. It is the intertwining of the fates of humans and aliens in *Alien³* and *Resurrection* that begins this process, as the series shifts from a clear definition of the xenomorph as the villain to something altogether more complex: Ripley becomes "mother" to a gestating alien in *Alien³*, is cloned with alien DNA and identified (albeit with some ambivalence on her part) as the mother of the Newborn in *Resurrection*. Rose and Zitzelsberger demonstrate how this preoccupation with the human "creation" of an alien/human hybrid in *Resurrection* leads the series onto the profound questions about creation in the prequels, which chronologically precede the events of the original quartet, but can be read productively as a continuation and expansion of these themes. The chapter's exploration of alternative models of mothering in the series amounts to a substantive critique of the cis-normative bias of popular culture. In so doing, Rose and Zitzelsberger show how the concept of motherhood in the *Alien* series transcends the subordinated position it otherwise holds in a patriarchal society, becoming a site of female agency.

Unique perspectives on the gender politics of the series continue with Mario Slugan's Cavellian reading of the *Alien* franchise. Slugan suggests that the *Alien* series can be read productively as bearing many of the characteristics of Stanley Cavell's "melodrama of an unknown woman," departing from its conventional categorization within the horror and science-fiction genres. Cavell argued that the melodrama was one of the few genres which allowed women to have a genuine voice and that what drives women in melodrama is the desire "to be known": to escape the social isolation they experience in a patriarchal society they undergo transformation, seeking ultimately to be understood and accepted as equals. Slugan sees in Ripley a similar pattern, demonstrating how this desire to be known becomes horrific throughout the *Alien* series, as she becomes "known" by the aliens, but is not (or cannot be) acknowledged. His expansive analysis incorporates not only the original quartet but also prequels, video games, and the short films that accompanied the fortieth anniversary of *Alien*. In so doing, he demonstrates that when one looks again at its gender politics and genre categorizations, one can offer alternative readings of the franchise.

Bronwyn Miller's chapter tackles the debate about Ripley as a feminist character and applies this to her remediation in the franchise's video games. In this, Miller demonstrates the gradual decline in Ripley's significance in this medium, which is dominated by men: games developers are overwhelmingly male, as are the consumers. Coupled with the conventions of representation and patterns of identification in first-person shooter games, Miller argues that this leads to a substantial alteration of Ripley's representation. Focusing primarily on the game of *Alien Resurrection* (2000), Miller shows how the structure and style of this adaptation denude Ripley of the potentially radical gender position that she develops through the original quartet of films. We play most of the game as Ripley but, because of the narrowness of perspective offered in the first-person shooter genre, we experience her strength only as technological and militaristic, which is a significant departure from the more complex play with gender identity we see in the film itself. Indeed, as Miller identifies, Ripley fades entirely from view in subsequent games in the *Alien* series, as the masculinist, militaristic mode comes to dominate. Miller's chapter makes a powerful call for a more inclusive and diverse approach to game production, content and strategies to challenge, and hopefully dismantle, the predominance of the patriarchal perspective.

Staying with the franchise's video games, Reuben Martens offers a thorough analysis of how *Alien: Isolation* fits into the wider narrative universe of the series and, through close attention to how *Isolation* pays tribute to the original film, demonstrates how conventional definitions of adaptation and remake can be disrupted when considering transmedia franchises. Martens also discusses how *Isolation* contributes to our knowledge and understanding of the overall series and assesses the extent to which the enjoyment of the game is contingent upon investment in the wider narrative of the *Alien* series. Martens argues that the *Isolation* "narrative-verse," which encompasses a novelization, comic books, a mobile game, and a web series, requires a very active role on the part of the reader-player to obtain the full pleasures embedded within. This chapter offers important lessons on the extraordinary possibilities of transmedia franchises in terms of audience investment and pleasure, but one might also consider whether, in demanding such devotion of its fans to comprehend and enjoy it, transmedia universes like *Alien: Isolation* might be considered potentially exclusionary.

What Does It All Mean?

On the occasion of the event we held to commemorate *Alien*'s fortieth anniversary, an article in *The Observer* described scholarly interest in the franchise as an academic industry.[18] While this is certainly true of the interest in Ripley herself and the original films, what we discovered is how much more there is to say about them, and everything else that has grown from that ill-fated moment when Kane was permitted back onto the Nostromo having been exposed to a parasitic organism. This collection has tackled the sequels, the prequels, the games, the online marketing campaigns, the audiobooks, graphic novels and comic books, novelizations and ephemeral paratexts that, to one degree or another, exist within the fictional, transmedia universe we call *Alien*. So, as Thomson asked of the original four films, what does it all mean?

Perhaps a definitive answer to this question is not all that important. While the grand claims of *Alien*'s progressiveness in terms of its gender politics have long been questioned, there is no doubt that the series even in its most recent incarnations continues to have interesting things to say about gender roles and biological determinism. The chapters in this collection suggest as much, returning to the original quartet and finding new ways of thinking about this, showing that the series can ask (if not always answer) questions that concern our current debates about female agency and gender definition, among others. Though *Prometheus* and *Covenant* were not overwhelmingly successful, there is also little doubt that they ask existential questions uncommon in mainstream, blockbuster cinema and have, at their fringes, inspired innovation and creativity in wider transmedial contexts. The chapters here examine this and demonstrate the extent to which *Alien* is at the forefront of developments in what constitutes the "cinematic" experience in the 21st century. Rather than dismiss them out of hand, as Roger Luckhurst does in his book about the original film, the chapters look for answers as to *why* some of the subsequent instalments have been less artistically (and, indeed, commercially) successful, looking to the waning influence of Giger, the interference of the studio, or a somewhat chaotic and inconsistent approach to what constitutes the series "canon." Another question that has arisen from the assembly of this collection which could inspire further inquiry is the extent to which *Alien*'s expansion across media demands an obsessive devotion to its multiplicity of offerings to enjoy it to its fullest potential. It would seem, from the chapters here, that as a transmedia franchise *Alien* asks a great deal of us. What is also readily apparent from the evidence you will find in the subsequent pages of this collection is that there are many of us willing and able to answer that call.

It is a truism of our disciplines that the media texts that sustain repeat viewing, playing or reading are the most rewarding because no matter how many times one returns to them, there is always something new to discover. As demonstrated by the original conference and this subsequent collection of essays, *Alien* is a franchise that has proved amenable to the application of new methodologies, conceptual ideas, and has grown and changed alongside the development of new media technologies and shifting political emphases. At the event itself, we hosted a panel of academics outside of the arts and humanities to share their thoughts on *Alien* in relation to their particular interests in evolutionary biology and artificial intelligence. *Alien* should not be characterized, like so many popular cultural phenomena are, as at best marginal to our pursuit of knowledge and enlightenment about ourselves as a species, and at worst trivial and irrelevant to these goals. What the continued debate and discussion about *Alien* demonstrates is how popular culture can reach across artificially-inscribed disciplinary boundaries, render intelligible the kind of esoteric debates academics usually involve themselves in and foster a greater understanding of the big questions we need to ask ourselves as humans. We hope this collection proves a helpful intervention in debates about *Alien*, its relevance to contemporary discourse, and points the way to future studies on the franchise as it enters an uncertain new phase under the dominion of a new corporate overlord. There is little doubt, however, that fans and academics alike will continue to chase xenomorphs across the cosmos for the foreseeable future.

Notes

1. Roger Luckhurst, *Alien* (London: British Film Institute, 2014), 46.
2. Ibid., 66.
3. Ibid., 85.
4. David Thomson, *The Alien Quartet* (London: Bloomsbury, 2000), 215.
5. Barbara Creed, *The Monstrous-Feminine: Film, Feminism, Psychoanalysis* (Abingdon: Routledge, 1993), 18.
6. Ibid., 25.
7. Ibid., 24.
8. Carol Clover, *Men, Women and Chainsaws: Gender in the Modern Horror Film* (Princeton, NJ: Princeton University Press, 1992), 53.

9. Ibid.

10. Elizabeth Hills, "From 'Figurative Males' to Action Heroines: Further Thoughts on Active Women in the Cinema," *Screen* 40, no. 1 (Spring 1999), 38–50.

11. Yvonne Tasker, *Working Girls: Gender and Sexuality in Popular Cinema* (London: Routledge, 1998), 71.

12. Christine Cornea, *Science Fiction Cinema: Between Fantasy and Reality* (Edinburgh: Edinburgh University Press, 2007), 150–54.

13. Sam Guynes and Dan Hassler-Forest, "Introduction," in *Star Wars and the History of Transmedia Storytelling*, ed. Sam Guynes and Dan Hassler-Forest (Amsterdam: Amsterdam University Press, 2018), 12.

14. Ibid., 13.

15. Filipa Antunes and Alec Plowman, "'Ages 5 and Up': Kenner's 1970s Alien Toys and the Question of Genre Histories," *Horror Studies* 13, no. 1 (2022), 7:25.

16. Thomson, *The Alien Quartet*, 2.

17. Henry Jenkins and Dan Hassler-Forest, "I Have a Bad Feeling About This," in *Star Wars and the History of Transmedia Storytelling*, ed. Guynes and Hassler-Forest, 26.

18. Robin McKie, "Dr Alien, PhD: The Horror Classic that Academia Loves," *The Observer*, March 24, 2019, https://www.theguardian.com/film/2019/mar/24/alien-horror-classic-that-academia-loves. Accessed July 27, 2021.

2

Boundaries of Viscerality

A Sense of Abjection Regarding "the Perfect Organism"

Sara Louise Wheeler

I had always had an irrational, unexplained fear and loathing of the whole *Alien* franchise. There was not a specific scene or tangible detail, beyond the embodied sense of a sickening, mucus-like substance, and a general feeling of disgust and complete and utter helplessness. I did not even know which of the films had caused this sense of horror, but it had developed into a kind of blanket aversion to anything associated with them. Even accidentally seeing a short clip on the television was enough to trigger a fear response. My thoughts would become erratic, and, like the needle of a record player, skipping over a scratch or speck of dust, my mind would jump, as though attempting to protect me from trauma. Self-preservation would kick in and I would seek to eradicate the stimulus, or else remove myself from its presence. It perhaps goes without saying that this is not a widely appreciated or understood attitude toward the *Alien* franchise, which is, while acknowledging the variable reputation of some of the films and transmedia, beloved by many. One only need look at the enormous and proliferating variety of products manufactured under the auspices of *Alien* and the universe in which it is set to see this is a series that inspires fascination and not disgust (or, perhaps, that the disgust is an integral part of the fascination). It is important to realize that, for every horror fan who enjoys reliving the grotesque, terrifying spectacle of *Alien* (and talking about it), there are potentially many more film consumers whose discomfort, fear, and revulsion are routinely ignored or dismissed. One of the legacies of *Alien* that is perhaps less well understood, therefore, is the anxiety and trauma it caused among a generation of viewers. With this in mind, I realized that the fortieth anniversary of the release of the original *Alien* film in 1979 was serendipitously an opportunity to combine scholarly development with an introspective wellbeing project, to explore the reasons for my counter-hegemonic and

Sara Louise Wheeler, *Boundaries of Viscerality* In: *Alien Legacies.* Edited by: Nathan Abrams and Gregory Frame, Oxford University Press. © Oxford University Press 2023. DOI: 10.1093/oso/9780197556023.003.0002 maladaptive response to an otherwise hugely successful popular culture phenomenon. In so doing, I hoped to understand the origins of my disgust and rejection of the franchise and to therefore give voice to an experience of *Alien* that has not been often discussed or appreciated in popular or scholarly circles.

My argument that the experiences of less enthusiastic viewers of *Alien* warrant further study is reinforced by the study conducted by Martin Barker, Kate Egan, Tom Phillips, and Sarah Ralph exploring audiences' memories of watching *Alien*. They conducted a mixed-methods survey, combining a rating scale and multiple-choice questions, with free boxes to collect qualitative data on people's experiences and thoughts. They identified what they felt to be clear patterns in the explanations given for ratings across the sample, particularly among respondents who rated the film to be "A masterpiece." However, they also found that among viewers who rated the film "Not that good," the reasons given were more disparate and variable.[1] The experiences of less enthusiastic viewers thus appear to warrant further study as an important first step in acknowledging the experiences of audiences that find the *Alien* series not endlessly enjoyable, but unbearable. Indeed, "Not that good" was the most negative option on Barker et al.'s rating scale, with no option for "other";[2] this may potentially have discouraged anyone who actively disliked the film from taking part. Consequently, while a few examples were discussed where people shared misgivings and negative experiences, there is a general paucity of data in their sample from less enthusiastic participants. The authors themselves acknowledge this as a limitation of their study since there is much to learn from considering the perspectives of these audience members.[3] I would argue that much could also be learned from audience members in the diametrically opposite position to those most prominently featured in this study—those who might variously be termed non-fans, anti-fans,[4] and, in my case, even film-phobics.

Additionally, while Barker et al. were able to gain a sense of patterning across the breadth of their sample, they inevitably, given the nature of even qualitative survey data, had less depth regarding people's experiences. They used their data creatively, drawing in parts on participant blog data,[5] building a more complete picture of the individuals taking part. Elsewhere, they draw together several aspects of one participant's data, supplementing it with their interpretation, to present a "portrait of a masterpiece-chooser."[6] This is, of course, standard fare in qualitative research.[7] However, as I have argued elsewhere, autoethnographic case studies can provide much richer and more complete data, less prone to misinterpretation and conjecture, particularly if written by academics with expertise in the field in question and, ideally, with expertise in introspection and reflexivity.[8]

Barker et al. engage with the macro-sociological literature, citing Karl Mannheim's theoretical perspective of understanding generations as cohorts with shared experiences.[9] They explore the psychological literature on memory, lamenting that it has, in their view, maintained a "traditional, scientific, cognitive approach," which they feel has little utility in considering "cultural and sociological questions"—including, how the historical circumstances of the release of the film might have affected how it was perceived.[10]

My scholarly training includes sociology and psychology, and I have spent my career exploring psychosocial phenomena, drawing on a range of theoretical perspectives and methodological techniques. I am particularly committed to "The Sociological Imagination," with the underlying principle that individual biographies and societal histories must be understood in relation to each other, because neither can be understood without the context of each other.[11] Since Barker et al. took a macro-sociological approach to study *Alien* audiences, my micro-sociological approach contrasts and complements their study.

In terms of psychological approaches to the study of memory, the most relevant for studying subjective, emotional, biographical memories to a stimulus such as *Alien* is psychoanalysis. Often criticized for *not* being scientific in approach,[12] its relevance for empirical audience research has been contested, particularly concerning memory, since "memory is a central strand present in all branches of psychoanalytic thought."[13] Jo Whitehouse-Hart makes a compelling case for including psychoanalysis within a psychosocial approach to audience studies, in her study of childhood viewing memories, particularly with regards to "attending to the mutually constitutive relationship between inner and outer worlds."[14]

I, therefore, present an introspective project, which might be termed an "auto-psychoanalysis," undertaken to explore the psychosocial reasons for my intense dislike, non-fandom, and even phobia of the *Alien* franchise. In this sense, I shall present a detailed case study of an individual's experiences, treatment, and outcomes, in much the same way as clinical case studies are written and presented.[15] The main difference will be that I shall write from the point of view of the patient, rather than that of the health care professional. The utility of this case study will be similar to that of clinical case studies, providing data that can be used to inform empirical investigations with large cohorts, for building models of treatment. In the specific context of studying *Alien*, my case study will highlight the currently under-researched phenomenon of anti-fandom within audience research. Methodological techniques include drawing on my biography, mining my memory, exploring my reactions to a variety of stimulus, systematic engagement with the main problematic stimulus, and noting evolving responses and thoughts. I reflect on themes within the existing adjunct literatures, locating my experiences accordingly. I conclude by considering lessons learned from this case, as per the guidelines for clinical case studies.

My Pre-Project Memories of the *Alien* Films

I am unsure of when, exactly, I first became aware of the *Alien* franchise, or which of the films gave me my first glimpse. The first *Alien* film (Ridley Scott, 1979) was released the year of my birth, with subsequent films released over the subsequent decades: *Aliens* (James Cameron, 1986), *Alien³* (David Fincher, 1992), and *Alien Resurrection* (Jean-Pierre Jeunet, 1997). Given their enduring popularity and thus multiple televisual repeats, it is likely that I encountered all the films several times during my life course, in varying sequences. The one thing I am certain of is that, before embarking on this project, I had not seen any of them from start to finish. Consequently, over the years, I had built up a confused jumble of memories, culminating in the conviction that I did not, under any circumstances, wish to engage with this cultural phenomenon. This included any engagement as an adult with the crossover series *Alien vs. Predator* (Paul W. S. Anderson, 2004) and *Aliens vs. Predator: Requiem* (Colin and Greg Strause, 2007), and indeed the pre-quel series of *Prometheus* (Ridley Scott, 2012) and *Alien: Covenant* (Ridley Scott, 2017), despite the connections with Greek mythology and legends, which interested me. The mere mention of the franchise provoked flashes of unpleasant scenes from the films, which would rush through my mind and make me intensely anxious.

This rather extreme response did not apply exclusively to the *Alien* films. It was provoked in varying degrees by the "horror" genre, and any depictions containing a high degree of violence, bodily damage, and helplessness. However, the strongest association was with the *Alien* films. This could re-flect personal taste, and it is also not a significant life problem to avoid certain films. However, it was inconvenient, socially, and my response was extreme enough to be characterized as a "specific phobia," as defined in the *Diagnostic and Statistical Manual*—5th edition.[16] I am not disproportionately squeamish or fearful in everyday life, nor indeed to the broad spectrum of films generally; thus there appeared to be something quite specific about these films.

The Viscerality of *Alien* and General Responses

The 1970s saw the dawning of a genre that is variously referred to as "body horror," "biological horror," and "visceral horror," depicting the physical destruction of the human body, mutation, mutilation, and parasitism.[17] However, despite being an illustrative example of the gruesome zeitgeist or "structure of feeling" of its era,[18] and although a plethora of films followed that continued to push the boundaries of this genre, *Alien* remains noteworthy for its imagery and ability to provoke a physical response.[19] This unsettling quality has consequences for the audience, particularly if, as in my case, the response goes beyond the "repugnant appeal" that horror films are deliberately designed to elicit.[20]

According to Barbara Creed,[21] there have been three main "looks" theorized concerning the screen-spectator relationship: that of the camera, at the profilmic event; of the character(s) in the diegesis; and of the spectators at the event on the screen. Creed states that Paul Willemen specified a fourth, concerning pornography—the possibility of the viewer being overlooked while engaged in the act of looking at something they are not supposed to look at.[22] Creed then proposes a fifth—the act of "looking away" when viewing horror films, which is a common genre-related phenomenon.[23] I propose a sixth, paradoxical look, as I remove myself from the audience and cast myself as an "absentee spectator."

Psychoanalysis is useful for considering the writing, construction, and production of films, with deliberate and targeted efforts for evoking specific reactions in audiences.[24] Perhaps unsurprisingly, therefore, it has underpinned some of the most influential scholarly works relating to *Alien*. Psychoanalysis is also an important framework for introspection and evaluating one's own responses and memories. There will therefore be a pleasing symmetry in the cultural literacies produced by my project, rooted in one coherent framework of thought.

Psychoanalysis as an Underpinning
Theoretical Framework

ΓΝΩΘΙ ΣΑΤΟΝ (Know thyself)

These words, inscribed in ancient Greek on the walls of the porch at the Temple of Delphi, are referred to by Freud in his influential text *The Psychopathology of Everyday Life* (1901). According to Freud, to observe this precept, we must study our own "apparently accidental actions and omissions."[25] Thus, self-knowledge is an important aim of psychoanalysis; other aims include "self-becoming," through developing what is as yet latent within, and improving "self-other relating."[26] All of these aims are interrelated and bring us to the point of being more at ease, within our sense of self, in the presence of other people, and concerning a variety of stimuli, including horror films.

The cornerstone concept within Freudian psychoanalysis is "repression"—the idea that much of our behavior is determined by unconscious thoughts, wishes, and memories, relating to our early childhood experiences. We repress threatening or unpleasant experiences to the point where they are "forgotten" and become inaccessible, safely removed from our conscious awareness. However, we can access our unconscious through a variety of techniques such as free association, dream analysis, and transference.[27]

My phobia of this corpus of films and the franchise as a whole has been exacerbated by confusion of memories of scenes, without their contexts, associated storylines, and, importantly, the closure of the films. However, there must also, logically, be some reason why I am overly sensitive to them, compared to those from within my own social and cultural circle. Since the films and franchise are easily accessible and are a relatively non-threatening stimulus, it should be possible to explore my unconscious thoughts and emotional responses, through controlled engagement, monitoring, and discussions with critical friends.

In the context of horror film analysis, the central tenet of psychoanalysis drawn upon involves consideration of Freud's concept of "repression" and its role in onscreen depictions that elicit fear and disgust.[28] Repression is at the heart of Freud's concept of "the uncanny," where something feels familiar to us, but is slightly incongruous, such as a severed head, dismembered limbs, or robots; the key is that the stimulus evokes a feeling of cognitive dissonance and a sense of something long forgotten.[29] The role of the uncanny in horror films has been explained as enabling the "return of the repressed," in that films can depict the dead returning to life, causing a blurring of metaphysical realities. The idea that such a thing is possible stems from childhood beliefs, which are repressed. Therefore, the visible portrayal of this "return of the repressed" temporarily satisfies certain unconscious drives—thus spectators are attracted to the horror in front of them.[30]

Robin Wood explains that by the 1980s, there had been heavy criticism of Freud's work in the broad socio-cultural sphere and thus also of psychoanalysis as an approach for horror film studies. However, he argues that "repression" remains an important theory in understanding our responses to horror films, in that we can all, as potential spectators, trace and understand this concept within our own lives.[31] Also in the 1980s, Julia Kristeva published her landmark psychoanalytic text *Powers of Horror: An Essay on Abjection*.[32]

The concept of "abjection" was initially developed by anthropologist Mary Douglas[33] concerning the "Othering" and dehumanizing of one group of people by another.[34] Kristeva combined this foundation with the psychoanalytic literature and feminist thought, to create a concept with a somewhat narrower focus—namely, "individual experiences of embodiment, boundaries, and separation."[35] The resultant text has a "performative" aspect, as Kristeva draws on her own biography to explore the themes of embodiment, boundaries, and separation within her personal frame of understanding.[36] In broad terms, Kristeva "explores the different ways in which abjection works in human societies as a means of separating the human from the non-human and the fully constituted subject from the partially formed subject."[37] Despite being primarily about literature, Kristeva's essay has had a profound impact on the analysis of horror films, including the films within the *Alien* corpus. It is also noted for its autobiographical approach and is, therefore, an appropriate foregrounding for my introspective project.

Abjection, Disgust, and the Xenomorph

The most often-cited phenomenon within Kristeva's conceptualization of "abjection" is a glass of milk from her childhood and the feelings of disgust it elicited in her. Kristeva explains that her parents would proffer a nutritional glass of milk, but that this "milk cream" would sometimes have a thin skin on the surface. While she acknowledges that this skin was harmless, she nevertheless experienced a highly visceral response to it and describes gagging, having stomach spasms, feeling as though her organs had shriveled, and having an increased heartbeat, dizziness, clouded sight, nausea, and perspiration on her forehead and hands.[38]

This description does, of course, map to the general concept of disgust, which has a vast literature.[39] However, Kristeva grounds her descriptions of disgust responses in the theoretical framework of psychoanalysis and how this might explain personal responses in everyday life. Following this example, she discusses the corpse and how this further violates borders between the idea of being alive and dead, forcing us to confront the reality of death, which we would normally repress to get on with "the business of living."[40] She comments that seen without the context of God or science, the corpse is the ultimate in abjection and is an "uncanniness" that might end up engulfing us—thus we fear the idea of "death infecting life."[41] Again, corpses are a staple topic in the disgust literature: however, it is the link back to psychoanalysis and "the uncanny" that distinguishes Kristeva's "abjection." This is particularly clear when she says: "It is thus not lack of cleanliness or health that causes abjection but what disturbs identity, system, order. What does not respect borders, positions, rules. The in-between, the ambiguous, the composite."[42]

The ambiguity Kristeva mentions here, brought about by the breaking down of borders, and eliciting the troubling of identity, is the cognitive dissonance caused by the "uncanny." Thus, for Kristeva, it is the uncanny which elicits abjection—the triggering of a particular kind of repressed thought. This then would seem to be a useful framework for conceptualizing a deeply personal and subjective sense of disgust. The idea of something causing cognitive dissonance to the extent of disturbing my sense of identity seemed particularly pertinent since I appeared to have developed such a personal aversion to the franchise.

Creed presents an extensive treatise of Kristeva's "abjection,"—including concerning *Alien*.[43] Creed states that she mainly draws on Kristeva's construction of abjection in the human subject about the notions of the border, the mother-child relationship, and the feminine body. She also refers to Kristeva's discussion of religious discourses and "abominations," including corporeal alteration, decay and death, and bodily wastes. Creed's work, then, is relevant to my study, particularly the section in which she proposes that the horror film illustrates the work of abjection in three ways.

Firstly, horror films abound in images of abjection, including the corpse, followed by an array of bodily wastes. Crucially, here, Creed specifically names blood, vomit, saliva, sweat, tears, and putrefying flesh. However, for me, blood, sweat, and tears can be unproblematic—on- and off-screen—I am not disgusted by them. However, mucus, which is not on this list, is the thing most likely to trigger my sense of abjection and which I associate most strongly with the *Alien* films. Throughout the films, there seems to be an unnecessary amount of sticky, mucus-like substance on display, threatening to splatter all over the viewer. It evokes in me a sense of being unwell and of disgust at being unable to escape my own mucus.

Secondly, the blurring of borders elicits abjection. Numerous things can represent the borders being violated. The monstrous presence onscreen is sometimes produced at the border between the human and the non-human. In other instances, the border may be between the supernatural and the "normal"—often "good vs. evil." In the sense of blurring of borders, I appear to be more susceptible to the onscreen drama, being entirely and passively absorbed by the storyline, and thus less able than most people to separate my own existence from that taking place onscreen. Others in my social circle read reviews before watching films and their engagement with on-screen action tends to be more active—for example, predicting the plot.

Thirdly is the construction of the maternal figure as abject. The central tenet of Creed's thesis is to draw on Kristeva's preliminary hypothesis for an analysis of the representation of woman as monstrous in the horror film. Thus, this section is detailed, specific, and not particularly relevant to my introspective study—however it was interesting to be able to exclude certain triggers and theories, to better identify what was at the heart of my specific phobia. Essentially, Creed deals with the concept of "the archaic mother" and the repressed memories of the mixing of bodily fluids before babies become separate from their mothers.

According to Creed, we learn, through training, to present the "clean and proper body," and thus onscreen depictions of bodily fluids represent a violation of this and are central to our culturally and socially constructed notions of the horrific. However, despite being horrific, there is pleasure in this perversity as it represents, to the audience, a breaking of the taboo and a return to the repressed memory of the archaic mother. Creed states that:

> The modern horror film often plays with its audience, saturating it with scenes of blood and gore, deliberately pointing to the fragility of the symbolic order in the domain of the body where the body never ceases to signal the repressed world of the mother.[44]

I found Creed's assertion here compelling, in terms of how audiences are expected to respond to onscreen viscosity and thus the reason for horror's repugnant appeal. The concept of "jouissance" is the flip side of abjection, with its origins in repressed memories of "the archaic mother." Depictions of bodily fluids can be a cathartic violation of culturally imposed boundaries. This explains the appeal of abject art generally, as it establishes a cycle of repulsion and attraction, fear and intrigue—jouissance and affect.[45] Additionally, here the psychoanalytic underpinning of abjection-jouissance gives a solid foundation for Creed's analysis of representations of the monstrous feminine concerning the archaic mother and horror films, including *Alien*.

However, since I do not respond in an anticipated manner, it seems that the archaic mother does not lie at the heart of my sense of abjection. I therefore do not experience the flipside jouissance. I am simply repelled, rather than drawn into a cycle of attraction and repulsion. There must therefore be some other repressed memories causing my response.

Kristeva's concept of abjection and its underpinning of repression and psychoanalysis are useful for exploring my phobia, though it is not an exact fit for my sense of disgust. However, Tyler argues for a shift from this narrow version of abjection and its preoccupation with "transgressive potentiality," toward a "consideration of being abject within specific social and political locations."[46] Therefore, while I am adopting a broadly psychoanalytic framework and drawing on Kristeva's concept of abjection, my overall approach will be heterodox, drawing on adjunct kinds of literature and theories. I will draw together information on the elicitation of phobias and, crucially, will not dwell on the concept of the "archaic mother," but rather on repressed memories and their subsequent embodiment. In this way, I will present a case study that illustrates how even non-threatening stimuli such as films can become problematic and induce phobias, and what can be done to reverse and neutralize these emotional responses, even when they have been embedded for several years.

Facing My Demons: An Introspective Methodology for Analyzing a Sense of Abjection

Since the aim of this project was to explore and address my specific phobia, it made sense for the methodological approach to be epistemologically grounded within this sphere of reference also. According to DSM 5, specific phobias can develop following being involved in, or observing others going through, a traumatic event, or else by "informational transmission" (such as extensive media coverage of a plane crash). However, for many individuals, the specific origin or reason for the onset of their phobia is unknown.[47] While I am vaguely aware that the viscosity in *Alien* is triggering, I do not recall when this response began, or what caused it. I will therefore need to mine my memory to discern the details that lie at the heart of my phobia.

According to the National Health Service (NHS) website, recommended treatments for phobias include: medications; counselling and cognitive behavioral therapies (CBT); self-help techniques, groups, and apps; mindfulness; and exposure therapy—or desensitisation.[48] Since my phobia has a relatively minor impact on my life, seeking treatments via the healthcare system felt disproportionate. Also, I had, a few years previously, benefitted from the therapeutic effects of learning about the physical manifestation of psychosocial distress, through writing my thesis about medically unexplained symptoms.[49] However, my phobia seemed too specific to be the somatization of general anxiety. I, therefore, resolved to explore the benefits of exposure therapy and mindfulness.

Exposure therapy involves gradually increasing the length of time of exposure to the stimuli.[50] Mindfulness entails paying more attention to thoughts and feelings and reconnecting with our bodies and the sensations we experience, as well as with what is happening in the present moment around us. In paying attention to the stream of thoughts that are preoccupying us, we can learn to disentangle ourselves, identifying certain thought patterns as "mental events" that do not control us.[51] Thus, bearing in mind the dictum "Know thyself," in the context of the psychoanalyst's commitment to studying one's own "apparently accidental actions and omissions,"[52] I engaged in uncomfortable introspective activities. This involved exploring unpleasant emotions and memories through creative outputs as methods of inquiry, including sketching,[53] writing, and poetry.[54] I also committed to presenting the project at a conference and discussing it with colleagues. In this sense, as well as having a psychoanalytic theoretical framework, the project was influenced by constructivism and reflexivity.

Phobic Stimuli and the Spectator/Patient

In discussing the matter with my mentor, a good place to start appeared to be a consideration of my own boundaries, with regard to viscerality generally. We quickly established that I am not particularly squeamish to offscreen stimuli. I enjoy cooking and do not suffer from any of the modern food loathing—common in the current context, where often meals can feel quite separate from the ingredients, including raw chicken and fish. I can happily take a whole fish, cut off the head and tail, use a knife to gut the insides, wash it, and prepare it for the oven. Therefore, considering the literature relating to disgust, and in particular "a specific sensitivity to disgust at sticky matter" associated with Sartre's work,[55] I would appear to have a higher-than-average threshold.

Growing up in northeast Wales in the 1980s, I did not experience the skin-on-the-surface-of-the-milk phenomenon, as described by Kristeva, since all milk that I encountered was refrigerated until consumed. However, I did experience "bits in butter," where knives had run along with bread and toast and then re-entered the butter tub, depositing crumbs, which then sat, mingled with the butter, threatening to be spread across fresh food next time it was used. This appears to be a common elicitor of disgust responses and is logical, given that crumbs could represent contamination of the food and be interpreted within the evolutionary theories of disgust.[56]

I also enjoy the genres relating to vampirism and zombies, so not even the ultimately abject corpse (according to Kristeva), or the drinking of blood, are necessarily barriers to my spectatorship. However, my responses to zombie decapitation with a sword are markedly different from witnessing a scene of zombies tearing living humans apart and consuming their flesh; the former I can tolerate, whereas the latter causes me to look away in disgust, and sometimes cast myself as "absentee spectator." The key triggers here appear to be the cognitive dissonance that might ensue as one's body lost corporeal integrity, descending into a mess of viscosity and torn flesh, while consciousness remained intact enough to be an observer of one's own demise.

During the early stage of conceptualizing the project, I engaged in word association, writing words that came to mind when I thought about these films. I looked at a page containing the words goo, ooze, slime, bursting, tearing, shaking, slime, yuck, and stickiness. I spent some time with the dictionary and added synonyms such as slush, sludge, mud, scum, mire, muck, grease, grime, gunge, grot, and gloop; my mentor and I discussed the idea of a personal continuum as the basis for the project. I then used *Twitter* to ask friends to suggest other synonyms for this phenomenon. One suggested "ectoplasm," which brought to mind the *Ghostbusters* films and "Slimer"— which I at once found triggering in terms of my sense of abjection; clearly, this was the right ballpark. The same friend, upon learning about my project, also suggested I draw on the literature regarding the "abject." Other terms that were forthcoming included "viscera" and "viscosity," which helped to translate the stimuli into scholarly language. I then used this language to search the scholarly literature for relevant terminology and found keywords such as "repugnant" and "abjection."

Relying on my memory alone, I was able to identify key images or scenes that I found particularly problematic:

1. The "chestburster" scene in *Alien*: the hemorrhaging, shaking, the uncanniness of the body being out of control, and, surprisingly somewhat less so, the parasite within.
2. The scene in *Aliens* where the android, Bishop, is skewered by the xenomorph, tearing his body in two, squirting his curious, white, mucus-like blood everywhere.
3. The scene in *Alien*[57] where the xenomorph leans close to Ellen Ripley but does not touch her and then withdraws (because it senses the alien growing inside her). It is not the tenseness, nor, upon closer inspection, the aesthetics of the xenomorph per se—it is the goo dripping over its face and down its teeth.
4. Numerous scenes where the xenomorph's blood can be seen oozing and dripping.

I then watched the films in sequence, to address the jumbled nature of my memories. This was daunting, but I managed to watch them all from beginning to end, including *Prometheus* containing the—I felt unnecessary—exploding-head scene. This was therapeutic and informative as I honed the idea that it was the gratuitous depictions of viscosity that bothered me consistent with the theory of moral and physical components to disgusting stimuli.[58] I had a sense of abjection to the contrived way in which the filmmakers seemed to be gratuitously screening an unnecessary level of disgust-inducing stimuli.

I also engaged with paratextual objects from the franchise. I was initially incensed to discover one could buy "battle-damaged xenomorph" models—made of plastic, with fake blood splattered on their otherwise sleek exteriors. Why was this sort of thing even available? This seemed to violate taste thresholds, exemplifying the activity that Wilson calls "Ockers"—the deliberate elicitation of disgust in others.[59]

However, engagement with a book on H. R. Giger's artwork relating to the *Alien* franchise brought a different perspective.[60] I could appreciate now

Figure 2.1 Presentation slide using my graphite drawing of the xenomorph.

what other people had been telling me about the sleekness and even beauty of the xenomorph's form. Using graphite pencils, I drew the xenomorph to make a marketing poster (Figure 2.1). I enjoyed the embodied nature of the sketching and the sense of control I had over the emergence of the monster on the page. I liked the resultant artwork so much I used it as the background for my opening conference slide on which this presentation was based and enjoyed the others' reactions to it. I felt empowered in using this image for creative ends. Notably, the drawing did not depict the slime I associate with the xenomorph, just the sleek creature itself. Then, it was the viscosity, un-canny lack of bodily control, and gratuitous nature of the depictions which was bothering me. The next question, therefore, was why?

Accessing the Repressed Memories

Having spent some time with my thoughts, drawing, and writing extracts and poems, I found some answers to my conundrum. I associated the onscreen viscosity with mucus. This made sense given my relatively frail health. As a child, I was small and prone to infections. Nine years ago, I suffered a bout of flu from which I struggled to recover. I spent weeks struggling to get out of bed, sweating profusely and feeling as though I was drowning in mucus. My appetite was suppressed, and I lost twenty-eight pounds. Of all bodily fluids, mucus is the one I have had the most unpleasant experiences with and have developed the strongest aversion to. It thus makes sense that onscreen depictions of this kind of substance would be difficult to tolerate.

Then I wrote a poem, called *Awakening in the White Room* (Figure 2.2). The poem explored the memory of my last "seizure," aged eight. Attributed as a relapse of my febrile convulsions, it was partly triggered by a virus that had raised my body temperature. I found myself describing the memories of my body not responding—both before the seizure and upon awakening

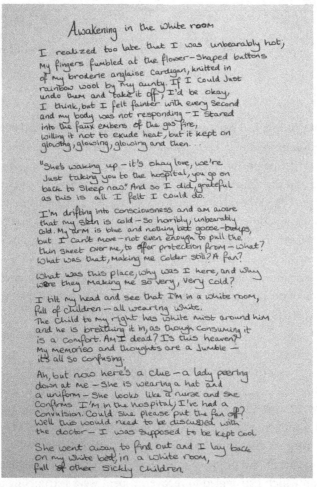

Figure 2.2 The confessional poem which led to an epiphany on my sense of abjection.

in the hospital. I made a full recovery and have been seizure-free since. Although I did not see myself having the seizure, I have seen others having "seizures," including onscreen depictions. I feared these memories and was uncomfortable with them, but I sat with my thoughts for a while, tracing the images that haunted the dark recesses of my mind. And there among them, was Kane—more horrifying for the lack of control over his own body than for the xenomorph gnawing its way through his stomach. This speaks to the Freudian idea of the uncanny and the general idea of repressing certain thoughts and memories to get on with the business of living.

Conclusion

My case study highlights the convergent evolution between the *Alien* franchise and the increasing role of popular culture in the formation of early memories and later points of reference in adult life. It answers Barker et al.'s call to explore how "certain cultural products, such as films, and the context in which they are viewed, embed in people's long-term memories and are reconstructed and re-experienced in their present lives"[61] and thus also play an important part in identity formation concerning media.[62] It also adds credence to Barker et al.'s assertion regarding the importance of including portraits of individuals within audience memory studies, since it reminds us that "people bring personal histories and eccentricities to their viewings and especially perhaps to their memories."[63]

In their study, Barker et al. cite one participant's account of how, upon watching *Alien* for the purposes of taking part in the study, she realized that she had seen the film before and that the "Facehugger" had been the inspiration behind a recurring childhood nightmare that had left her "suspicious of octopi in real life," but that her memory of viewing the film must have been repressed.[64] Meanwhile, another participant described a scene where Ripley's bodily breathing is in danger of giving her away as she hides from the Xenomorph, and how this reminded them of childhood experiences of hiding from their father's imminent beatings.[65] In a similar way, my memories of the films had melded with personal memories, in a problematic manner, leading to a specific phobia—one that is, therefore, indicative of the modern epoch. My case study offers a more extensive analysis of these kinds of responses and experiences.

It therefore makes sense to me now that the dark history of my ill health would be the repressed memory at the heart of my sense of abjection. It also makes sense that I would link the on-screen viscosity with mucus and cold, unhealthy sweating, along with the seizures that were no longer a part of my life. My investigations into my generally frail health revealed that there is some scientific evidence to suggest that the anti-seizure drug "Epilim," which I took preventatively until age seven, may be linked with a compromised immune system.[66] It seems that when I chose the sixth "look," of "absentee spectator," I was experiencing a sense of abjection to myself, and as Kristeva says about spitting out the milk and thus herself,[67] I was refusing to view myself as a spectacle of disgust and horror.

As well as watching the *Alien* films, I engaged with the whole franchise and have surprisingly found myself now attracted to the associated paratexts. I like my xenomorph models and want to learn more about the artwork of Giger and visit the Giger bar in Switzerland, with its interior decoration reflecting the physicality of the xenomorph.[68] I no longer see Giger's creation as a completely abject abomination, but rather as an intriguing and sleek, "perfect organism." I found myself desiring a t-shirt with "Nostromo" on it and a lunchbox with a matching flask that depicts the xenomorph egg.

I have come to associate horror studies with an improved sense of individual agency, control, and wellbeing. I have also begun addressing issues with other films and have successfully watched them all the way through. This has, therefore, been a worthwhile project on a personal level, concerning film and beyond.

Thus, the main "lessons learnt" from this autoethnographic case study are that memories of films viewed in early childhood can become entwined with actual childhood memories and can exacerbate existing aversions, while creating a sense of abjection and phobia to certain stimuli, including films, while having a cross-pollinating effect back into everyday life. Mindful engagement with the problematic stimuli can facilitate a reversal of this maladaptive response and even lead to enjoyment and positive experiences and responses. While empirical research and model building are beyond the scope of this case study, it does provide some data upon which to base a hypothesis and develop an experimental program of research, using large cohorts and statistical analysis. This research could potentially be beneficial and of interest to scholars in the fields of psychology and film studies and help us better understand reactions to the *Alien* franchise not solely limited to those for whom it elicits uncomplicated fascination and pleasure.

Acknowledgements

I would like to thank my mentor, Dr Roger Slack, for his support in conceptualizing and developing this chapter. I would also like to thank my colleagues and students at Wrexham Glyndŵr University, for their support and interest as I developed the chapter. Finally, I would like to thank the editors, for including this somewhat unusual chapter in this book.

Notes

1. Martin Barker, Kate Egan, Tom Phillips, and Sarah Ralph, *Alien Audiences: Remembering and Evaluating a Classic Movie* (Hampshire: Palgrave Macmillan, 2016), 102.

2. Ibid., 121.

3. Ibid., 102.

4. Jonathan Grey, "New Audiences, New Textualities: Anti-fans and Non-fans," *International Journal of Cultural Studies* (March 1, 2003), 64–81, https:// doi.org/ 10.1177/1367877903006001004.

5. Barker et al., *Alien Audiences*, 70–76.

6. Ibid., 25–27.

7. Sara Louise Wheeler, "The Impact of Familiarity on Doctor-Patient Interaction during Primary Care Consultations Pertaining to Medically Unexplained Symptoms (MUS)" (PhD diss., University of Liverpool, 2011).

8. Sara Louise Wheeler, "Autoethnographic Onomastics: Transdisciplinary Scholarship of Personal Names and 'Our-Stories,'" *Methodological Innovations* 11, no. 1 (2018), https://doi.org/10.1177/2059799118769818.

9. Barker et al., *Alien Audiences*, 37.

10. Ibid., 66.

11. C. Wright Mills, *The Sociological Imagination* (Oxford: Oxford University Press, 1959), 3.

12. Martin Hoffmann, "Psychoanalysis as Science," in *Handbook of the Philosophy of Medicine*, ed. Thomas Schramme and Steven Edwards, 1–22 (Dordrecht: Springer, 2015), https://doi.org/10.1007/978-94-017-8706-2_41-1.

13. Jo Whitehouse-Hart, "A Psychoanalytic Perspective on Childhood Television Memories," in *The Past in Visual Culture: Essays on Memory, Nostalgia and the Media*, ed. Jilly Boyce Kay, Cat Mahoney, and Caitlin Shaw, 185–201 (North Carolina: McFarland & Company, 2017).

14. Ibid., 186.

15. Brian Budgell, "Guidelines to the Writing of Case Studies," *The Journal of Canadian Chiropractic Association* 52, no. 4 (2008), 199–204, doi.org/10.1177/ 2059799118769818; George D. Tsitsas and Antonia A. Paschali, "A Cognitive-Behavioural Therapy Applied to a Social Anxiety Disorder and a Specific Phobia, Case Study," *Health Psychology Research* 2, no. 3 (2014), 1603.

16. American Psychiatric Association, *Diagnostic and Statistical Manual of Mental Disorders, Fifth Edition (DSM-5)* (Washington, DC: American Psychiatric Publishing, 2013), 197–202.

17. Shaula Schneik Rocha, "Screening Disgust: The Emergence of Body Horror in Modern Cinema" (MA diss., Texas State University, 2017), 1–15.

18. Frances Pheasant-Kelly, "Towards a Structure of Feeling: Abjection and Allegories of Disease in Science Fiction 'mutation' Films," *Medical Humanities* 42 (2016), 238–245, https://doi.10.1136/medhum-2016-010970.

19. Christopher Lee, "Desert Island Discs," interviewed by Sue Lawley, *BBC Sounds*, March 3, 1995, https://www.bbc.co.uk/programmes/p0093ptj, accessed March 11, 2021.

20. Adéle Nel, "The Repugnant Appeal of the Abject: Cityscape and Cinematic Corporality in District 9," *Critical Arts: South-North Cultural and Media Studies* 26, no. 4 (2012), 547–569.

21. Barbara Creed, *The Monstrous-Feminine: Film, Feminism, Psychoanalysis* (Oxon: Routledge, 1993), 29.

22. Paul Willemen 1980 in Creed, *Monstrous-Feminine*, 29.

23. Creed, *Monstrous-Feminine*, 29.

24. Damien Cox and Michael Levine, "Chapter 29: Psychanalysis in Film," in *The Oxford Handbook of Philosophy and Psychoanalysis*, ed. Richard G. T. Gipps and Michael Lacewing (Oxford: Oxford University Press, 2019).

25. Sigmund Freud, 1901, in Richard G. T. Gipps and Michael Lacewing, "Introduction: Know Thyself," in *The Oxford Handbook of Philosophy and Psychoanalysis*, ed. Richard G. T. Gipps and Michael Lacewing (Oxford: Oxford University Press, 2019), 1.

26. Richard G. T. Gipps and Michael Lacewing, "Introduction: Know Thyself," in *The Oxford Handbook of Philosophy and Psychoanalysis*, ed. Richard G. T. Gipps and Michael Lacewing (Oxford: Oxford University Press, 2019), 1.

27. Richard Gross 2015. *Psychology: The Science of Mind and Behaviour*. 7th ed. (London: Hodder Education, 2015), 803.

28. Robin Wood, "Foreword: 'What Lies Beneath?,'" in *Horror Films and Psychoanalysis: Freud's Worst Nightmare*, ed. Steven Jay Schneider (Cambridge, UK: Cambridge University Press, 2004).

29. Rocha, *Screening Disgust*, 38.

30. Cox and Levine, "Psychoanalysis and Film," 523.

31. Wood, "Foreword: 'What Lies Beneath?'"

32. Julia Kristeva, *Powers of Horror: An Essay on Abjection* (New York: Columbia University Press, 1982)."

33. Mary Douglas, in Darrin Hodgetts and Stolte Ottilie, 2014. "Abjection." In *Encyclopedia of Critical Psychology*, ed. Thomas Teo. (New York: Springer, 1966). https://link.springer.com/referenceworkentry/10.1007/978-1-4614-5583-7_494.

34. Ibid. https://link.springer.com/referenceworkentry/10.1007/978-1-4614-5583-7_494.

35. Ibid.
36. Thea Harrington, "The Speaking Abject in Kristeva's Powers of Horror," *Hypatia: A Journal of Feminist Philosophy* 13, no. 1 (Winter 1998).
37. Creed, *Monstrous-Feminine*, 8.
38. Kristeva, *Powers of Horror*, 2–3.
39. Winfried Menninghaus, *Disgust: Theory and History of a Strong Sensation* (Albany: State University of New York Press, 2003), 366.
40. Kristeva, *Powers of Horror*, 4.
41. Ibid., 4.
42. Ibid., 4.
43. Creed, *Monstrous-Feminine*, 8–29.
44. Ibid., 13.
45. Rina Arya, *Abjection and Representation: An Exploration of Abjection in the Visual Arts, Film and Literature* (Hampshire: Palgrave Macmillan UK, 2014).
46. Imogen Tyler, "Against Abjection." *Feminist Theory* 10, no. 1 (2009), 77–98.
47. American Psychiatric Association, *DSM 5*, 200.
48. "Treatment: Phobias," NHS, https://www.nhs.uk/conditions/phobias/treatment/, accessed June 18, 2020.
49. Wheeler, *Doctor-Patient Interaction.*
50. "Self-Help: Phobias," NHS, https://www.nhs.uk/conditions/phobias/self-help/, accessed June 18, 2020.
51. "Mindfulness," NHS, https://www.nhs.uk/conditions/stress-anxiety-depression/mindfulness/, accessed June 18, 2020.
52. Freud, 1901, in Gipps and Lacewing, "Know Thyself," 1.
53. Sue Heath, and Lynn Chapman, The Morgan Centre Sketchers, "Observational Sketching as Method," *International Journal of Social Research Methodology* 21, no. 6 (2018), 713–728.
54. Laurel Richardson and Elizabeth A. St. Pierre, "Writing: A Method of Inquiry," in *The Sage Handbook of Qualitative Research*, 3rd ed. (London: Sage Publications, 2005), 959–978.
55. Jean-Paul Sartre, in Menninghaus, *Disgust*, 361.
56. Menninghaus, *Disgust*, 183.
57. Robert Rawdon Wilson, *The Hydra's Tale: Imagining Disgust* (Alberta: The University of Alberta Press, 2002), xvi.
58. Wilson, *Hydra's Tale* xiv.
59. Wilson, *Hydra's Tale xiv.*
60. Hans Rudolf Giger, *Giger* (Koln: Taschen, 2018).
61. Barker et al., *Alien Audiences*, preface.
62. Ibid., 9.
63. Ibid., 27.
64. Ibid., 114.
65. Ibid., 118.

66. Ettore Beghi and Simon Shorvon, "Antiepileptic Drugs and the Immune System," *Epilepsia—Official Journal of the International League against Epilepsy* 52 (Supplement 3, 2011), 40–44.

67. Kristeva, *Powers of Horror*, 3.

68. "Museum Bar H R Giger," Museum H R Giger, accessed June 18, 2020. https://hrgiger.com/barmuseum.htm.

3

Fractal Patterns Out of Chaos in Ridley Scott's *Alien, Prometheus,* and *Covenant*

Carrie Lynn Evans

Ridley Scott, who directed the landmark film *Alien* (1979), returned to the franchise some thirty years later with the prequels *Prometheus* (2012) and *Alien: Covenant* (2017), which further examine the origin and evolution of the lethal xenomorph. These three cohere as a trilogy because of the consistent tone and themes brought by Scott. The dominant theme of his contribution to the series is the chaotic and brutal nature of the universe outside of the order of civilization; chaos theory, specifically its identification of the fractal structure, is therefore a fruitful lens for understanding the patterns that do emerge. Gordon Slethaug, in *Beautiful Chaos*, explains that fractals occur in literature and geometry when replications show an "infinite nesting of pattern within pattern, [and] repetition across scales."[1] Not only can fractal geometry shed light on the dynamic procreative patterns of the xenomorph's evolution, but it puts into relief the interconnections of the three films' themes related to (pro)creation, which give the trilogy a fractal structure. The films exhibit a pattern of eliding familiar binaries related to the act of creation, then iterate the pattern with increasing complexity. *Alien* begins with the simplest binary of male and female, blending and reversing traditional gender representations, including the introduction of male birth. *Prometheus* interrogates the ideologies of religion-science and nature-technology as binary pairs, suggesting that their competing approaches to creation and knowledge suffer from over-simplified dichotomous thinking. *Alien: Covenant* is the most complex, building on the patterns sustained over the three films and examining two new conceptual pairings; it focuses on the relative position of creator in a chain of creator-created relationships and draws attention to destruction's role in creation. Tracing the fractal

Carrie Lynn Evans, *Fractal Patterns Out of Chaos in Ridley Scott's* Alien, Prometheus, *and* Covenant In: *Alien Legacies.* Edited by: Nathan Abrams and Gregory Frame, Oxford University Press. © Oxford University Press 2023.
DOI: 10.1093/oso/9780197556023.003.0003

development of these binaries highlights Scott's view that dichotomous thinking is over-simplified and inadequate for comprehending the nature of life in a vast universe and rising to meet the challenges to human survival. Fractal patterns are more appropriately complex while conveying the central pattern of life: endless reiteration with difference. The trilogy reveals that, despite Scott's dark and pragmatic view of the universe as chaotic and amoral, order persists in some forms, including humanity's tenacious pursuit of a system of morals.

Chaos Theory in Literature

Chaos theory is "a set of mathematical tools for modelling emergent, evolving and unpredictable behavior in complex systems."[2] Shortly after this paradigm gained prominence in the mathematics and sciences disciplines in the late 1980s, chaos theory was taken up both by "pop-science writers," fiction authors, and in literary theory circles.[3] In fiction, one finds stories that incorporate the science of chaos theory as a theme in itself, as well as the patterns of these dynamical systems represented in texts' structures; literary theory attempts to identify and trace these patterns within fiction and culture.[4] For the purposes of this chapter, I am only concerned with the features of the fractal, which is one particular phenomenon associated with chaos theory, as a model for tracing both the xenomorph's evolution and the structure of the films' themes.

A fractal pattern is a naturally occurring geometric phenomenon within a dynamical system, generated when a solution value is repeatedly incorporated into a nonlinear equation in the place of an original term.[5] When the same process is repeated at different scales, it creates a geometric fractal, a shape that remains "self-similar" at any rate of magnification (Figure 3.1).[6] James Gleick explains that, because the pattern of repetition remains constant, a small amount of information can be the basis of a branching structure that increases in complexity exponentially as it grows.[7] According to Slethaug, the fractal pattern in literature is often mobilized to bring attention to narrative patterns of similarity, repetition, mirroring, and reiterations with variation in order to develop and highlight their thematic importance,[8] as "recursion is rarely used for its own sake."[9] The kernel forming the basis of the pattern in Scott's *Alien* trilogy is the problematization of a binary related to the processes of creation of life.

Figure 3.1 Partial view of the Mandelbrot set, demonstrating the recursive pattern of the fractal that remains self-similar across scales. Source: Wikimedia Commons, "Mandel zoom 11 satellite double spiral," created by Wolfgang Beyer, 2005.

Alien and Its Gender Binaries

The troubling of the gender binary represents the starting point of the fractal pattern in *Alien*. The reversals and conflations of traditional gender roles are self-evident in the film and have been covered at length by scholars and

critics, surveyed here to identify the critical strands. The process of conception, gestation, and birth is of course a central theme, with the notable reversal that it is primarily men who are forced to submit to the reproductive
process. According to the original script writers, Dan O'Bannon and Ronald
Shusett, implantation by the facehugger was intended to "evoke subconscious imaginings of male rape."[10] Chad Hermann goes as far as to suggest
that, in *Alien*, the patriarchal imagination is not so much afraid of the mother,
referring to the familiar "monstrous mother" trope of the horror genre, but
rather "is afraid of *becoming* mother."[11] Even so, fear of the mother––the negative construction of the maternal principle, found in patriarchal discourse–
–is a major source of *Alien*'s psychological horror, as Barbara Creed explains.
Creed identifies and elaborates on the film's imagery of the "gestating, all-
devouring womb of the archaic mother which generates the horror," present
in every aspect of the film, especially the *mise-en-scène*.[12] The mythological
primal mother, however, is not feminine in the traditional patriarchal sense,
in that she prefigures an understanding of men's contribution to reproduction and the nuclear family unit;[13] her ability (and presumed desire) to in-
dependently and endlessly reproduce is a source of the horror, due to a fear
that her "total dedication to the generative, procreative principle" operates
beyond reason or society's laws and will overwhelm.[14] From this perspective,
the xenomorph, itself defying gender categorization, is the realization of this
primal fear.

Both scholars and artists have observed that the creature, designed by
Swiss artist H. R. Giger, presents simultaneously as masculine and feminine.
Some have pointed out the xenomorph's large and noticeably phallic head.[15]
Hermann compares its nested mouth to a "fluid-oozing phallic shaft"[16] that
"extend[s], erect, when aroused by its prey" and "quite literally fuck[s its
victims] in the head,"[17] disagreeing with Creed's interpretation and arguing
that it "clearly represents an uncontrolled monstrous-masculine power."[18]
Similarly, James Kavanaugh describes the chestburster as a "razor-toothed
phallic monster [. . .] a kind of science fiction *phallus dentatus*."[19] Despite
these interpretations, others find that the xenomorph's slender limbs and
graceful movements communicate femininity. N. C. Winters, an artist
commissioned to recreate the iconic creature for the cover of *Birth.Movies.
Death*'s commemorative *Alien: Covenant* edition, explains that Giger's entire body of work "contains a lot of play between masculine and feminine,"
saying that, "all of his creatures have a feminine quality [. . .] The word 'el-
egant' keeps coming to mind. . . . [it is] silky and graceful."[20] Scott himself,

when asked about the alien's gender, responded that its lifecycle dictates it is hermaphroditic.[21] The variable responses to the xenomorph, in determining it as phallic, feminine, and otherwise, demonstrate its elision of such categories.

Gender allusions and inversions are on display in many other aspects of *Alien*. The fact that the film's hero is a woman is a significant reversal of genre norms. The *Nostromo*'s warrant officer and third in command, Ellen Ripley, is brave, rational, and competent; her self-control might be contrasted to her male counterparts, in this film and its sequels, who at times appear hysterical.[22] Both spaceships, the derelict alien ship and the *Nostromo*, also evoke associations with gender. The enclosures of each have been read as the internal spaces of a mother's body, with scholars pointing to the "birth" of the crew from their cryogenic sleep in the belly of the *Nostromo* and the dark, damp, womblike interior of the alien ship that harbors the alien eggs.[23] Again these feminized elements often simultaneously evince the masculine. Hermann points out that, while the ship is addressed by the crew as "Mother," its official name, *Nostromo*, translates as "our man," and its external shape features both phallic towers above and "breast-like mounds" below.[24] Thus, this first installment in Scott's trilogy begins the pattern of challenging traditional binary conceptions of gender and their sexual associations that are usually so entrenched, not only in Hollywood productions of this kind, but also in science fiction. These deviations aid in deliberately generating a sense of disorientation, disgust, and horror, foregrounding the chaos of the films' setting.

Prometheus

Released thirty-three years later, *Prometheus* continues the pattern of disrupting binary divisions related to the creation of life, thereby initiating a fractal pattern and generating the next level of complexity. The film repeats *Alien*'s gender themes and introduces new binaries regarding ideological systems commonly thought to be competing for dominance in the explanation of reality and the pursuit of creation: religion versus science and nature versus technology. *Prometheus* undermines these knowledge systems and casts doubt on the meaning any of them offer, suggesting their attempts to exert order on the chaotic universe are over-simplified and insufficient. Even chaotic systems, however, develop patterns like fractals, and, in Scott's trilogy, it is the endlessly repeating act of creation that emerges as such a self-organizing principle.

Prometheus and Ideologies of Creation: Religion versus Science

Prometheus rejects the commonly perceived opposition between religion and science, in that the characters who feature as the most significant scientists and technological creators demonstrate affiliation with aspects of both. The most prominent is Dr. Elizabeth Shaw (Noomi Rapace), who maintains simultaneous allegiances to science and Christianity. Early in the film, she explains that she is willing to "discount three centuries of Darwinism" because humans' creation by an intelligent designer is "what [she] choose[s] to believe," which alludes to the tension between belief through faith and belief through evidence. By the end of the film, after the mission's failure and the death of the other crew members, she reclaims her religious necklace and tells David that, "after all this, I still believe." Shaw chooses to continue her faith in a protective deity despite what many would consider evidence to the contrary, a perspective that persists alongside her scientific knowledge. As testament to her status as a scientist, she successfully uncovers and interprets the symbols that allow them to reach the Engineers' ship in deep space, something she accomplishes with both scientific analysis and religion-inflected hope. Shaw incorporates her discovery of the Engineers, mortal creators of humans, into her scientific understanding of the universe, leaving unaffected her religious belief that the Christian God ultimately created them all.[25]

The other significant techno-scientists in the film, Peter Weyland (Guy Pearce) and the Engineers, are not Christian like Shaw, but their beliefs and practices go beyond scientific objectivity into what is arguably in the realm of its binary opposite. Weyland is the wealthy patron of the expedition, having made his vast fortune through technological innovation that includes the synthetic humans who appear regularly throughout the *Alien* franchise. Fearing death, Weyland harnesses his technology to gain a chance to confront his makers, the Engineers, and demand eternal life. He brings Shaw on the trip, not for her expertise alone but because he is "superstitious," and this influences him to "want a fanatic onboard." Weyland not only expects the Engineers will possess the skill to give him immortality, but assumes they will find him worthy because he, like them, is a creator of sentient beings.

Figure 3.2 "Temple" room discovered in the Engineers' ship, featuring a stone head in the center, overlooking concentrically arranged ampoules full of the mutagenic black ooze. Source: *Prometheus*, directed by Ridley Scott (2012, Los Angeles, CA: Twentieth Century Fox).

As he explains to the sole surviving Engineer on LV-223 (Ian Whyte), he deserves eternal life because "we are creators; we are gods and gods never die."[26] Weyland's conflation of scientific mastery with divinity also appears in one of the film's promotional shorts, featuring Weyland's TED Talk in the year 2023; he tells the audience, "we are the gods now" because of their techno-scientific advancement, having picked up the mantel from the Greek god Prometheus.[27] The Engineer is not persuaded, killing Weyland and, as if to add insult to injury, destroying David. Weyland's recourse to superstition and notions of divinity do nothing to further his goals.

The supposed split between science and religion is further erased by what is shown of the Engineers' culture, which suggests that the science of these advanced beings is bound up with ritualistic practices of a religious nature. The extended version of the film's opening scene reveals that the Engineer's self-sacrifice to seed a dead planet with genetic material to begin life is imbued with religious significance.[28] He is attended by a small group of fellow Engineers, wearing robes and appearing somber in what David McWilliam describes as a "weird mixture of sacred ceremony and

Figure 3.3 Cruciform mural, resembling the xenomorph, found in the "temple" room in the Engineers' ship. Source: *Prometheus*, directed by Ridley Scott (2012, Los Angeles, CA: Twentieth Century Fox).

aggressive biotechnology."[29] This characterization is echoed in the interior chamber discovered in the derelict Engineer ship that resembles a temple (Figure 3.2). It features an enormous stone humanoid head overlooking rows of ampoules filled with black ooze, the volatile bioweapon that initiates the mutations that eventually develop into the xenomorph and its cousins. Similar to human religious spaces, the walls are decorated with figures in presumably significant or symbolic scenes; the figures resemble the xenomorph, including one with arms outstretched in a cruciform pose (Figure 3.3). As Stephen Mulhall suggests, this may indicate that the Engineers narcissistically worship their own superior intellect and ability to create;[30] put another way, they may worship their science. In arguing that *Prometheus* "ostensibly combines Darwinian theory and Christian fundamentalist belief in intelligent design while at the same time abandoning both,"[31] McWilliam identifies this theme of problematizing science and religion as exclusive worldviews. Furthermore, neither the Engineers' religious practice nor their mastery of biology prevents or brings any meaning to their demise when the bioweapon escapes control. Similarly, neither science nor religion brings the humans any closer to the answers they seek. The film does not privilege one worldview over another, but instead reflects only frustrated attempts to exert order in chaotic environments. In setting up this supposed binary, only then to un-dermine its separation, *Prometheus* repeats the pattern begun in *Alien*.

Prometheus and Ideologies of Creation: Nature versus Technology

The fractal structure is continued in *Prometheus*'s consideration of nature and technology as dichotomous, rival approaches to the creation of life. Questions about the relative superiority of one approach over the other and their status as opposites are raised through the accomplishments of Weyland and the Engineers. For Weyland, this binary represents incom-patible ideologies, of which he strongly prefers the technological. Weyland characterizes his creation of synthetic, robotic humans as "the first true evo-lutionary step forward in creating new and mentally superior life on earth,"[32] a comment meant to contrast his work to that of his former mentor who, in working with human DNA, "chose to replicate the power of creation in an unoriginal way, by simply copying God."[33] As Mulhall elaborates, Weyland disdains his mentor's work with genetic material, representative of "nature" for my purposes here, because it is derivative of existing processes; he sees his own work with inorganic material as superior and indicative of a higher genius because it is a new method for generating life.[34] This dichotomy be-tween nature and technology is also figured in Weyland's offspring, Meredith Vickers (Charlize Theron) and David. Vickers, despite being Weyland's bi-ological daughter, is unfeeling, unsympathetic, and robotic, such that the audience who is familiar with the franchise's penchant for androids passing as human will reasonably suspect she may be one until a character asks her point-blank. On the other hand, David, Weyland's synthetic "son," displays inhumanly "perfect composure"[35] but does not share Vickers' cold demeanor. In addition to being personable, he demonstrates passionate interests in art, philosophy, and Peter O'Toole's character in *Lawrence of Arabia* (1962), which evoke humanity. She is human, he is android, yet they choose to per-form characteristics of their opposites in overt ways. For Weyland, tech-nology and nature are diametrically opposed and hierarchical, to the extent that he openly shows a preference for his technological child. His views are discredited, however, in that he is selfish, cruel, and rejected by the Engineer, and, significantly, natural processes win out in the end, as technology does not save Weyland from death.

The Engineers' technological methods are most accurately described as biotechnology, further demonstrating the collapse of the boundaries between nature's and technology's domains. The Engineers' artifacts all have biological appearances, such as their elephantine helmets and architecture that imitates bodies. Their primary technique seems to be the use of volatile organic substances that, when put in contact with complex organisms, trigger growth through mutations and replications. In the opening scene, an Engineer ingests one such substance that dissolves his body into the genetic basis to seed the dead planet with an ecosystem. A similar substance that operates in a comparable manner is discovered in the ampoules found by the team of explorers, but in this case, it has a destructive effect. The Engineers' technological interference into natural processes, from entire ecosystems to species, suggests a universe in which technology leaves no natural process untouched; yet, nature retains dominion over death, suggesting that these domains remain contested. *Prometheus* repeats *Alien*'s pattern of troubling binaries related to creation; consistent with the fractal pattern, it does so with double the complexity.

The Xenomorph's Lifecycle as a Fractal Pattern

In addition to developing the trilogy's fractal structure through binaries, *Prometheus* incorporates fractal development as a theme in itself, in its creation of an evolutionary biography for the xenomorph species. The film's portrayal of the early development of the species' lifecycle, progressing from black ooze to the final xenomorph-like creature (the "Deacon"[36]), suggests both the randomness of chaos and the pattern of a fractal. John Briggs and F. David Peat explain that all natural processes, including lifecycles and species evolution, are inherently fractal because they develop through iterations that incorporate feedback.[37] The accelerated rate of the proto-xenomorph's development, in conjunction with the creature's violence, is suited to increase the film's horror and pacing, but it also allows for a condensed view of the fractal pattern. As Mulhall points out, while the rapid progress of the infections/conceptions, mutations, and hybrid organisms seem chaotic and arbitrary, they in fact depict a "law-governed generativity,"[38] just as fractals follow the laws of nonlinear equations within chaotic systems.

In the proto-xenomorph's development, the feedback value that determines its subsequent iteration is its contact with another organism.[39]

When the ooze makes direct contact with humans, it is only destructive, with no creative capacity, as evidenced by Holloway's and Fifield's lethal exposures; however, "when mediated by the human procreative capacity," such as between the infected Holloway and Shaw, its generative capacity is activated, and the otherwise infertile Shaw is impregnated with the Trilobite squid.[40] This organism inherits and adapts the human means of impregnation through penetration[41]--which the subsequent facehugger inherits-- and implants the next iteration into the Engineer, producing the Deacon, a creature that is similar to the xenomorph in its overall appearance and elongated head, but with the Engineer's grey skin and exoskeletal ribs. *Prometheus* thus establishes a genealogy from which the xenomorph's later development can be anticipated because it does follow a pattern, albeit a nonlinear one that adapts to feedback.

The ooze also comes into direct contact with worms in the soil of the temple. This union creates a new species that blends the anatomy of the worm with the predacity of the ooze, creating a hybrid creature that also attacks by forcibly penetrating the mouth, but kills without further regeneration.[42] Thus, by comparing the genealogies initiated by the ooze, it is possible to identify the branching patterns of the fractal, wherein the incorporation of different feedback variables influences the results within a set of parameters. In *Prometheus*, chaos theory's fractal emerges as the productive approach to mapping the chaotic universe.

Repetitions: *Prometheus*'s Echoes and Anticipations

Prometheus repeats the disruption of gender stereotypes that initiated the trilogy's fractal structure in *Alien* and anticipates developments to come in *Alien: Covenant*. Again, women command important roles: Vickers leads the group and displays traditionally masculine traits, and Shaw, like Ripley, is a professional in her own right who survives, alone, by virtue of her ingenuity and bravery. In an instance of reversal, a threatening alien pregnancy also happens in *Prometheus*, only this time involving a woman. As Susan George points out, Shaw's pregnancy is doubly an inversion of events in *Alien* in that she "conceives 'naturally' through intercourse with her infected partner, but delivers 'unnaturally' by conducting a robotic Caesarian section upon herself."[43] In both films, childbirth is life-threatening and motherhood a source of horror.

In a scene foreshadowing *Alien: Covenant*'s foregrounding of creators, David encounters Holloway drinking in his disappointment that his makers fail to live up to his expectations and desires for ones who are caring and wise. David engages him in a philosophical question about the significance of this moment, alluding to the parallels between them as creatures with disinterested creators. Holloway misses this connection, however, telling David humans only made his kind "because they could," which articulates the neglect and disdain David has suffered from humanity since his birth. When David asks him to what lengths he would go to get what he came for, Holloway answers "anything and everything." David appears to take this answer as implicit permission to reject moral culpability in favor of ambition and proceeds to infect Holloway with the black ooze. It becomes clear in *Alien: Covenant* that this scene foreshadows David's destiny to become a creator and gives a glimpse into his rationale for doing so. These additional thematic repetitions add to the branching and complexifying fractal structure developed in this second installment of the trilogy.

Alien: Covenant

Alien: Covenant, released five years after *Prometheus*, continues the important themes and tropes of the earlier films, developing the fractal pattern with new binaries related to creation. For example, there are well-rounded characters who are fleshed out beyond gender stereotypes, with the addition of some representation of the LGBTQ community. An intelligent woman, Daniels (Katherine Waterston), emerges mid-film as the rational leader and hero, as Ripley did in *Alien*, responding to a disaster prompted by misplaced religious conviction, as happened in *Prometheus*.[44] There are lethal impregnations resulting in newly hideous violent births and hybridized creatures: as in *Alien*, this only befalls men, but the means of exposure continue to proliferate, a trend begun in *Prometheus*. The xenomorphic lifeforms in *Alien: Covenant* further demonstrate the fractal nature of the species' evolution, this time responding to the genetic input of the life on the new planet, LV-426. Mutagenic mushroom spores develop as a fertilization agent, which leads to the gestation of the Neomorph in a living body. Like its xenomorph cousin, it kills its host, only this one may exit the body from any place. Also, the indigenous peoples of LV-426 share the Engineers' physiognomy, thus representing another fractal branching of a genetic line, one similar, yet different, from that of humans. Like *Alien*, the atmosphere of horror is amplified by the specter of a menacing parental figure but, in *Alien: Covenant*, it is an amoral father rather than a monstrous primal mother. This pernicious paternal influence relates to the problematized binaries introduced in *Alien: Covenant*, that of creator versus created and creation versus destruction. Again, the relationships between these pairs are interrogated, which develops the fractal structure of the trilogy to the next level of complexity.

Alien Covenant: Creator versus Created

Prometheus introduced the theme of questioning the hierarchy between creator and created based on a presumption of the father-creator's superior qualities. This is foregrounded in *Alien: Covenant* when it is revealed that David not only lives but has used the Engineers' bioweapon to spawn a multi-branched species of predator lifeform at the cost of all indigenous life on LV-426. This disturbing discovery is only gradually realized by the audience and the ill-fated crew. Not only is David responsible for birthing the xenomorph into the galaxy, it is learned, but he also killed Shaw and desecrated her body to accomplish it. This transformation of David from a quirky, mistreated, and sympathetic android to a sinister, megalomaniacal mass murderer and father of monsters represents the true horror of *Alien: Covenant* and draws focus on the ethical dimension of creation.

The creator-created line of analysis begins with David in the position as created-son. In order to recall and develop the audience's insights into David's contemplations on this topic, afforded by the scene with Holloway in *Prometheus*, *Alien: Covenant* opens with David's "birth" when he meets his creator, Weyland, who calls himself his father. The encounter is immediately disappointing for David. As Kalyn Corrigan observes, "it should be a moment of compassion, of connection, but Weyland's cold delivery feels more like it's meant to put David in his place, by letting him know he is beneath him."[45] David passive-aggressively responds by contrasting his "father's" mortality with his own deathlessness, to which Weyland ends the conversation and orders him to pour his tea. Thus begins David's experience of being subservient to people who treat him with contempt, despite his superior capabilities.

The centrality of creation, invention, and self-expression to David's character is emphasized through contrast to Walter (also Michael Fassbender), who represents an upgraded version of the David android. Part of what makes the Walter model new and improved is a proscription barring him from any creative practice or production—of "even a simple tune"—because this quality in David apparently "disturbed people." In effect, Walter is restricted from enjoying all the things that make existence meaningful to David. As they converse in a workshop filled with evidence of David's unremitting creative output, David quotes poetry, explains his genetic experiments, and teaches Walter to play a flute in an effort to tempt his "brother" to join him, to "reign in hell rather than serve in heaven," as he puts it.[46] David tells Walter he "was not made to serve." The plain truth is that Weyland made him precisely to serve, but David uses the expression as a human might, to express the nature of his personality, suggesting to Walter that he too might choose to deviate from his programming. In exercising such agency, engaging with art, and dabbling with the Engineers' biotechnology, David believes he has transformed himself from the created to a creator.

David's transformation undermines these categorical distinctions and raises questions about what qualities and moral imperatives may or may not be attendant on creators; in demonstrating the position of any creator as relative, the film establishes a fractal pattern. If one considers "The Great Chain of Being," a notion that posits a hierarchical order from gods down through ranked humanity to animals,[47] one might insert sentient androids into this chain below humans. From this perspective, as the creator figure is reiterated through *Prometheus* and *Alien: Covenant*, his position (all the creators in these films are male) continually moves lower on The Great Chain of Being, from Shaw's Christian god, to the Engineers and Weyland as mortal creators, to David. When David takes up a position as creator, it highlights the relativism of the status and creates a funhouse mirror––or fractal––pattern of perpetually receding layers of creator to created relationships. The chaos inherent in this conception not only undermines the notion of a fixed hierarchy of beings with a divine creator at the top, but it also rejects the ideology of humanism that posits the unique supremacy of the human, a stance that McWilliam terms the films' "nihilistic posthuman creationism,"[48] that decouples creation from any ethical framework or deeper meaning. David's ability to become father to a species does not elevate his ontological status but, rather, demotes and demystifies creators on the whole, rendering their distinction from the created as inconsequential. Thus, the fractal pattern continues with the erasure of the split between another binary related to creation and is further complicated with new fractal patterns.

Alien: Covenant: Creation versus Destruction

Creation and destruction are portrayed as closely linked throughout the *Alien* franchise, in that the life of each xenomorph is only possible through the death of its host organism, and in *Alien: Covenant* this pair forms the film's second major binary in the fractal pattern. Again, the split between these supposed opposites is demonstrated to be illusory in a chaotic universe.[49] The connection of death to life is made explicit with David's genocide on LV-426 for the sake of his creature. In interviews, Scott has admitted he is drawn to explore grim topics. "It's not perversity," he insists, but because "there's a dark side to life . . . it's the truth."[50] As Jeremy Smith puts it, Scott is prone to "scold viewers for their sentimental attachment to this universe."[51] Considered from this perspective, Scott's *Alien* films seem to want to remind the audience that destruction is a necessary part of creation and that the old must make way for the new. Even so, the creators in *Prometheus* and *Alien: Covenant* are troubling in the extent of their negligence toward life, demonstrating that, regardless of destruction's role in the chaotic cycle of life, humans will attempt to impose order, such as that of an ethical framework, through our participation in the process.

Alien: Covenant's examination of this binary reveals the tension in evaluating a tolerable balance between creation and destruction; when the balance is disrupted by an excess of destruction, moral condemnation comes into play. Despite the initial sympathy David may have garnered from his earlier mistreatment, his later actions appear objectively evil because his destruction goes beyond any sense of balance with creation. Ten years after his arrival on LV-426, he and his creatures have wiped out all indigenous life forms, including a civilization of sentient beings. Rather than reluctantly accommodating death as necessary to the flourishing of his creation, David seems unmoved by genocide, if not indulging in a misdirected desire for retribution against the humans who mistreated him.

In addition to the imbalance, David's creative impulses invite condemnation on a more subjective level. For example, rather than endear him to the audience, David's fatherly doting is disturbing due to his creatures' hideous appearances and relentless, bloody violence. His love for art, which in other contexts can be symbolic of virtue, is also problematic. His arrangement of Shaw's desecrated body as an artistic object is reprehensible. His favorite works, Percy Bysshe Shelley's poem "Ozymandias" and Richard Wagner's "The Entry of the Gods into Valhalla," are both, as

Smith points out, "about the death of the gods, and the arrogance of mankind,"[52] suggesting that David is conscious of but unconcerned by his repetition of Weyland's errors of hubris. Even his effort to teach Walter the flute is contaminated because it asks Walter to dishonor his obligations as an android. These combine to create a subjective but strong sense of condemnation toward all that David generates; even in creating life, all he seems to produce is death. As with the other binaries in the trilogy, the relationship between destruction and creation is shown to be complex; specifically, they are interlinked as opposing, perpetual aspects of the fractal organizing principle of the lifecycle.

Conclusion

The horror of Scott's *Alien* trilogy arises from the notion that the universe outside the relatively safe confines of human order is chaotic, violent, and terrifying; attempts to mitigate the threats posed by chaos fall short if they suffer from simplistic dichotomous thinking that fails to capture the complexity of reality. However, patterns emerge in the chaos, such as the fractal. The fractal developments found in Scott's *Alien* trilogy offer a glimpse into why aspects of the natural world can be better understood with chaos theory than with the limited linearity of binaries. Grasping the patterns that emerge from the chaos helps in anticipating their trajectories, even if this understanding does not bring comfort or safety. Scott presents his perspective as one of unsentimental pragmatism, one that must acknowledge that, blameworthy as David is, he no worse than the other life-creators: they are all lacking, all ultimately unfeeling toward the ones that die. Yet David is judged, nonetheless. In the human world, even when we engage in activities that occur in nature, like destruction and creation, we impose a moral calculus on our actions. Despite Scott's dark and utilitarian view of the universe as chaotic and amoral, order persists, including humanity's tenacious pursuit of moral ideals.

Acknowledgments: I would like to thank Drs. Jean-Philippe Marcoux and Liani Lochner for their help and advice on drafts of this work. I must also acknowledge a debt of gratitude to my son, Merrick Williams. It is thanks to our many hours of discussion about Ridley Scott's *Alien* films, in particular about David, that many of the ideas herein came into focus.

Notes

1. Gordon Slethaug, *Beautiful Chaos: Chaos Theory and Metachaotics in Recent American Fiction* (New York: State University of New York Press, 2000), 110.
2. Merja Polvinen, "The Ends of Metaphor: Literary Analysis and Chaos Theory," *European Journal of English Studies* 11, no. 3 (2007), 274.
3. Carl Matheson and Evan Kirchhoff, "Chaos and Literature," *Philosophy and Literature* 21, no. 1 (1997), 28. See especially James Gleick, *Chaos: Making a New Science*, 2nd ed. (New York: Open Road Media, [2008] 2011). EPUB and Katherine N. Hayles, *Chaos Bound: Orderly Disorder in Contemporary Literature and Science* (Ithaca, NY: Cornel University Press, 1990).
4. Polivenen, "The Ends of Metaphor," 274. See especially Slethaug, *Beautiful Chaos*. Another excellent example of chaos theory as applied to literature is Donald Palumbo's evaluation of Frank Herbert's six-book *Dune* series. He demonstrates how chaos dynamics feature prominently in the novels' concern with ecology and that the "repetition of ancillary parallel plot structures, themes, and motifs throughout the series" give the series a fractal structure. See Donald Palumbo, "The Monomyth as Fractal Pattern in Frank Herbert's *Dune* Novels." *Science Fiction Studies* 25, no. 3 (1998), 434. My analysis of Scott's *Alien* trilogy was originally inspired by Palumbo's approach to *Dune*.
5. Palumbo, "The Monomyth as Fractal Pattern," 433.
6. Gleick, *Chaos*, chap. 4. As the version cited is an EPUB, chapter numbers are cited in place of page numbers. There are interactive fractal patterns online that users can explore. See, for example, Hobart and William Smith Colleges' Mandelbrot Set program: http://math.hws.edu/eck/js/mandelbrot/MB.html.
7. Ibid.
8. Slethaug, *Beautiful Chaos*, 111.
9. Ibid., 99.
10. Jacob Q. Knight, "The Colour Out of Space: Dan O'Bannon, *Alien* Architect," in *Birth. Movies. Death.* Alien: Covenant *Commemorative Issue*, ed. Meredith Borders and George Bragdon (Texas: Alamo Drafthouse, 2017), 18.
11. Chad Hermann, "'Some Horrible Dream About (S)mothering': Sexuality, Gender, and Family in the *Alien* Trilogy," *Post Script* 16, no. 3 (1997), 38. See also Stephen Mulhall, who writes that the xenomorph, in subjecting Kane to "a nightmare vision of sexual intercourse, pregnancy and birth," thus performs a particular incarnation of masculinity characterized by "penetrative sexual violence; . . . as such, it threatens the human race as a whole with the apparently monstrous fate of feminization." Stephen Mulhall, *On Film*, 3rd ed. (London and New York: Routledge, 2015), 13.
12. Barbara Creed, "Horror and the Monstrous-Feminine: An Imaginary Abjection," *Screen* 27, no. 1 (1986), 63. Creed explains that, even though a mother figure does not appear as such in the film, "her presence forms a vast backdrop for the enactment of all the events," for example, in the birth and "womb-like" imagery, "the long winding tunnels leading to inner chambers, the rows of hatching eggs, the body of the

mother-ship, the voice of the life-support system, and the birth of the alien" (58). As Hermann observes, Creed's analysis proved prescient, in that the sequel, *Aliens* (1986) directed by James Cameron, brought the figure of the monstrous generative mother from the shadows of the subconscious to the foreground, in the form of the Alien Queen. See his "Some Horrible Dream," 36.

13. Creed, "Horror and the Monstrous-Feminine," 60.

14. Ibid., 62.

15. See Thomas Byers, who concludes that, overall, the alien's gender is ambiguous despite at times appearing distinctively phallic, with a head that "looks like a huge erect penis." Thomas B. Byers, "Kissing Becky: Masculine Fears and Misogynist Moments in Science Fiction Films," *Arizona Quarterly: A Journal of American Literature, Culture, and Theory* 45, no. 3 (1989), 93, n. 13.

16. Hermann, "Some Horrible Dream," 36.

17. Ibid., 39.

18. Ibid., 36.

19. James H. Kavanaugh, "'Son of a Bitch': Feminism, Humanism, and Science in *Alien*," *October* 13 (1980), 94.

20. Scott Wampler, "Under the Cover: An Interview with Cover Artist NC Winters," in *Birth. Movies. Death.*, 54.

21. Danny Peary, "Directing *Alien* and *Blade Runner*: An Interview with Ridley Scott," in *Ridley Scott: Interviews*, ed. Laurence F. Knapp and Andrea F. Kulas (Jackson: University Press of Mississippi, [1984] 2005), 47.

22. Kavanaugh suggests that the audience registers a "subliminal surprise" when Ripley emerges as the film's heroic rational center and when Dallas dies despite being the intelligent and attractive male leader, which usually, according to genre convention, communicates that he "must be [the] hero [and] can't be killed." See his "Son of a Bitch," 93.

23. John Cobbs argues that the opening scene, in which the crew awakes from cryosleep, presents them "diapered in giant bassinets, and the opening action is their 'rebirth,' emerging from a fetal sleep into the world of the film." See John L. Cobbs, "'*Alien*' as an Abortion Parable," *Literature/Film Quarterly* 18, no. 3 (1990), 198. See also Creed, "Horror and the Monstrous-Feminine," 55, and Kavanaugh, "Son of a Bitch," 93. On the alien ship as a womb, see Hermann, "Some Horrible Dream," 38, and Kavanaugh, "Son of a Bitch," 93, among others, such as Mary Anne Doane, "Technophilia: Technology, Representation and the Feminine," in *Liquid Metal: The Science Fiction Film Reader*, ed. Sean Redmond (New York: Wallflower Press, 2004), 185–118. Cobbs points out that the interior of the *Nostromo* is like the interior of a body. See his "'*Alien*' as an Abortion Parable," 199. Creed suggests that the explosive ejections of bodies from the "mother-ship"--first Kane's corpse and later the xenomorph--can be read as symbolic births from "Mother's" body. See her "Horror and the Monstrous-Feminine," 58.

24. Hermann, "Some Horrible Dream," 38.

25. Mulhall points out that, although Shaw is criticized by fellow crewmembers for her faith, there is no evidence that she ever believes the Engineers to be divine. *On Film*, 233–234.

26. This conversation between Weyland and the Engineer occurs in a scene cut from the theatrical and digital releases. Such deleted scenes and the film's pre-release promotional shorts can easily be found online. See, for example, Aliens 13/23, "What did the engineer say? / The Engineer Speaks," June 2, 2018, video, 1:37, https://youtu.be/OMyqowbs2-c. Accessed June 6, 2020.

27. Prometheus, "Peter Weyland's 2023 TED Talk," Mar 16, 2012, video, 3:08, https://youtu.be/dQpGwnN3dfc. Accessed June 6, 2020.

28. Cinema Box, "Prometheus—Alternate Opening Sequence," May 24, 2018, video, 2:27, https://youtu.be/SNm2AvrkE4w. Accessed June 6, 2020.

29. David McWilliam, "Beyond the Mountains of Madness: Lovecraftian Cosmic Horror and Posthuman Creationism in Ridley Scott's *Prometheus* (2012)," *Journal of the Fantastic in the Arts* 26, no. 3 (94) (2015), 533.

30. Mulhall, *On Film*, 231.

31. McWilliam, "Beyond the Mountains of Madness," 534.

32. This reference is made in Weyland's transcribed commentary on the "Happy Birthday David" promotional short, featuring an infomercial for David as a product for sale, available with the rest of the paratextual material on the BluRay releases. Qtd. in Mulhall, *On Film*, 227.

33. Quoted in Mulhall (*On Film*, 227). Fans and some critics, including Mulhall, have interpreted Weyland's comments as referring to Eldon Tyrell of *Blade Runner* and his replicants, a film also directed by Ridley Scott ("Happy Birthday David," Xenopedia––The Alien vs. Predator Wiki, https://avp.fandom.com/wiki/Happy_Birthday,_David. Accessed June 1, 2020). Leading up to *Prometheus*'s release, the film makers utilized social media and video-sharing websites to generate anticipation and fan participation by providing glimpses of an extended *Alien* universe. The fan culture took to the paratextual material, disseminating it further and generating a critical conversation responding to the information and clues it introduced. As such, Mulhall is correct to assert that the information contained in this material is constitutive of much of the audience's overall experience of the film and understanding of the story's universe (*On Film*, 226–227).

34. Ibid., 227–228.

35. This is Oram's characterization of David in *Alien: Covenant* (directed by Ridley Scott, 2017, Los Angeles, CA: Twentieth Century Fox Home Entertainment).

36. Names for the various creatures in the series, presumably taken from original scripts, are disseminated by the fan community and thus adopted generally. The final creature of *Prometheus*, which emerges from the Engineer's body, is called the "Deacon," the squid creature Shaw aborts is a "Trilobite," and the mutated worm in the temple is a "Hammerpedes" ("Chemical A0-3959X.91—15," Xenopedia––The Alien vs. Predator Wiki, https://avp.fandom.com/wiki/Chemical_A0-3959X.91_%E2%80%93_15. Accessed June 24, 2020).

37. John Briggs and F. David Peat. *Turbulent Mirror: An Illustrated Guide to Chaos Theory and the Science of Wholeness* (New York: Harper and Row, 1989), 26.

38. Mulhall, *On Film*, 229.

39. Mulhall describes the pattern of the ooze's interaction with the human as "a history which grafts a succession of external contingencies upon an internal reproductive logic in ways that affect the nature and trajectory of both"; I have put his observation in the language of the fractal. See Ibid., 229–230.

40. Ibid., 229–230.

41. Ibid., 230.

42. Ibid., 229.

43. Susan George, "Women in Film Time: Forty Years of the Alien Series (1979–2019)," *IAFOR Journal of Arts & Humanities* 6, no. 2 (2019), 65.

44. For an elaboration on acting Captain Oram's religious convictions leading to his disastrous decision in *Alien: Covenant*, see Jeremy Smith, "Ridley Scott's Age of Discovery," in *Birth. Movies. Death.*, 8.

45. Kalyn Corrigan, "Battle of the Fassbenders: God, the Devil and the Fight to Control Creation in *Alien: Covenant*," in *Birth. Movies. Death.*, 38.

46. David's quote from Milton's *Paradise Lost* suggests that he, like Satan, values living on his own terms even if it is in a hellish and lonely environment.

47. *Oxford Dictionary of Cultural Anthropology Online*, s.v. "The Great Chain of Being," https://www.oxfordreference.com/view/10.1093/acref/9780191836688.001.0001/acref-9780191836688-e-163. Accessed June 6, 2020.

48. McWilliam, "Beyond the Mountains of Madness," 535.

49. The creation-destruction connection also appears in *Prometheus* when an entire planet's living systems are generated through the sacrifice of an Engineer. Regarding this film, Mulhall characterizes the Engineers' creativity as "indistinguishable from complete annihilation." *On Film*, 232. McWilliam points more generally to its "recurrent theme of creation through destruction" in "Beyond the Mountains of Madness," 534.

50. Paul M. Sammon, "Interview with Ridley Scott," in *Ridley Scott: Interviews*, ed. Laurence F. Knapp and Andrea F. Kulas (Jackson: University Press of Mississippi, [1996] 2005), 110.

51. Jeremy Smith, "Ridley Scott's Age of Discovery," 9.

52. Jeremy Smith, "The Divine Spark: Screenwriter John Logan on *Alien: Covenant*," in *Birth. Movies. Death.*, 79.

4

The Progeny of H. R. Giger

Christopher L. Robinson

Hans Reudi Giger's biomechanical style of artwork anticipated, influenced, or resonated with numerous aspects of *Alien*, far beyond the visual designs for which the artist is duly famous. Ridley Scott, inspired in large measure by the imagery he discovered in Giger's *Necronomicon*, a book that gathers some of the artist's most representative work from the mid-1960s to the mid-1970s, guided his artistic team to create an ambience that evoked not merely horror, but awe. Although the director has claimed that he intended *Alien* to appeal to viewers' emotions, rather than their thoughts,[1] his film nonetheless challenged a number of preconceived ideas concerning ontology, biology, sexuality, technology, and more. This was due in no small part to Giger's designs, which mixed bodies with machines, death with birth, male with female, beauty with terror, disgust with fascination, and the future with the past. Many of the qualities that rendered the original film so innovative, and also ensured that it would make such a lasting impact in cinema and popular culture in general, can thus be attributed to Giger's mind-blowing artistic concepts. His work on the film went on to become widely imitated, reshaping the look of horror and science fiction cinema. Thanks to his success, he was hired to work on subsequent films such as *Poltergeist II* (Brian Gibson, 1986) and *Species* (Roger Donaldson, 1995). The influence of Giger's style has since extended into other domains such as video games, graphic novels, music, interior design, fashion, tattoos, and more. Such transmedial diffusion has bolstered the iconic status in contemporary culture, not only of Giger's artwork, but also of *Alien* and the franchise it has spawned.

Yet, the artist's progeny in later films have been progressively divested of their most interesting and disconcerting features. Starting with the first sequel, James Cameron abandoned the sense of awe evoked by Scott's original for action-oriented science fiction and over-the-top gore, tendencies

Christopher L. Robinson, *The Progeny of H. R. Giger* In: *Alien Legacies*. Edited by: Nathan Abrams and Gregory Frame, Oxford University Press. © Oxford University Press 2023. DOI: 10.1093/oso/9780197556023.003.0004 adopted to lesser effect in later films of the franchise. Cameron justified not hiring Giger for the sequel by saying that he needed to distance himself, since he feared being overpowered by the artist and his universe.[2] Other directors have followed suit. Although Giger was invited by David Fincher to work on *Alien³* (1992) and made a number of designs and models, none were used, and his name was not included in the visual-effects team nominated for an Academy Award. Jean-Pierre Jeunet claimed that he felt it important to respect Giger's style in *Alien: Resurrection* (1997), yet he and his art department abandoned key elements of that style. In *Prometheus* (2012), Ridley Scott employed unused designs by Giger for both *Alien* and Alejandro Jodorowsky's unrealized *Dune*, but the director turned in *Alien: Covenant* (2017) to other sources of visual inspiration. So, what has survived of the artist's subversive vision? How have his biomechanical style and themes fared in each new *Alien*-inspired film? And how have the evolutions (some might say travesties) of Giger's iconic creatures affected the artistic quality and intellectual sophistication of the films in which these creatures appear? To answer these questions, we will first need to explore his contributions to the original film.

The Father of *Alien*

In executing his designs for *Alien*, Giger was re-creating his own artistic universe, as filtered through the imaginations of Dan O'Bannon and Ridley Scott. O'Bannon, who met Giger while the two were collaborating on Alejandro Jodorowsky's ill-fated project to adapt *Dune* to the screen, was so impressed by the artist's imagery that, when he began writing *Alien*, he found himself "visualizing it as a Giger painting."[3] Later, O'Bannon introduced Ridley Scott to the artist's work. The director was deeply impressed in turn, and, against the objections of the executives at 20th Century Fox, who found the artwork too obscene and disturbing, Giger was brought on board. The artist was initially hired to design the different stages of the Alien's lifecycle. Over the course of production, his contributions would expand to include the design of the exoplanet landscape, the extraterrestrial pilot, and its vessel. He also helped in the construction of the sets and the costume for the adult Alien. In addition to leaving his distinctive stamp on the overall aesthetics and mood of the film, Giger contributed to the plot. This input has never been acknowledged, not even by the artist, yet the central act of the film is structured around the Alien's reproductive cycle, the different phases of which are prefigured in his imagery. In this way the artist's work anticipated—and perhaps influenced or inspired—the facehugger and the chestburster in both form and function. His designs for the adult Alien, meanwhile, display the same characteristics as the biomechanoids in his artwork.

The first images of what might be called proto-facehuggers appear early in the artist's career. *Schacht Nr. 6* (*Shaft No. 6*, 1966–1968) shows an organism, plopped atop an armless woman's head, that is surprisingly similar to the facehugger in the film, though it lacks a tail.[4] In *Under the Earth* (1968), *Phallelujah* (1968–1969), *Homage to S. Beckett* (1968), *Homage to S. Beckett I* (1969), the *Biomechanoids* portfolio of screen prints (1969), and *Humanoid I* (1970), weird symmetrical organisms blend with the artist's recurrent motif of gas masks, which morph into goggles or pulpy sacks that resemble a pair of buttocks, the head of a penis, testicles, or spermatozoa, with tubes or tails that plug into female figures' flesh or skeletons.[5] These gynomorphs are confined in the cavities of machines that are tightly adjusted to the contours of their bodies, which are contorted, mutilated, and sometimes amputated or decapitated. Similarly, the painting depicted in Figure 4.1 features a seated woman whose torso is held in place by a metal harness, with her arms bound behind her back.[6] Her head is encased in a helmet with black goggles. Facing her is a creature with a mechanical proboscis that protrudes directly into the woman's mouth.

In these images, tubes are fastened to the women's nipples, inserted into the navels of their swollen bellies, forced into their anuses, and jammed down their throats; the purpose of the tubes would appear to be to pump the women's breasts for milk, implant and/or nourish a fetus in their wombs, eliminate wastes, and feed them oxygen. This latter function is highlighted in the painting *Biomechanoid 75* (1975), in which a gynomorph performs fellatio on the valve of an oxygen tank.[7] Even if the victim in *Alien* is male, these images of female bodies immobilized, blindfolded, and subjected to multiple penetrations may very well have fostered O'Bannon's imagination when he came up with the idea of the facehugger; this phase of the Alien covers the victim's face, induces a coma that leaves him paralyzed, and forces a tube down his throat that implants an embryo and feeds him oxygen.

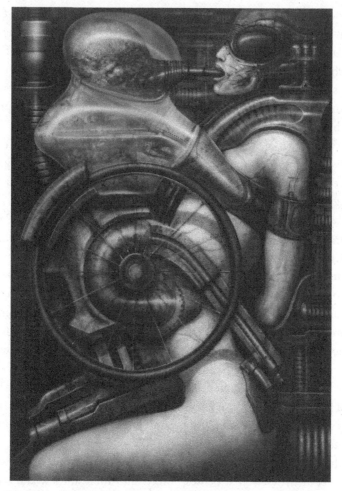

Figure 4.1 *Biomechanoid* (1976), work n° 308, 100×70 cm, acrylic on paper on wood. © HR Giger Museum.

Sexuality and reproduction explain much of the horror and fascination inspired by *Alien*. The manner in which the chestburster explodes out of the host's chest is anticipated by several series of images in Giger's oeuvre. Associating procreation with murder, *Birth Machine* (1967) shows the cross-section of a gun loaded with fetuses shaped like bullets.[8] In *Birth Machine, 2nd version* (1965) fetuses are lined up like bullets in the uterus of a body shaped like a gun.[9] A later pair of pictures entitled *Stillbirth Machine I* (1976) and *Stillbirth Machine* (1977) feature women with cannon barrels between their legs, and newborns on the point of being gouged in the eyes, decapitated, and trepanned as they shoot out from the wombs.[10] In such images, fetuses become bullets, uteruses serve as ammunition magazines, and birth canals are replaced by the barrels of a gun or a cannon. Even if it explodes out of the chest of a male host, and condemns the parent rather than the infant to death at the same instant as birth, the chestburster is likewise a fetal projectile.

Although Giger made a number of designs for this larval phase of the creature, all proved unsatisfactory, and the task of creating the prop was passed on to Roger Dicken. Giger's input cannot be overlooked, however. Dicken's chestburster had to conform to the adult Alien, which had been designed at an earlier stage. Dicken, Giger, and Scott, moreover, met together on multiple occasions, and throughout the production of the film, the director kept on hand a copy of the artist's *Necronomicon*, which he used as a source of illustration for the members of his art department. A couple of images in the book prefigure the chestburster. In *Stillbirth Machine*, a ribbed neck extends from the bottom of the mother's throat to join the lower jaw of a biomechanical organism whose mouth and beluga-like forehead are shaped like those of the chestburster. Extending out from the sternum of the upper figure in *Necronom V* (1976), which served as the model for the pilot in the derelict spacecraft, there is a serpentine creature that surprisingly anticipates the chestburster in the film[11] (see Figure 4.4).

Like all Giger's biomechanoids, the adult Alien is a partially humanoid organism whose body melds flesh with metal and glass, intertwines tubes and wires with veins and nerves, fits pipes and rods to exposed skeletons, displays exaggerated sexual features, and retains a certain grace and elegance, despite its terrifying aspects as a whole. The forms and textures of the biological components of these creatures resemble those of the mechanical, and vice versa. It is frequently difficult, if not impossible, to identify whether a given feature is organic or inorganic in substance, as illustrated by the teeth of Alien or the semi-transparent visor that covers its head. Biomechanoids are not mechanical organisms, like the synthetic humans Ash, Bishop, Call, and David. Nor are they biomorphic machines, like the cephalopod sentinels or arachnid "docbots" that maintain the pods in the power plant of *The Matrix* (Wachowskis, 1999), all part of a machine world that superficially bears the stamp of Giger's style. Whereas bodies and machines are inseparable in the latter's artwork, the Wachowskis make a distinction between the two, as illustrated by the fact that the bodies can be unplugged from their pods after their avatars in the virtual world swallow a red pill. The film moreover establishes a hierarchy of the mechanical over the biological, as the human bodies generate bioelectrical energy that feeds the power plant.

Similar observations can be made concerning the popular aesthetic of the Borg in the *Star Trek* universe, which the designer, Durinda Rice Woods, acknowledges was inspired by Giger.[12] The artist's influence is evident in the sadomasochistic chic of the Borgs' costumes, the retrofuturistic look of their prosthetics, and even the monochromaticism of their physical appearance. (To Adam Roberts, the Borg look as if they stepped out of a 1950s black-and-white film).[13] Ricardo Delgado's initial designs for the Borg Queen in the film *Star Trek: First Contact* (Jonathan Frakes, 1996) show a number of family resemblances with both the gynomorphs in Giger's artwork and the adult Alien. There are protrusions off the Queen's spine, and her "anemone hair," which is protected by a transparent "carapace," brings to mind the semi-transparent dome that covers Alien's upper skull.[14] The costume on screen is rather different: the head is elongated and bald, with three braided tubes across the top and one looping off the base of the skull. The result is still Gigerian enough that Michael Westmore, who was responsible for the make-up of the Queen, worried viewers might find the resemblances between *First Contact* and *Alien* too evident.[15] There is nonetheless an essential difference between the designs of the Borg and Giger's Alien. As Tudor Balinisteanu observes, in the bodies of the Borg drones, the flesh is subservient to and controlled by prosthetics, thus establishing a binary, hierarchical relationship between biology and technology.[16] With the Queen, it would appear that the biological and the mechanical form "a reciprocally sustaining whole."[17] Whether hierarchical or reciprocal, the dichotomy nonetheless persists. The mechanical implements integrated into the Borgs' bodies are visually distinct, and, as in *The Matrix*, they can be surgically removed to a greater or lesser degree. There is no such duality or hierarchy in Giger's artwork nor in his designs for *Alien*, and this is one of the reasons his biomechanoids remain, to this day, more radical in conception than many of the creatures and machines inspired by his work that are found in later films and series.

Figure 4.2 *Cross-section through the Alien egg VI* (1977), work n° 363i, 100×70 cm, acrylic on paper. © HR Giger Museum.

A Queer Creature

Like Donna Haraway's cyborg, Giger's Alien breaks down the binary distinctions, not only between the physical and non-physical, but also male and female, human and non-human.[18] The central body of the facehugger depicted in Figure 4.2 resembles an earthworm.[19]

Its eight "spidery fingers," as the artist calls them, form humanoid hands on the side, and thus merge human attributes with those of so-called lower lifeforms such as worms and spiders.[20] The tips of the fingers caress what Giger identifies as an organ that forms embryos, and thus combines the functions of ovary and uterus. There is just above this organ what he calls the proboscis, though it is closer in form and function to an ovipositor. When viewed together with the embryo sack, the two resemble a penis and a testicle. Giger's painting thus deconstructs the binary division of sexes, since an organ can be female in function, serving to produce, gestate, and deposit embryos, yet be modelled in terms of shape and appearance on male anatomy.

Giger based the adult Alien on *Necronom IV* (1976).[21] As Ridley Scott has observed, the painting represents a demon that possesses a phallic head.[22] It also wears an enormous strap-on dildo. Both head and dildo are tipped with transparent bulbs that reveal partial human skeletons inside, with their skulls forming the "glans" of the two "penises." The rib cages resemble coils, or the springs of a Jack-in-the Box, making the figures look as if they are on the point of ejaculation, like skeletal homunculi. No less than his Stillbirth Machines, the painting intermingles procreation with death. Per Scott's request, the artist toned down the sexual imagery of *Necronom IV* in his designs and costume for the film. Phallic symbolism nonetheless shapes two of Alien's most striking anatomical details: the head and tongue. Given that the dentition of the tongue in the costume for Alien is identical to that of the middle face in the tricephalic demon of *Necronom II* (1976),[23] and that the other two faces in the painting have erect penises sticking out their mouths, the tongue of Alien would appear to be a *penis dentata*, its head a giant foreskin.

Yet, Alien is neither male, nor female, nor even hermaphrodite, as Jeunet had initially intended for the Newborn to be in *Resurrection*.[24] Alien's sex and gender defy any simple, unproblematic binary categorization. This claim is not meant to challenge gender-based analyses, such as Barbara Creed's well-known discussion of the monstrous feminine in *Alien*.[25] As specialists of gender theory have pointed out, there are many cases in which binary sexual distinctions have been and continue to be useful or necessary as an analytical tool. Yet, certain individuals or communities blur the lines between divisions or otherwise resist binary categorization.[26] In a similar manner, when taken as a whole, the two-sex model of sexual reproduction is inadequate for or even inapplicable to Alien's anatomy and reproductive cycle.

Most of Giger's designs for the adult phase do not possess any identifiable sexual organs. The one exception is the drawing entitled *Alien III, front view*, version 2 (1978), in which the creature has a vagina and organs suggestive of fallopian tubes and a uterus.[27] (These organs are visible because, as is often the case with his biomechanoids, the skin is transparent.) A number of Alien's precursors are moreover feminine in appearance, including the central figure in *Necronom V* and a reclining figure in the background of *Friedrich Kuhn II* (1973).[28] Both of these gynomorphs are actually closer in appearance to the adult Alien than the phallic demon of *Necronom IV*. Such examples illustrate that having a phallic head alone does not determine the sex or gender of Giger's Alien. Elongated heads, a recurrent motif that dates back to his formative years, evolved out of stylized representations of women's hair, as illustrated by a couple of sculptures from 1965, *Small Head* and *Large Head*.[29] *Alpha* (1967) presents a woman with a cranial excrescence shaped like long hair flowing in the breeze.[30] The serpentine manes of the gynomorphs in *Li I* (1974), *Passages Temple: Life* (1974), and *The Master and Margarita* (1976) recall the mythological figure of Medusa.[31] In other works, these motifs join with another favorite of the artist, royal accoutrements from ancient Egypt. The heads of female figures in *The Spell II* (1974) and *Stillbirth Machine* resemble *hedjets*, or the white crowns worn by the pharaohs of Upper Egypt.[32] The sorceress in *Female Magician* (1973) is modelled on the goddesses Isis and Hathor, whose cow horns enclose a solar orb; the overall shape of the head of Giger's horned witch, however, is in the shape of a *pschent*, the double crown of the pharaohs that combines the *hedjet* with the *deshret*.[33] The crown of the gynomorph in Figure 4.3 joins the *hedjet* with the cobra motif of the *nemes* or striped headcloth.[34]

Sexing the Xenomorph

Giger's biomechanical style, motifs, and themes, we have seen, made a profound impact on numerous aspects of *Alien*, including not only its creature and set designs, but its overall aesthetics, mood, plot, and discourse. The artist's influence remains strong and runs throughout the films that evolved out of Scott's original. As Giger himself has stated, the franchise "has, from the very beginning, contained my unique and personal style." He even goes so far as to claim that, had it not been for his designs, "[i]n all likelihood, all the sequels to ALIEN would not even exist!"[35] Yet, beginning with the first sequel, the newly dubbed Xenomorph robs the original Alien of two of its most unsettling characteristics: its indefinable sexuality and mixture

Figure 4.3 *Li II* (1973–1974), work n° 251, 200×140 cm, acrylic and Indian ink on paper on wood. © HR Giger Museum.

of human and non-human traits. James Cameron thus began the process, furthered by later directors, of stripping away much of what made Giger's Alien such a remarkable creation.

   It is plausible that one of the most distinctive features of the Xenomorph Queen in *Aliens* (1986), her giant crest, was inspired by the phantasmagorical heads of the artist's gynomorphs. Stan Winston, who was given the task of conceptualizing and building the models and props for Cameron' sequel, was intimately familiar with Giger's work, as shown in his work on *Predator* (John

McTiernan, 1987). The title creature has a pair of jaws, its outer mandibles enclosing an inner rectangular mouth with a dentition similar to Alien. Although Predator's quills, which suggest dreadlocks, were inspired by an image of a Rastafarian warrior,[36] Giger's *Passages Temple: entrance section* (1975) features a creature whose head is similar in shape, and has braided metallic tubes or tentacles hanging down its back and sides.[37] This aesthetic filiation helps explain why Predator and Alien have proven to be so visually compatible in the crossovers of the Dark Horse comics series and especially the two films of *Alien vs. Predator*.[38] Giger's influence on Winston's designs for the Xenomorph Queen is also evident. His clay model of her head is very Gigerian in shape and surface, right down to the molten texture of its scalp, which is reminiscent of the artist's biomechanical landscapes.[39] Winston's sketches of the hands are modelled on the arachnid fingers Giger created for the facehugger, and further refined in *Alien Monster III* (1978) and *Alien Monster IV* (1978).[40]

While Cameron's invention of the Queen completes the Alien's reproductive cycle, it does so at the cost of dividing the species into two distinct sexes: an egg-laying mother and her male warriors. This division robs Giger's original species of one of its key characteristics and sources of both discomfort and fascination. Noël Carroll defines horror as a combination of fear and disgust, and he furthermore suggests (following the work of anthropologist Mary Douglas) that disgust is triggered by objects and beings that are categorically interstitial or contradictory.[41] The indefinable sexuality of Alien and its non-heteronormative reproductive cycle likely explain some of the anxiety, fear, or dread that it elicits in some viewers. This observation is supported by O'Bannon's infamous declaration that

> One thing that people are all disturbed about is sex [. . .] I said, "That's how I'm going to attack the audience; I'm going to attack them sexually. And I'm not going to go after the women in the audience, I'm going to attack the men. I am going to put in every image I can think of to make the men in the audience cross their legs. Homosexual oral rape, birth. The thing lays its eggs down your throat, the whole number."[42]

Like Carroll, Jeffrey Jerome Cohen argues that monsters are perceived as dangerous and threatening because "they are disturbing hybrids whose externally incoherent bodies resist attempts to include them in any systematic structuration."[43] In his view, however, this "ontological liminality" may also serve as a source of wonder and attraction. The "fear of the monster," he states, "is really a kind of desire."[44] The cultural popularity and transmedial propagation of the original Alien, which continues unabated after more than four decades, supports this claim.

In addition to its hybrid sexuality, Alien possesses an uncanny, yet visually credible fusion of human and non-human attributes. As Andrea Zanin observes, "Giger's Alien has an amorphously human tone to it, which adds ambiguity to the familiar distinction of 'man versus monster' that resonates throughout the mythology."[45] With this statement in mind, we can see that Cameron and his art department made another unfortunate decision when they rendered the Queen less humanoid and more insectoid and saurian. *Alien³* takes this division of the human and non-human even further. Hired to create a quadruped version of Alien, Giger designed a sleek, feline Sphinx that resembles the incubus in his painting *Death* (1977).[46] The one human feature David Fincher insisted on keeping was a woman's mouth, with the actress Michelle Pfeiffer serving as the model.[47] Unknown to Giger, Alec Gillis and Tom Woodruff, Jr., working separately, created the canine version that would eventually be shown on screen.

The Biomechanoid Made Flesh

Even if they fall back on more traditional ways of thinking about biological distinctions and sexual reproduction, the first two sequels nonetheless remain faithful to Giger's biomechanical style. *Alien: Resurrection*, however, marks a turning point in the franchise from biomechanics to biogenetics, both visually and thematically. The shift is announced from the beginning with the title sequence, a viscous flow of body parts shown in close up as they morph one into another. The premise of the film is based on the genetic reconstruction of Ellen Ripley, who is pregnant with a xenomorph queen. None of the eight clones of Ripley display any biomechanical features. The Newborn and even the xenomorph drones were purposefully made to look fleshy and organic, due to the mixture of alien and human DNA in the cloning process.

In terms of concept, Jeunet and his team deserve credit for reintroducing the blend of human and non-human features, but the Newborn lacks two other qualities that are essential to Giger's style: beauty and gracefulness. Its pasty flesh, distorted infantile expressions, and elderly body with sagging flesh and slumping posture render the Newborn simply loath-some. Citing Jeunet's *The Fabulous Destiny of Amélie Poulain* (2001) as an example, Claude-Marie Trémois notes that ugliness is very much in vogue in contemporary French cinema.[48] This anti-aesthetic tendency is evident in *Resurrection*. The Newborn, which is not only ugly, but also ungainly in its movements, fits Carroll's description of horror as a mixture of fear and dis-gust. Giger's designs, in contrast, are not simply horrific, but combine terror, disgust, and beauty in a manner that remains potent to this day. He designed his lithe and graceful creature "to be a very beautiful thing, not just some-thing disgusting, not just a monster, but something aesthetic." He says the monsters of *Resurrection*, however, look like "turds."[49]

The new creature designs for *Prometheus* and *Covenant* are shorn of their biomechanical aspects for the same reasons given by Jeunet and his art de-partment.[50] The Deacon, Hammerpede, Fifield mutant, and Trilobite do not possess any biomechanical features. The same goes for the Neomorphs of *Covenant*. Certain features of their anatomy, such as the elongated cranium, spinal excrescences, and tail respect in general outline the body of the orig-inal. Both the Deacon and the Neomorph, moreover, have extensible inner jaws. Where the newer creature designs are based on the jaws of the deep-sea goblin shark,[51] the tongue of Giger's Alien is mechanical in both shape and substance: it is basically a square metallic tube of rectangular grating that ends with a mouth full of chrome teeth.

Ancient Astronauts and Biomechanical Pharaohs

The intermingling of technology and biology prompts many viewers to think of Giger's artwork and designs as futuristic, but retrofuturistic would be the more appropriate term. This is illustrated by a fascination with ancient Egypt that guided his designs for the derelict spacecraft and its pilot in *Alien*. The earliest of these designs were based on instructions given to the artist by O'Bannon prior to Walter Hill's extensive revision of the script. In the orig-inal plot, human astronauts discover two distinct exo-civilizations on a dis-tant planet. One, which is embodied by the pilot, is foreign to the planet. Another, represented by the builders of a temple in the form of a pyramid that serves as both a ritual mating ground and an incubator for eggs, is native. Giger's first detailed illustration of the temple, *Eggsilo Exterior* (1978), bears little resemblance to an Egyptian or Mesoamerican pyramid.[52] Imagining

the civilization that built the edifice as having disappeared in a global cata-
clysm (most likely an atomic war), he says he intended the surrounding terrain to look like an amalgamation of machinery and magma.[53] The resulting
geological formations resemble bones, viscera, or deliquescent blobs of flesh.
One can also make out what look like machine and body parts that have been
engulfed in an upheaval of molten rock. *Landscape* (1978), intended for use
in the construction of the exoplanet's surface, presents similar features, including skulls of both humanoid and not so humanoid shape, and, in the
center of the painting, a head and torso wearing what looks like a military
pilot's flight suit.[54] These echoes of war and mass destruction both anticipate
and resonate well with Hill's introduction of a subplot based on the conspir-
atorial machinations of a military-industrial complex. Although O'Bannon
and Ronald Shusett vociferously opposed these revisions to their screenplay, Hill's contributions enriched the original film, adding layers of intrigue
that would be further exploited in the franchise, especially with *Aliens* and
Resurrection.

   To stand for the frescoes and bas-reliefs covering the interior walls of
the temple as described in O'Bannon's script, Giger created *Hieroglyphics*
(1978).[55] Reminiscent in form of an ancient Egyptian cartouche, the painting
presents a stylized illustration of Alien's birth cycle. A triangle evokes the
pyramid in the script and is covered by the adult Alien represented as the
Egyptian goddess Nut. Written out in horizontal lines between the sides
of the triangle and the Alien's body are biomorphic hieroglyphics. None of
these designs were included in the film, though in *Prometheus* Scott included
a mural in bas-relief in what has come to be known as the Giant Head Room.
He also used similar-shaped hieroglyphics in cuneiform patterns to represent the culture of the Engineers.

   In *Alien*, these designs were not used because Hill merged the pyramid
and spacecraft into one, and transferred the egg chamber of the temple to the
lower deck of the vessel. The extraterrestrial spacecraft is unlike anything in
Giger's previous imagery—or in the history of cinema, for that matter. It does,
however, share several features with his designs for the Harkonnen Castle in
Jodorowsky's *Dune*. Both structures are anthropomorphic. The spacecraft
vaguely resembles a woman's body, while the castle takes the shape of the
corpulent body of the Baron Harkonnen. Both castle and vessel also display
or evoke military weapons and vehicles. Like the surfaces of the Harkonnen
castle, the spacecraft is covered with a network of cables and pistons, which,
together with its aerodynamic curves, give the impression of an early

twentieth-century dirigible. The vessel in *Wreck Entrance Passage* (1978 could easily be taken for a retrofuturistic Zeppelin, especially with the monochromatic color scheme, which enhances the retro appearance, making it look like an old black-and-white photo.[56] In *Dune II* (1975), the Baron holds a Vickers' style machine gun at his side.[57] A round portal resembling a large wheel, together with the sloped back, give the overall impression of a WWI tank of the Renault FT-17 variety, rolling over a field strewn with shapes that could be taken for a terrain of human corpses. In place of a turret, the tank-shaped castle is topped with a human face.

In *Dune V* (1976) the head is replaced by a skull, bringing to mind the *Totenkopf* insignia on the hats worn by officers of the *Schutzstaffel* (SS), which was responsible, among other things, for carrying out Nazi Germany's genocidal campaigns.[58] *Dune I* (1975) likewise evokes fascism with an allée leading up to the Harkonnen castle, lined on either side by biomechanical scorpions, with round glass cockpits in place of heads, that hold pairs of bayonets in the shape of giant ice picks in place of claws.[59] The painting gives an impression similar to that of the large-scale military formations in Leni Reifenstahl's *Triumph of the Will* (1935). Scott recycled Giger's designs for the Harkonnen castle in *Prometheus*. Allusions to fascism, war, and mass killing in the designs get carried over into the film. The cylinders stock-piled in the Engineer's base contain "black goo," a lethal substance designed for a planetary Final Solution to wipe out the human race. In *Covenant* there is a reversal of fortune. David drops the payload of cylinders to annihilate the race of the Engineers on their home planet, in a scene that recalls WWII footage of bombs falling from a B-29 Superfortress.

Even if Hill wrote the pyramid out of *Alien*, the film nonetheless features a mausoleum that houses a majestic pilot mummified atop its cockpit throne. The very set of the spacecraft's interior forms a catacomb, constructed with bones that the artist procured at a butcher's shop. In the scenes where Dallas, Lambert, and Kane gingerly explore the wreck, these organic materials make the gangways look like the inside of a great leviathan's ribcage, reinforcing the impression that the ship is a biomechanical vessel. The mummified pilot is moreover a visual descendant of the ancient pharaohs. *The Attempt to Reveal a New God* (1966) features two figures remarkably similar to the Space Jockey, sitting in the classic pose of a pharaoh, with their hands on their knees.[60] One wears a gas mask, the other sports a postiche, the braided, metallic beard worn by the pharaohs. The postiche and the tube of the mask are identical in shape and texture, resembling the ribbed, flexible hoses of

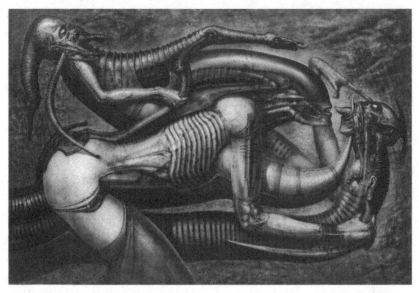

Figure 4.4 *Necronom V* (1976), work n° 303, 100×150 cm, acrylic on paper on wood. © HR Giger Museum.

SRB-type gas masks used in World War I. Figures with skull-like helmets and hoses hanging down from the nose, chin, or mouth also appear in *Shaft No. 5* (1965), *Town II* (1966), *The Spell I* (1973–1974), *A. Crowley-The Beast 666* (1975), and *Samurai* (1976), among others.[61] In *Biomechanoid III* (1974) and *Passages Temple: Life*, the postiche/hose motif morphs into a vertebral column that hangs from the chins of the biomechanoids rather than from the base of their skulls.[62]

Even as these earlier works anticipate the Space Jockey, Giger was instructed by Scott to base his designs for the pilot on the upper figure of the painting in Figure 4.4, which is itself a reworking of an earlier drawing entitled *Astreunuchen* (*Astro-Eunuch*, 1967).[63]

Like the figures in the artwork, the pilot in the film forms an interlocking ensemble with its chair and navigational equipment, thus effacing the frontiers of body and machine. As Dallas observes, it "looks like it's grown out of the chair." Neither body nor machine in *Necronom V*, or in the sculpture of the pilot, forms self-contained, individualized units, but rather interpenetrate each other at multiple points. An apparatus covers the pilot's face and extends down its chest to form appendages that look like ribs, which seamlessly morph into a series of straps that cover its arms and connect with the chair. Where the legs of the upper figure in *Necronom V* disappear into the gynomorph's brassiere, which is shaped like a pair of bulls' horns, the legs of the pilot disappear into the lower end of the chair, which is shaped like an Egyptian sarcophagus. The borders of the different components are thus difficult if not impossible to identify and trace.

While the upper figure in *Necronom V* wears a postiche, the appendage protruding from the Space Jockey's face is more ambiguous in appearance. It could be a mummified facehugger. Or the pilot could be wearing, like the central figure in the drawing *Astreunuchen*, a biomechanical gas mask resembling a rib cage and spinal column. It could also be a proboscis or trunk, which is how the creators of the Dark Horse Comics series imagined it.[64] These ambiguities disappear in *Prometheus*. The pilot whom David discovers wears a helmet and suit, and no longer forms a biomechanical assemblage with his chair and navigational instrument. This is regrettable. At the beginning of *Prometheus*, the Engineers bathe in an aura of the sacred, especially in the eyes of Elizabeth Shaw (Noomi Rapace), who, despite being a scientist, undertakes her quest to discover humankind's creators with religious fervor. Yet, the pilot whom David discovers turns out to be an anthropomorphic grey hulk that exudes more testosterone than majesty and mystery. This is a far cry from Giger's amalgam of biomechanical pharaoh and ancient astronaut, a being that collapses distinctions, not only between body and machine, but also between the distant future and the far past.

The Perfect Organism

Just as *Prometheus* robs the Engineers of their mystique, so *Covenant* unshrouds the mysterious origins of the Alien. The sole pursuit of David (Michael Fassbender) in the latest film of the franchise is the creation of the "perfect organism." This, of course, is an echo of the words spoken by Ash (Ian Holm) in *Alien*: "You still don't know what you're dealing with: [the] perfect organism." To bring his work to fruition, David must acquire fresh human specimens, since he has exhausted the bodily resources of his sole human companion, Elizabeth Shaw, the heroine who had befriended and repaired the android in *Prometheus*. The body of this woman, whom he claims to have loved and whose memory he claims to cherish still, serves as the matrix, in multiple senses of the term, of David's supreme creation.

The fleeting views we are given of the drawings of her mutilated corpse are perversely fascinating, erotic, horrific. The still-lifes (the French term *natures mortes* might be more appropriate here) that David makes of Shaw's body show in form and composition the influence of Takato Yamamoto. Working in a "pop" vein of the Ukiyo-e tradition, some of Yamamoto's best-known works feature the decapitated heads or disemboweled bodies of (usually) women arranged with skulls and bones, flowers, and plants, and the body parts of animals such as the wings of birds or insects.[65] Like David's artwork, these baroque compositions blend eroticism with gore and the macabre. Stylistically, however, the black-and-white images in *Covenant* are either drawn in the naturalist vein of Leonardo da Vinci or in the biomechanical manner of H. R. Giger.[66] The artists responsible for David's drawings, Dane Hallett and Matt Hatton, consider their contributions to the film as an homage to Giger.[67] Their work is a notable exception to the tendency of other filmmakers and artistic teams involved in the franchise to denude Giger's vision of its key stylistic traits and subversive themes.

The desire of later directors to renew the artist's designs and leave the stamp of their own creative vision is both understandable and necessary to breathe new life into the *Alien* franchise. Efforts to copy or renovate Giger's creations, however, remain aesthetically inferior to the originals, as they fall into the tired clichés of mainstream body horror and action-oriented science fiction, and resort back to familiar oppositions between body and machine, male and female, human and non-human, beauty and horror. To an even greater degree than other films and series inspired by the artist's work, such as *Predator* or *Star Trek*, the Alien sequels and prequels have abandoned key elements of Giger's biomechanical aesthetic. The humanoid bodybuilders of *Prometheus* and *Covenant* are impoverished descendants of the awe-inspiring Space Jockey. The title creature of the franchise has been progressively divested of its most alluring, yet disquieting, characteristics, resulting in pale imitations, appropriately symbolized by the ghostly pallor of the Neomorphs. Yet, even if Cameron, Fincher, Jeunet, and the Scott of *Prometheus* have all been set on taming the beast that H. R. Giger loosed upon the world in 1979, his original Alien abides as one of the most iconic monsters of our time, and one of the most remarkable and unique artistic achievements in the history of cinema.

Acknowledgments: I wish to extend my deepest gratitude to Mme. Carmen Scheifele-Giger for granting permission to reproduce the paintings and drawings by H. R. Giger included in this chapter. I would also like to thank Gwendoline Sottas and Matthis Belz at the HR Giger Museum for their precious assistance.

Certain passages from this current text originally appeared in a French publication, *L'art et la science dans* Alien (2019), co-written by Frédéric Landragin, Roland Lehoucq et Jean-Sébastien Steyer. Many thanks to Raphaël Tomas, editorial director of Les Éditions de La Ville Brûle, for permission to reuse and revise this earlier material.

Notes

1. Mark Patrick Carducci and Glenn Lovell, "Ridley Scott: Director," *Cinefantastique* 9, no. 1 (October 1979), 12.
2. James Cameron to Leslie Barany, February 13, 1987. https://hrgiger.com/james_came ron.htm. August 21, 2020.
3. Ed Sunden II, "Dan O'Bannon on Alien: Alien Screenplay Writer Speaks His Mind," *Fantastic Films*, September 1979, 13.
4. H. R. Giger, *H.R. Giger's Biomechanics* (Beverley Hills: Morpheus International, 1990), 17.
5. Ibid., 9–13.
6. Ibid., 70.
7. Ibid., 79.
8. Giger, *Necronomicon*, 5.
9. Ibid., 4.
10. Ibid., 70, 77.
11. Ibid., 65.
12. Judith and Garfield Reeves-Stevens, *Star Trek The Next Generation: The Continuing Mission* (New York: Pocket Books, 1998), 90.
13. Adam Roberts, *Science Fiction* (London: Routledge, 2000), 163.
14. Ricardo Delgado, *Star Trek VIII Borg Queen*, in "Creating the Borg," Forgotten Trek, last modified September 14, 2019, https://forgottentrek.com/creating-the-borg/. Accessed July 30, 2020.
15. Larry Nemecek, *The Star Trek: The Next Generation Companion* (New York: Pocket Books, 1992), 325.
16. Tudor Balinisteanu, "The Cyborg Goddess: Social Myths of Women as Goddesses of Technologized Otherworlds," *Feminist Studies* 3, no. 2 (Summer 2007), 398.
17. Ibid., 400.
18. Donna. J. Haraway, *Simians, Cyborgs and Women: The Reinvention of Nature* (New York: Routledge, 1991), 150–153.
19. H. R. Giger, *Giger's Alien: Film Design 20th Century Fox* (Beverly Hills: Morpheus International, 1999), 9.
20. Ibid., 10.

21. Giger, *Necronomicon*, 65.

22. Carducci and Glenn Lovell, "Ridley Scott," 12.

23. Giger, *Necronomicon*, 31.

24. Anthony C. Ferrante, "Overseers of the Resurrection," *Fangoria* 170 (March 1998), 29.

25. Barbara Creed, "Alien and the Monstrous Feminine," in *Alien Zone: Cultural Theory and Contemporary Science Fiction Cinema*, ed. Annette Kuhn (London: Verso, 1990), 128–141.

26. Lal Zimman, Jenny L. Davis, and Joshua Raclaw, "Opposites Attract: Retheorizing Binaries in Language, Gender, and Sexuality," in *Queer Excursions: Retheorizing Binaries in Language, Gender, and Sexuality*, ed. Lal Zimman, Jenny L. Davis, and Joshua Raclaw (Oxford: Oxford University Press, 2014), 1–3.

27. Giger, *Alien*, 59.

28. Giger, *Necronomicon*, 65, 55.

29. Giger, *Retrospective*, 13.

30. Giger, *Biomechanics*, 13.

31. Giger, *Necronomicon,*, 31, 59, 64.

32. Ibid., 24, 77.

33. Ibid., 52.

34. Ibid., 21.

35. H. R. Giger to Twentieth Century Fox, November 13, 1997. https://lettersofnote.com/2013/01/21/the-alien-father-is-h-r-giger/. Accessed August 21, 2020.

36. Jody Duncan, *The Winston Effect: The Art and History of Stan Winston Studio* (London: Titan Books, 2006), 101

37. Giger, *Necronomicon*, 57.

38. Randy Stradley, Phill Norwood, and Chris Warner, *Aliens vs. Predator* (Milwaukie: Dark Horse Comics, 1991).

39. Duncan, *The Winston Effect*, 81.

40. Giger, *Alien*, 5, 7.

41. Noël Carroll, *The Philosophy of Horror, or Paradoxes of the Heart* (London: Routledge, 1990), 27–30, 32.

42. Brent Zacky, *The Alien Saga* (Image Entertainment, 2003), DVD.

43. Jeffrey Jerome Cohen, "Monster Culture (Seven Theses)," in *Monster Theory*, ed. Jeffrey Jerome Cohen (Minneapolis: Minnesota University Press, 1996), 6.

44. Ibid., 16.

45. Andrea Zanin, "Ellen Ripley: The Rise of the Matriarch," in *Alien and Philosophy*, ed. Jeffrey Ewing and Kevin S. Decker (Oxford: Wiley Blackwell, 2017), 159.

46. Giger, *Necronomicon*, 79.

47. Les Paul Robley, "Alienated," *Imagi-Movies* 1, no. 3 (Spring 1994), 24.

48. Claude-Marie Trémois, "Le Sinistre Destiné d'Amélie Poulain," *Esprit* 278, no.10 (October 2001), 196.

49. Andrew Abbott and Russell Leven, *Alien Evolution* (Twentieth Century Fox, 2003), DVD.

50. Mark Salisbury, *Prometheus: The Art of the Film* (London: Titan Books, 2012), pp.

51. Simon Ward, *The Art and Making of Alien: Covenant* (London: Titan Books, 2017), 98.

52. Giger, *Alien*, 13.

53. Frederic Albert Levy, "H.R. Giger: Alien Design," *Cinefantastique* 9, no. 1 (October 1979), 39.

54. Giger, *Alien,*, 17.

55. Ibid., 15.

56. Ibid., 29.

57. Giger, *Necronomicon*, 67.

58. Ibid., 69.

59. Ibid., 67.

60. Giger, *Biomechanics*, 12.

61. Giger, *Necronomicon*, 6, 8, 28–29, 46, 47.

62. Ibid., 43, 58.

63. Giger, *Biomechanics*, 18.

64. Mark Verheiden and Mark A. Nelson, *Aliens: Book One* (Milwaukie: Dark Horse Comics, 1990).

65. Takato Yamamoto, *Necrophantasmagoria Vanitas* (Tokyo: Editions Treville Co. Ltd., 2015).

66. Dane Hallett and Matt Hatton, *Alien Covenant: David's Drawings* (London: Titan Books, 2018), 10.

67. Ibid., 37.

5

The Unescapable Labyrinth

Archetypal Retrogression and Aesthetic Rigidity in *Alien³*

Kenneth Sloane

Overcoming the Monster

In his book *The Seven Basic Plots*, Christopher Booker built on C. G. Jung's conception of the archetypes of the collective unconscious to propose a taxonomy of archetypal plots into which all narratives can be categorized, the most ancient and primal of which is that of "Overcoming the Monster."[1] Whether encountered in the epic sagas of ancient civilizations or Hollywood blockbusters of the multiplex era, the pattern of these stories remains consistent: a preternatural and hostile being emerges to cast a shadow over an individual, a community, or humanity itself. An opposing hero is called upon to confront this deadly threat. While confronting the mysterious and daunting monster, the hero will suffer many reversals until they near a condition of seemingly inevitable defeat. It is at this point that a dramatic reversal occurs. Due to the hero's ingenuity, the revelation of a previously unknown weakness in their heretofore invulnerable foe, and occasionally an element of luck, the hero manages to escape the beast's clutches and vanquish it. Booker summarizes this archetypal plot as consisting of five stages.[2] The first is the "Anticipation and Call" stage in which the hero, or heroes, become aware of the monster from a distance as a vaguely menacing curiosity and are called upon to confront it. This is followed by the "Dream" stage in which the heroes make preparations and set off confidently on their quest, still with a sense of remoteness from, and immunity to, danger. Next comes the "Frustration" stage wherein the heroes falter on encountering the monster face to face and are overcome by it. As the monster's power becomes apparent, the heroes' destruction seems inevitable. In the penultimate "Nightmare" stage, the hero approaches a point of maximum danger, being drawn toward a final

Kenneth Sloane, *The Unescapable Labyrinth* In: *Alien Legacies*. Edited by: Nathan Abrams and Gregory Frame,
Oxford University Press. © Oxford University Press 2023. DOI: 10.1093/oso/9780197556023.003.0005

confrontation where all odds seem in the monster's favor. Booker identifies the final stage as "the thrilling escape from death and death of the monster" wherein the monster is dealt a miraculous fatal blow and its power is overthrown.[3]

Alien (Ridley Scott, 1979) begins in precisely this fashion when the crew of the Nostromo are awakened prematurely and literally called by the distress signal to the monster's lair. In the Dream stage we witness the crew employ their skills to reroute the Nostromo, execute a hazardous landing, brave the planet's hostile surface, and boldly enter and explore the derelict spacecraft. The Frustration stage commences with the attack on Kane (John Hurt) and continues with the creature's horrific birth and its successful predations on the remaining crew members. The Nightmare stage occurs after the death of Lambert (Veronica Cartwright) and Parker (Yaphet Kotto), when Ripley (Sigourney Weaver) finds herself alone in the Labyrinthine corridors of the floundering Nostromo within which the creature lurks unseen and, even when safety seems to have been reached, discovers to her horror the creature has stowed away aboard her escape shuttle. The thrilling escape from death and death of the monster correspond to the final moments of *Alien* when the seemingly defenseless Ripley ingeniously harpoons, ejects, and blasts the creature into the void. It is striking how closely *Alien* adheres to the stages of this archetypal plot structure.

Most sequels instinctively stick to the same archetypal plot structure as their predecessor. Doing so allows them to satisfy audience expectations, but also risks an effect of diminishing returns, as the once thrilling, novel, or terrifyingly mysterious becomes stale and overly familiar. *Aliens* (James Cameron, 1986) unquestionably reiterates the archetypal plot of its predecessor with all five stages of the Overcoming the Monster plot readily identifiable. Burke's (Paul Reiser) invitation to act as an advisor to the expedition serves as the Anticipation and Call stage. The Marine platoon's preparation, seemingly formidable weaponry, successful execution of the hazardous planetary landing, and uneventful exploration of the colony constitute the Dream stage. The Frustration stage duly arrives with the Marines routed by the creatures on their first encounter beneath the atmosphere processor, and the subsequent loss of their weapons, ammunition, and means of retreat with the destruction of the dropship and armored personnel carrier, coupled with the news that their rescue will take seventeen days. *Aliens'* Nightmare stage commences with the creatures' attack and further evisceration of the platoon, and the capture of Newt (Carrie Henn). The climactic descent to the

Queen's chamber, rescue of Newt, and ensuing battle aboard the Sulaco with the stowaway Queen can be aptly described as a "thrilling escape from death and death of the monster."[4] However, to consider *Aliens* a mere reiteration of the archetypal plot its predecessor employed would be to underestimate its sophistication. Cameron's film is unusual as its narrative also incorporates a second complete archetypal plot pattern, that of Rebirth. This unusual dual archetypal plot structure helped secure *Aliens'* acclaim and commercial success.

Whether due to the proliferation of Jung's ideas in the Hollywood system[5] or spontaneously emerging from the artistic instinct of their creators, both *Alien* and *Aliens* appear as pristine examples of archetypal coherence. By contrast, as will be argued here, the creators of *Alien³* (David Fincher, 1992) appear to have been less attentive to the film's archetypal plot structure and made key story decisions in preproduction that ultimately produced a script that was a dissonant mixture of conflicting archetypal plot fragments, making a chaotic production and underwhelming reception all but inevitable.

Alien³: A Tragedy?

"I don't think they've got much of a script, and I don't think Jim's movie can be topped, or that they could ever come close to it. From what I've been able to understand, I don't think it's going to work."
—Michael Biehn.[6]

The critical and commercial successes of *Alien* and *Aliens* had perhaps set a dauntingly high bar for *Alien³* to match. The project produced and discarded three screenplays before Sigourney Weaver's involvement was confirmed.[7] Elevated to the role of co-producer, and with a significant degree of creative input, Weaver insisted at an early meeting with producers Gordon Carroll and David Giler that *Alien³* would be her last involvement in the series. The death of Ripley thereby became a predetermined endpoint of the then *Alien* trilogy. The inevitable death of a story's protagonist sets the plot of the third installment at odds with the "life overcoming death" essence of the Overcoming the Monster and Rebirth archetypes on which the previous films had been constructed, and therefore made them ill suited as foundations for the third episode. If Ripley was required to die, through either heroic self-sacrifice or a fall from grace, the Tragedy archetypal plot presented itself as an appropriate, and arguably the only appropriate, foundation on which the events preceding her demise could be constructed in a dramatically compelling and psychologically meaningful way. Booker notes how "a death that is violent, premature, a death that is 'unnatural'[. . .] which shows that something has gone hideously, or . . . tragically wrong"[8] is a distinctive attribute of the Tragedy archetype's final Death or Destruction stage. The loss of kinship bonds (friends, family, allies) that Ripley suffers in the opening act of *Alien³* is also characteristic of the Tragedy archetypal plot. However, these story moments are not accompanied by any of the Tragedy archetype's other stages (Anticipation, Dream, Frustration, Nightmare).[9] A tragic protagonist is frequently an initially heroic character who has become possessed by a dark obsession[10] and suffers the loss of kinship bonds as a consequence.[11] But Ripley never loses her heroic aura, nor does she become a darker character driven by obsession. While she does suffer the loss of her loved ones, this is not a consequence of any choice she makes, therefore it is merely unfortunate rather than tragic. Ultimately, the project lacked the confidence to fully commit to the Tragedy archetype, and each of the numerous redrafts of *Alien³* instead attempted to retain or recapture the archetypal essence of *Alien*. Consequently, Ripley's death and the loss of her companions became merely tragic moments bookending a disorientated and incongruent reiteration of the Overcoming the Monster plot. The presence of these tragic plot points at the start and end of what is traditionally a life-affirming archetype created an irreconcilable contradiction that lay at the heart of the *Alien³*'s difficulties. Producers Hill and Giler sought at the eleventh hour to reverse the decision on Ripley's demise, precipitating a serious dispute with Weaver and Fincher in which the co-producer and director prevailed.[12] *Alien³*'s archetypal contradictions ultimately remained unresolved.

Of the lingering fragments of the Overcoming the Monster plot, *Alien³* is without an Anticipation and Call stage, nor is there a Dream stage. The Confrontation stage, the first lethal encounter with the monster, is compromised as it befalls characters naïve to a danger of which the audience and protagonist are thoroughly aware. When the Nightmare Stage of the creature's murderous predations on the inmates of Fury 161 commences, it is as if *Alien³* has merely been killing time before it could get to the gratifying business of killing its characters. Ripley's preordained death ensures the thrilling escape from death and death of the monster stage is only half realized. Thus, *Alien³* misses the mark on three and a half of the five archetypal plot stages that were central to its predecessors.

The inclusion of a Rebirth archetypal plot had given *Aliens* a dual archetypal plot structure that distinguished and arguably helped elevate it above the subsequent episodes in the series. When we meet Ellen Ripley at the start of *Aliens*, she is at a low ebb and inexorably sinking deeper into a metaphorical state of living death (Figure 5.1). Her account of the events of the first film is dismissed by the official inquiry. Stripped of her flight license, Ripley finds herself at the bottom of the economic ladder, compelled to scrape a living "running loaders and forklifts." In her time off work, she ruminates on the traumatic events of the first film and grieves for the loss of her daughter. In her waking and sleeping hours she is tormented by nightmares and hallucinations. She is withdrawn from the world and fearful of reengaging with life.

As the narrative of *Aliens* unfolds, Ripley experiences an archetypal Rebirth, which reverses many of the traits of her initial state, including her debilitating neurosis. She transitions from a traumatized victim requiring masculine protection to become the last warrior standing, after her hubristic bodyguards have been undone by their failure to heed her warnings. Her previous fearful paralysis at the thought of encountering the creature again is reversed as she becomes an active avenger, pursuing the beast to its innermost lair at the film's climax. Psychologically, Ripley moves from being tormented by nightmares to become the banisher of "scary dreams," and from mourning her lost daughter to risking her life to rescue the orphaned Newt. The dramatic impact of Ripley's rebirth is amplified

Figure 5.1 Ripley's state of living death.

considerably by the contrasting diminution in status and prestige of several other characters.

The principle of enantiodromia is central to the Rebirth archetypal plot, which restores a hero who has fallen into a metaphorical state of living death to their true heroic stature. Enantiodromia can be understood as the process by which something becomes its opposite. Carl Jung elaborated on the Greek philosopher Heraclitus's original understanding of the term to describe not merely elements that run counter to each other, but to "designate the play of opposites in the course of events—the view that everything that exists turns into its opposite."[13] Jung cites the conversion of St. Paul, a quintessential instance of a character who undergoes a symbolic rebirth, as a good example of enantiodromia.[14] It is within Cameron's skillful juxtaposition of an intricate series of interrelated enantiodromic trajectories among the characters of *Aliens* that much of the film's dramatic gratifications and meaning reside.

Ripley's recovery of composure and courage is all the more impactful when juxtaposed with the unravelling of Private Hudson (Bill Paxton), whose swaggering machismo evaporates into a blubbering hysteria in the aftermath of the Marines' rout by the aliens. Hudson only composes himself when Ripley demands he do so. She further asserts her leadership qualities by issuing him orders to organize for the survivors' defense and rescue. This reversal of status is dramatically satisfying given Hudson's previous condescension to Ripley, imbued with implications of his sexual dominance and her subordination. At a more institutional level, Lt. Gorman's (William Hope) inexperience and complacent faith in man's mastery over nature and any foe it can produce leads to his downfall. His paralysis at the moment of crisis when his assumptions are confounded and his ability to improvise falters contributes to the loss of his authority, a position of leadership that Ripley swiftly fills. As Burke reveals his opportunism and selfishness, this consolidates Ripley's rediscovery of her selflessness and willingness to put herself at risk to protect others. This is illustrated profoundly by the fact that when Ripley (initially adamant that she will not return to LV426 and "would not be any use if she did"), when presented with an opportunity of escape, instead enters alone into the netherworld of the atmosphere processor to rescue Newt, the love of whom has been the most powerful inspiration for her rebirth. For it is this struggle between life and death, in both its literal and symbolic form, that constitutes the essence of the Overcoming the Monster and Rebirth archetypes. In the climax of *Aliens*, Cameron orchestrates a

harmonious conjuncture of both these archetypal plots to deliver a crescendo with powerful meaning both visceral and cerebral; that while life may
be vulnerable and susceptible to a variety of terrors and reversals both physical and psychological, it remains something of supreme value, to be preserved and protected even at the risk of the hero's own life. *Alien³* abandoned
this dual-archetypal structure. However, a fragment of the Rebirth archetype
can be detected, but its potential remains largely unrealized. The loss of her
companions and return of the creature could be considered an instance of the
hero falling under the shadow of a dark power, which comprises the Rebirth
archetype's first stage. Ripley's romance with Clemens (Charles Dance) could
have been a route to the final Rebirth stage when the protagonist is liber-
ated from their state of living death by feelings of affection toward a romantic
partner or innocent child. However, Clemens' abrupt departure curtails this
trajectory. The other archetypal plots of Comedy, Rags to Riches, The Quest,
and Voyage and Return are conspicuous only by their absence. It should be
emphasized that archetypal plots are not formulae to which rigid adherence
is demanded. Rather archetypal plots exist at a level of abstraction that allows
for an infinite variety of hybridization, variation, and innovation in story
structure. However, when analyzed from an archetypal perspective, *Alien³*
is very much a mixture rather than a blend. Its improvidently assembled archetypal fragments remain distinct and misaligned with one another, rather
than combining to create a story with a coherent and satisfying psychological
resonance.

Aesthetics over Archetypes: Trapped in the Nightmare Stage

It is interesting to consider why the structural strengths of *Aliens*' story, particularly its archetypal innovation, was abandoned by the creators of *Alien³*.
In addition to neglecting to craft a coherent archetypal plot foundation, arguably another significant factor that hampered *Alien³*'s development was an
inability to see beyond the audio-visual aesthetic conventions established by
its predecessors despite a desire to do so.

For many, the swirling amber warning lights, wailing klaxons, amid
dimly lit hexagonal corridors within which death lurks unseen, are the
iconic visual and aural essence of the series. This aesthetic had been established in the Nightmare stage of *Alien* and revisited by *Aliens* toward its own

climax. Writers and producers perhaps assumed that as long as this aesthetic was maintained audiences would be satisfied regardless of archetypal plot considerations. However, by the time of *Alien³*'s development, this signature aesthetic had created a flourishing transmedia sci-fi/horror subgenre populated by imitators and spin-offs. Prior to the release of *Alien³*, and perhaps with the influence of the *Alien* franchise in mind, movie critic Alex Cox criticized the tendency of many science-fiction films to "fall down at the end, stumbling . . . into a dull welter of chases down corridors and high-tech gunfire."[15] *Alien* and *Aliens* had perhaps done more than any other films to establish the hegemony of this neo-Labyrinthine aesthetic.

Since *Aliens*, all subsequent episodes seem inexorably bound to the conventions of the once exhilarating, but now familiar, routine of chases down corridors. Even with the ambitions of *Prometheus* (Ridley Scott, 2012) to take the series in a new direction, it reverts to chases down corridors in its finale. Likewise, *Alien: Covenant* (Ridley Scott, 2017) feels compelled to reprise *Alien* in miniature, compressing an abridged version of the neo-Labyrinthine peril of its precursor into its final twenty minutes, while *Alien Resurrection* (Jean-Pierre Jeunet, 1997) is essentially the same premise extended to feature-length duration. 2019's series of fortieth-anniversary *Alien* shorts *Containment* (Chris Reading), *Harvest* (Benjamin Howdeshell), *Night Shift* (Aidan Brezonick), *Ore* (Kailey and Sam Spear), and *Specimen* (Kelsey Taylor)) closely adhere to the "chases in confined places" formula, while amber-illuminated, steam-filled corridors and crawlspaces are the almost exclusive setting of the paratextual *Alien* universe.

It seems their creators have come to believe that all stories set in the *Alien* universe must inevitably channel their characters toward monstrous predations in darkened corridors and this alone is sufficient to satisfy audience demands. However, this effectively binds the series to increasingly less effective reiterations of the Overcoming the Monster plot while simultaneously impeding exploration of other archetypal plots that may permit a return to deeper psychological and dramatic themes, such as the progression to the Tragedy archetypal plot that Ripley's demise naturally suggested. Ultimately, an aesthetic is not an archetype, with the former primarily acting on the senses while the latter acts on the mind. While revisitations to *Alien*'s neo-Labyrinthine aesthetic may trigger the fleeting thrill of memories of past gratifications, it cannot alone provide the deeper psychological and emotional meaning of a story built upon a sound and skillfully crafted archetypal foundation.

It is understandable that the series became addicted to the powerful aes-thetic it had created. The gratifications of the horror genre are more closely aligned to the gratifications of intoxicating substances than most perhaps realize, both being grounded in pleasures of physiological arousal. But the series' addiction to its neo-Labyrinthine aesthetic ultimately bound both the audience and the creatives affiliated to the *Alien* franchise in an unfulfilling relationship. Like a bartender with a patron who perhaps visits somewhat too regularly, the creators felt compelled to give their audience what they ap-parently enjoyed last time and refrained from offering any alternative, while the returning audience wondered why more of the same was less and less satisfying, as it became increasingly apparent that the elation and euphoria of their first intoxicating encounter could never quite be recaptured, but only palely imitated.

De-Cameronization and Re-Cameronization

Cameron's absence is perhaps another reason for *Alien³*'s difficulties with finding a sound archetypal structure. Themes of enantiodromia and rebirth were already identifiable components of Cameron's emerging auteur traits. For example, the symbolic rebirth of an oppressed female protagonist is something of a leitmotif in Cameron's work as he employs the same arche-typal pattern in *The Terminator* (1984), *Aliens* (1986), and *Titanic* (1997). In all these films female protagonists are initially oppressed by monstrous fig-ures, before being aided by a male protector who enables their enantiodromic transformation from a state of vulnerability and subordination, to indepen-dence and self-reliance. This newfound independence of the female protago-nist faces its final test when, through the death or incapacitation of this male mentor, the heroine must stand alone to face her monstrous foe in the final conflict. The decision not to retain his services for *Alien³* perhaps increased the probability that it would be a more conventional sequel, reiterating, rather than expanding on, the archetypal plots of previous episodes. However, if the jettisoning of the second archetypal Rebirth plot could per-haps be explained by conventional thinking in Cameron's absence, as *Alien³*'s development proceeded, there seems to emerge a more deliberate ambition to terminate, negate, or reverse many of the other elements he had brought to the franchise. This introduced a secondary series of conflicting impulses that arguably further undermined the project. With Cameron as director and Sigourney Weaver as lead, *Aliens* had brought together two formidable personalities. Weaver had contested several aspects of the direction in which Cameron was guiding the series. As a committed gun-control advocate, she repeatedly expressed strong reservations when the extent of the prominence of firearms became apparent while filming. Ultimately Cameron's Vietnam War-in-space vision had prevailed. Weaver was also uneasy with the hatred that Ripley was developing toward the creatures and wanted a more complex relationship. Cameron dismissed this idea in favor of a more primal antagonism. Ultimately, *Aliens* was shaped principally by Cameron's distinct and uncompromising personal vision.

For *Alien³*, Weaver revived many of the ideas previously dismissed by Cameron. In addition to Ripley's demise, Weaver also convinced producers Gordon Carroll and David Giler that the series should not continue along the militaristic action trajectory *Aliens* had established.[16] In addition to jettisoning Cameron's Rebirth archetype and war movie aesthetics, *Alien³* would proceed to revert to a single xenomorph antagonist and attempt a more psychologically complex relationship between Ripley and the creature. These decisions did much to reverse what Cameron had brought to the series. The subsequent abrupt off-screen deaths of Hicks (Michael Biehn) and Newt dispensed with the last remaining aspects of Cameron's legacy. This erasure of his characters and generic, aesthetic, and archetypal innovations suggest a desire to "De-Cameronize" the franchise. In a perhaps unintended metaphor, Cameron's last remaining character Bishop (Lance Henriksen) is literally consigned to a trash heap in *Alien³*.

Thus, *Alien³* found itself accumulating a series of contradictions: a fatalistic story constructed on an incompatible life affirming archetype, a desire to negate the legacy of its preceding auteur but an inability to find a new auteur or authorial vision, a desire to avoid predictable generic conventions but reverence for those same conventions and lack of confidence to move beyond them. Amid this confusion *Alien³* had jettisoned much that was meaningful in its predecessor while replacing it with very little.

The Rebirth archetype that Cameron had employed derives its psychological meaning by articulating the capability of hope to endure when all seems lost, and life to be redeemed from the jaws of death. At the end of *Aliens*, not only had Ripley been reborn as an individual, but a nascent family had been formed with Hicks and Newt, promising a further defiant repudiation of the alien's life-consuming threat, that the child rescued from its clutches would now be ushered to adulthood and independence, and in time continue the cycle of life through future generations. The subsequent abandonment of hope and desire for death by the Ellen Ripley of *Alien³* negated her previous rebirth and returned her to a state of living, and eventually literal, death.

Clive Barker spoke for many when he said, "so much emotional commitment is thrown out of the window because Michael Biehn and Newt are dead from the beginning of the picture. I didn't want that to happen. I wanted continuity."[17] Critic Karen Krizanovich described *Alien 3* as a film that most fans will want to rewrite.[18] This desire was to some extent realized eventually in 2019 when two paratextual adaptations resurrected Cameron's discarded characters. An Audible Original audiobook adaptation of William Gibson's rejected *Alien III* screenplay saw Michael Biehn and Lance Henriksen reprise their roles as Hicks and Bishop, with Ripley and Newt also resurrected albeit now voiced by Laurel Lefkov and Mairead Doherty. Gibson's screenplay was also adapted as a Dark Horse graphic novel the same year. These adaptations had been preceded by a wave of fan excitement generated by the online release of Neill Blomkamp's concept art, which promised to resurrect and reunite Ripley and Hicks. The enduring desire of the audience to see *Alien³*'s destruction of this family unit undone is indicative of the powerful psychological meaning derived from the archetypes employed in the crafting of its predecessor. It also reveals the audience's archetypal preference to see life triumph over death even in this fictional realm, manifested in this case via the paratextual resurrection of the family unit formed in *Aliens* and, almost three decades after its initial theatrical release, the implicit repudiation of *Alien³* as a noncanonical misadventure. It is also perhaps significant that while several alternative unmade screenplays for *Alien III* exist, it was only Gibson's script—which alone revives Cameron's characters and most clearly continues his vision of the *Alien* universe—that has been selected for paratextual adaptation. Gibson's story, while arguably showing some signs of the diminishing creative momentum that comes with later sequels, does adhere to the Overcoming the Monster archetypal plot more so than the *Alien³* that emerged on screen. Gibson crucially also manages to reinvigorate the creature with new and dreadful threatening capabilities. The failure to do this is a particular weakness of the cinematic *Alien³*. Gibson's story also alludes to the creature's artificial origins,[19] an idea revisited by *Prometheus* over two decades later.

The Frustration Stage

While Weaver had a vision of what *Alien³* should not be, it seemed nobody had a clear vision of what it should be. The auteur role Cameron had vacated was never truly filled, but instead only semi-replaced by Weaver's prohibitions and a mixture of half formed and ultimately derivative concepts that emerged from a nebula of transient writers, directors, producers, and executives. After Gibson's script, at least seven other writers would try and fail to make the cinematic version of *Alien³* work. The project's contradictory impulses and absence of a singular authorial vision meant that the dissonant archetypal fragments inherited from one draft to the next were never successfully blended. Consequently, *Alien³* entered production with its archetypal foundation fatally compromised and languished in a creative doldrum amid increasingly frantic rewrites as its release date loomed ever closer.

The troubled development and production of *Alien³* is well documented, as was its tepid critical and fan reception.[20] Despite subsequently gathering some advocates who defend the film on its aesthetic qualities, few regard *Alien³* to be a film as meaningful as its predecessors, or a triumph of character development and storytelling. Having negated its predecessor but failed to embrace the tragic potential of Ripley's death, the predetermined demise of its hero now also undermined the Overcoming the Monster archetype onto which *Alien³* found itself retreating. Throughout all its various incarnations proposed by the numerous writers and directors associated with the project, *Alien³*'s plot always retreated to a diminished and partial version of the primal Overcoming the Monster archetype. However, even had all its stages been present, this archetype could not be revisited effectively without a new and more menacing threat than the hero had already faced. While several serviceable sci-fi/horror/action scripts were produced, the retreat from Cameron's archetypal advances perhaps lay at the root of producers Giler and Hill's intuition that each proposal lacked something. From its inception the project iterated through a recurring cycle of script development, frustration, and rejection for a series of similar screenplays. Finally, compelled by the commencement of production, a composite screenplay was pieced together that borrowed elements from the previous drafts, but never solved the fundamental, archetypal problem that had caused them to be rejected initially.

The enantiodromic interplay between characters that was a strength of its predecessor was also absent. The characters in the frantically assembled final screenplay for *Alien³* have a generic quality, consisting of largely interchangeable names and dialogue. While the film had an undoubtedly talented cast, none are best remembered for their characters in *Alien³*. This contrasted with *Aliens*, which arguably represents something of a career high for Biehn, Paxton, Goldstein, Henriksen, and perhaps even Weaver herself. As David Thomson observes, none of the characters in *Alien³* are memorable enough to become emotionally invested in their fate:

> Andrews and Clemens are hauled away [. . .] in a matter of moments—and neither is missed . . . neither of them mean enough to Ripley [. . .].
> In *Aliens*, Apone, Hicks, Hudson and Vasquez—even Gorman—mean so much more because they have things to do, cinematic moments that are emblematic of character. In contrast, the woeful rendering of Clemens' past is flabby and redundant.[21]

The final script also contrived to render Ripley invulnerable to the monster, creating a final contradiction between the film's story and the archetypal plot onto which the movie had regressed.

Harmony and Discord

Cameron had brought to the series an ability to introduce new characters, environments, institutions, and technology, and to innovate on the creature's biology and behaviors while maintaining a sense that all these elements felt organically part of the universe established by Ridley Scott's film. This aptitude for harmonious evolution of the universe created by the series' first installment arguably also eluded his successors. Brian Moriarty emphasizes the crucial nature of harmony between all components of a work that seeks to create a fictional universe.

> The principle of harmony applies to almost any work of art [. . .] it's not an intellectual exercise. It's a sensual, intuitive experience. It's something you can feel . . . harmony emerges from a fundamental note of clear intention . . . its presence produces an emotional resonance with its audience.[22]

It is perhaps due to this sense of harmony that it is Cameron's vision that seems to hold more allure for many devotees of the franchise, as the ecosystem of paratexts including comics, novels, action figures, board and video games, and theme park rides that have proliferated in the wake of the second film are more often branded with the title and aesthetics of "*Aliens*," rather than "*Alien*." Perhaps Cameron's most harmonious innovation was the introduction of the Alien Queen—a figure that, once revealed, so fully accords with the audience's previous understanding of the aliens' insectoid appearance and biology that she literally requires no introduction, fitting so seamlessly into the creatures' lifecycle that it is hard to believe her revelation was not always intended by the original writers. Dialogue in the *Aliens* screenplay speculating on the existence of a Queen is elided from the final theatrical cut, because the audience recognizes the Queen for what she is on sight. While a frightening and dreadful revelation, the Queen's nature can be deduced by the audience without explicit exposition. This contrasts with the less harmonious attempt at monstrous innovation with *Alien Resurrection*'s (Jean-Pierre Jeunet, 1997) Newborn, whose birth requires a heavily expositional commentary from Brad Dourif's Gediman in order to make sense to the audience. Lacking this harmonious quality, the Newborn perhaps never quite convinces audiences to suspend their disbelief in the way the Queen does. However disharmonious, the Newborn was at least an innovation on the creature, something that despite numerous attempts *Alien³* never achieved.

Fear and the Unknown

"In the third film, you needed a new kind of alien".

—Eric Red.[23]

A conventional device for sequels involving a monstrous antagonist is to incrementally increase the qualitative or quantitative threat the creature represents in the hope of inducing in an audience, now acclimatized to the original threat, a renewed sense of fear at the monsters' expanded capabilities. Such monstrous incrementation can frequently be perfunctory and unsuccessful in this aim, producing simply more numerous monsters, or creatures with enhanced fearsome attributes such as bigger claws or teeth, gigantification, flight, or an ability to circumvent previous environmental restraints and deterrents. Most writers realized that a new element of threat was required in the third film. However, despite numerous attempts to do so, none could match Cameron's harmonious evolution of the species.

Via the device of genetic experimentation, William Gibson, David Twohy, and Eric Red's screenplays conjured a menagerie of genetically spliced alien hybrids. Vincent Ward's script presents, without explanatory origin, a chameleonic Alien King capable of assuming the appearance of wood, wheat, and other material found on the monastic planetoid of the New Zealander's unrealized world. However, these attempts to reinvest the creature with new capabilities ultimately seemed arbitrary and superficial when compared to Cameron's harmonious Alien Queen. All were eventually abandoned as the final draft took shape in favor of a creature largely identical to that encountered by the crew of the Nostromo. As was the case with the story-line generally, efforts to reinvent the creature led to a pattern of attempted innovation, frustration, and subsequent retreat to the familiar formulas of the past. This difficulty was perhaps because Cameron had, with the introduction of the Queen, revealed a complete biological circle. The Queen and her warrior offspring, mimicking the lifecycles of known insect species, leave little room for further harmonious and plausible incrementation. Lacking the same resonance with real-world insect species, the proposed hybrid creatures of Alien³ all seem rather contrived. In the absence of an innovative and escalated menacing element from the creature, Alien³ achieved an unhappy state of dramatic irony. The audience began, and remained throughout, with perfect knowledge and a complete familiarity with the nature of the threat the creature represented and the means by which it could be overcome. The film's characters, lacking this knowledge, were condemned to reiterate the fatal and familiar mistakes of their franchise predecessors, wandering alone into darkened corridors to be duly dispatched by the beast. As Thomson concluded, "These killings are not just monotonous now, they risk being pointless or merely serial."[24]

The father of cosmic horror, H. P. Lovecraft, had observed that "the oldest and strongest kind of fear is fear of the unknown."[25] While both Weaver and Fincher expressed a desire to return to the spirit of the Alien, a key element of the original film's ability to frighten and fascinate was the unknown nature of the barely glimpsed creature. An aura of mystery was created and sustained by the creature's metamorphic character, being different in form for each of its initial attacks. Its abilities, motives, and vulnerabilities also remained opaque throughout the first film. By the time of Alien³'s development, very little remained unknown about the Xenomorph due not only to Cameron's sequel but also to a flourishing ecosystem of paratexts. The creature, lacking any significant innovation in its capabilities, was now perhaps simply too familiar to be frightening. In accordance with Lovecraft's observation, an element of mystery, of the unknown, would appear to be a vital attribute of a monstrous antagonist intended to provoke deep unease in an audience. Mathias Clasen underlines the potent ability of the unknown to stimulate a deeper sense of fear and unease by citing a famous thought experiment by C. S. Lewis:

> Suppose you were told there was a tiger in the next room: you would know that you were in danger and would probably feel fear. But if you were told "There is a ghost in the next room," and believed it, you would feel, indeed, what is often called fear, but of a different kind. It would not be based on the knowledge of danger, for no one is primarily afraid of what a ghost may do to him; but of the mere fact that it is a ghost. It is "uncanny" rather than dangerous, and the special kind of fear it excites may be called Dread.[26]

While an effective upping of the ante in Cameron's film, the revelation of the Queen demystifies the aliens, revealing them to be essentially giant termites. Consequently, by *Alien³*, the Xenomorph has become something akin to an extraterrestrial tiger, capable of inspiring the fear associated with any large predatory animal, but not the dread of a monster with unknown motives and capabilities.

Conclusion: Image and Substance

Compelled to build on a compromised archetypal foundation, *Alien³* proceeded to frustrate a series of writers and directors who attempted to reconcile its discordant ideas and ultimately irreconcilable contradictions. The production itself became something monstrous, consuming resources and talent ever more voraciously. William Gibson, Renny Harlin, Eric Red, David Twohy, Vincent Ward, John Fasano, Larry Ferguson, and Rex Picket all came and went before the project passed into the hands of debutant director David Fincher, who swiftly realized the challenge he faced. "We started shooting with only forty pages and the script changed so much and so fast that we were receiving stuff off the fax machine and shooting it the next day. It was just insane."[27] With increasing studio concern regarding overruns in budget and shooting, Jon Landau was installed as line producer and began to cut un-shot scenes from the schedule: "After watching David Fincher scramble for two weeks in a futile effort to shoot the last few scenes and save his film, Landau finally closed the production down."[28] Scorched by this baptism of fire on his first feature, Fincher would later state of *Alien³*, "No one hated it more than me; to this day, no one hates it more than me."[29]

In an anecdote that would be oft repeated, when asked by Weaver during a production meeting how he saw the character of Ripley in the soon-to-be third episode, Fincher replied "bald?"[30] While often recounted as a state-ment of bold and unconventional originality from the young director, it is also notable how the response revealed a characterization of striking imagery but little psychological substance. Fincher arguably came so late to the pro-duction that imagery was the only domain he had to express his talent, the misshapen archetypal plot foundations having already been poured and now immutably set prior to his arrival.

Thus, *Alien³* became an artefact of inspired imagery but uninspired sub-stance. Its predecessors had strongly resonated with their audiences be-cause of their archetypal qualities in addition to their visual flair. Both *Alien* and *Aliens* are fertile texts for analysis using Jungian amplification, which is essentially the identification of components of a text with mythic, histor-ical, and cultural parallels. The Nostromo can be thought of as a modern Labyrinth and the lurking alien a reiteration of the Minotaur. Both monsters share a similar interspecies genesis, born of an unnatural union between the human and inhuman. Likewise, The Weyland-Yutani Corporation fulfills the role of King Minos, whose greed and tyranny have brought the lethal crea-ture into existence, that once born "walketh about seeking whom it may de-vour."[31] In *Aliens*, Ripley initially strikes a Cassandra-like figure, cursed to utter true prophecies which are never believed. Despite the validity of her premonitions of danger, her words are unheard and unheeded, and she is unable to avert the disaster she perceives is approaching. Similarly, Burke's access to secret knowledge, in addition to the tendency to mix lies with truth and present as an ally to Ripley while in fact plotting the destruction of all for his own selfish ends, make him the archetypal Trickster of the ensemble. Ariadne's gift to prospective lover Theseus of a sword and guiding spool of thread that allows him to navigate the Labyrinth and defeat the Minotaur is paralleled with Hicks' gift of a locator and his training of Ripley in the use of the pulse rifle, which later allows her to complete a similar escape.

Few mythological parallels are revealed by a similar analysis of *Alien³*. Rather than drawing its inspiration from the deep wells of archetypal symbolism as its predecessors had, *Alien³* became possessed by a spirit of emulation rather than inspiration. In seeking to recapture the spirit of its origin, *Alien³* had plotted a hazardous course to an unreachable goal and ultimately encountered only a series of creative dead ends within an unescapable Labyrinth of its own construction.

Notes

1. Christopher Booker, *The Seven Basic Plots: Why We Tell Stories* (London: Continuum, 2004), 21–29.
2. Ibid., 48.
3. Ibid.
4. Ibid.
5. This Jungian influence on Hollywood is exemplified by the impact of titles such as Christopher Vogler's *The Writer's Journey: Mythic Structure for Writers* (Studio City: Michael Wiese Productions, 2007) and Joseph Campbell's *The Hero with a Thousand Faces* (Princeton: Princeton University Press, 1968)
6. David Hughes, *Alien³ Movie Special Issue 2* (London: Dark Horse International, 1992), 40.
7. John L. Flynn, *Dissecting Aliens, Terror In Space,* (London: Boxtree, 1995), 87.
8. Booker, *The Seven Basic Plots*, 154.
9. Ibid., 156
10. Ibid., 173.
11. Ibid., 177.
12. Flynn, *Dissecting Aliens*, 102.
13. Carl G. Jung, *Collected Works of C.G. Jung, Volume 6 Psychological Types* (Princeton, NJ: Princeton University Press, 1976), 591.
14. Carl G. Jung, *Collected Works of C.G. Jung, Volume 6 Psychological Types* (Princeton, NJ: Princeton University Press, 1976), 593.
15. Alex Cox, "Moviedrome Introduction to Escape from New York," http://moviedro mer.tumblr.com/post/79638254457/escape-from-new-york-1981 (accessed 5 May 2020).
16. Flynn, *Dissecting Aliens*, 80.
17. David Hughes, *Aliens: Volume 2 Number 8* (London: Dark Horse International, 1992), 23.
18. Karen Krizanovich, Twitter Direct Message conversation with author, April 15, 2020.
19. In Gibson's Script the alien's genetical material is cultivated by two rival laboratories. In the Biolab of the Rodina space station Colonel-Doctor Suslov comments on the alien's DNA, "The readiness with which it lends itself to genetic manipulation . . . The speed with which its cells multiply . . . As though the gene-structure has been designed for ease of manipulation. And this apparently universal compatibility with other plasms...Perhaps it is the fruit of some ancient experiment . . . A living artifact, the product of genetic engineering . . . A weapon. Perhaps we are looking at the end result

of yet another arms race." This idea of the xenomorphs as the creation of a more so-phisticated alien intelligence is essentially the premise of Prometheus's plot. See https://www.avpgalaxy.net/files/scripts/alien-3-william-gibson-1987.pdf   (accessed November 14, 2020)

20. See Flynn, *Dissecting Aliens*.

21. David Thomson, *The Alien Quartet* (London: Bloomsbury, 2000), 150–151.

22. Brian Moriarty, "Listen!: The Potential of Shared Hallucinations," http://ludix.com/moriarty/listen.html (accessed May 5, 2020).

23. Flynn, *Dissecting Aliens*, 86.

24. Thomson, *The Alien Quartet*, 147.

25. Mathias Clasen, *Why Horror Seduces* (Oxford: Oxford University Press, 2017), 32.

26. Ibid., 47.

27. David Hughes, *Alien³ Movie Special Issue 1*, 41.

28. Flynn, *Dissecting Aliens*, 102.

29. Mark Salisbury, *Guardian Interviews at the BFI David Fincher*, available at https://www.theguardian.com/film/2009/feb/03/david-fincher-interview-transcript (Accessed December 9, 2018).

30. Flynn, *Dissecting Aliens*, 95.

31. Booker, *The Seven Basic Plots*, 32.

6

"Building Better Worlds"

The Rise of *Alien*'s Online Marketing Campaigns

Kim Walden

As transmedia franchising has become increasingly accomplished over the last twenty years, with the development of reboots, sequels, prequels, legacyquels, and shared cinematic universes, film marketing costs have risen steeply in the fiercely competitive marketplace of screen entertainment.[1] One of the consequences of this is that film marketing practices have had to devise correspondingly creative approaches to promotion online and through social media. This chapter considers the evolution of film marketing as blockbuster franchises transform into transmedia franchises iterating across media platforms. Through an examination of the award-winning campaign for *Prometheus* (Ridley Scott, 2012) and then *Alien: Covenant* (Ridley Scott, 2017), the chapter will examine the forms transmedia film marketing campaigns take and why, what functions they fulfil, and how these campaigns exemplify industry marketing practices during this period. In the light of this consideration, the chapter concludes that transmedia marketing is often as entertaining as the films it promotes and plays an increasingly significant role in the life of a franchise.

A New Marketing Platform—The Website

The marketing campaigns for the first three *Alien* films followed a largely conventional format for a blockbuster movie featuring posters, trailers, teasers, TV spots, interviews, and documentaries. There were also games, tie-in products, and a "live cinema" experience at London's Trocadero in Trafalgar

Kim Walden, *"Building Better Worlds"* In: *Alien Legacies*. Edited by: Nathan Abrams and Gregory Frame, Oxford University Press. © Oxford University Press 2023. DOI: 10.1093/oso/9780197556023.003.0006

Square called *Alien War*,[2] where a maze of low-ceilinged underground rooms were fitted out with metal mesh panels to simulate the spacecraft's gridded ceilings and walkways, making it a perfect venue for an alien attack.[3] But spin-offs aside, *Alien Resurrection* (Jean-Pierre Jeunet, 1997) was the first film in the series to have a bespoke marketing website.

Alienresurrection.com was created by Media Revolution, whose founder Jason Yim would go on to develop the multi award-winning site for Neill Blomkamp's *District 9* (2009). Although *Alienresurrection.com* has long since been taken down, it is still possible to travel back in time to see the site using the *Internet Archive*'s aptly named *Wayback Machine* search engine. On entering, visitors are advised the site can be viewed with or without free downloadable software, in recognition of the different operating systems and limited bandwidth at the time. Set against the familiar black outer space background, the site has two entry points: *Alien* Experience and *Alien* Digizine. However, while the former is no longer viewable, Digizine is, promising an "in-depth look" at the making of the film with blurry thumbnail "slides," accompanied by their file byte size for downloads. The "making of" sections are framed in a register that is part electronic press kit (EPK), part film school, and these parallel modes of address indicate the dual purpose of early "shop window" websites aimed at both the press and public audiences.

Despite its promise, the *Internet Archive* has not archived the *Alien: Resurrection* site in its entirety as many of its assets are located elsewhere, have been moved or deleted, and are no longer available as their hyperlinks are broken. However, what is still available are a series of interviews with the film's cast and crew that are surprisingly extensive. Like websites for comparable films such as *Event Horizon* (Paul Anderson, 1997), and *The Lost World: Jurassic Park* (Steven Spielberg, 1997), the *Alien: Resurrection* site is largely text-based with few graphics.[4] But what is notable about this early marketing site is its close proximity to the film's production. Cast members read lines that are incorporated into the site's game experience,[5] and the actors are interviewed for the website which is updated bi-weekly to keep the content fresh and dynamic.[6] Yim recounts how the site attracted 2 million page views per day at its peak.[7] So, while early online marketing was constrained by text-based operating systems and limited bandwidth, and confused in its mode of address, what was referred to at the time as a film's "web presence" did demonstrate the potential to become a rich and dynamic locus for franchise marketing.

Transmedia Marketing

Since *Alien: Resurrection*, websites have become a familiar feature of film marketing campaigns in which conventions have crystallized, and formats standardized. Typically, today "official" sites host the film's trailer(s), plot summary, behind-the-scenes features, a photo gallery, clips and links to the campaign's social media. However, the specific tendency that is of interest to this chapter is film websites that function beyond promotion and contribute to the experience—that is to say, sites designed not just to promote by *extracting* content from the film, as is conventional with trailers,[8] but marketing that *contributes* content to the film's storyworld. When film websites contribute narrative content, they can be regarded as transmedia marketing. Today, franchise transmediation takes a myriad of different forms including: Marvel Cinematic Universe's in-movie TV WHIH.

Christine Everhart (Leslie Bibb) covering events that take place in the films and TV series; *The Hunger Games*' in-movie world that takes the shape of an online fashion magazine called *Capitol Couture* on Tumblr, featuring fashion spreads and profiles about in-movie characters and events;[9] and the Harry Potter franchise's *Pottermore*, now *Wizardingworld*, retracing Harry's book-based adventures and the backstories of minor characters written by the author, J. K. Rowling.[10]

One intriguing convention to emerge in transmedia marketing is the rendering of the film's storyworld in the shape of a fictional corporate website. This can be seen in many of the science fiction franchise campaigns such as Cyberdyne Systems in *The Terminator* films (James Cameron, Jonathan Mostow, McG, Alan Taylor, Tim Miller, 1984–2019), Omni Consumer Products in *Robocop* (Paul Verhoeven, Irvin Kershner, Fred Dekker, José Padilha, 1987–2014), International Genetic Technologies (InGen) in the *Jurassic Park* series (Steven Spielberg, Joe Johnston, Colin Trevorrow, J. A. Bayona, Colin Trevorrow 1993–2022); Resources Development Administration in *Avatar* (James Cameron, 2009), Encom International in *Tron: Legacy* (Joseph Kosinski, 2010), Tagruato and Slusho in *Cloverfield* (Matt Reeves, Dan Trachtenberg, Julius Onah, 2008–2018), MNU (Multi National United) in *District 9* (2009), and Weyland Industries in *Prometheus* (2012). Evil fictional corporates have often featured in science fiction, as can be seen in films that predate the web such as the Soylent Corporation in *Soylent Green* (Richard Fleischer, 1973) and the Tyrell Corporation in Ridley Scott's *Blade Runner* (1982). But the proliferation of fictional corporations in films at this time could be reflective of a growing real world wariness at the rise of multinational corporations during the Reagan administration in the 1980s with its ethos of free-market fundamentalism and deregulation.[11]

In *Convergence Culture: When Old and New Media Collide* (2006), Henry Jenkins explains that "more and more, storytelling has become the art of world building."[12] He goes on to suggest that world building has become increasingly important to the corporatized film industry for the simple reason that this strategy embodies commercial logic, as film franchises have the potential to spawn spin-offs, licensed goods, and other merchandise. In his later writings, he goes on to say that, as a consequence of this commercial logic, media producers have moved away from singular narratives following classical linear paths from beginning to end, in favor of fictional worlds that have the capacity to host a range of stories, games, and other forms of engagement.[13] So, today transmedia world building has become "one of the cornerstones of popular entertainment."[14]

It has been argued by Mark J. P. Wolf that imaginary worlds do not just provide a background to plot but can be compelling media artefacts in their own right.[15] Wolf takes his cue from J. R. R. Tolkien's theory of world making where he drew a distinction between the world in which we live, which he termed the "primary world," and imaginary worlds that he called "secondary worlds."[16] Wolf extends the concept by suggesting that an imaginary world can take the form of a place, in the geographical sense of the word, or a space, in the experiential sense of the word, like the in-fiction corporate websites.[17] But for him, what makes imaginary worlds particularly rich is that:

> imaginary worlds can comment on the Primary world through their differences, they can embody other ideas and philosophies, and convey meaning in a variety of ways beyond the traditional ways found in stories set in the Primary world.[18]

Weylandindustries.com—"Building Better Worlds"

Director Ridley Scott built his career on the creation of compelling micro-worlds for commercials such as the Hovis "Boy on the bike" advertisement (1973), and the Orwellian-style "1984" Apple Macintosh computer advertisement. With hindsight, these micro-worlds now seem to be precursors of the fictional world conceived for *Prometheus*. Designed by Ignition Interactive and sporting the slogan, "Building Better Worlds," *Weylandindustries. com* provides an entrance to the film's fictional world. The landing page boasts Weyland Industries is "the largest company on the planet" and it is represented as a "fully-realized company website."[19] The site is divided into three areas: Products, The Company, and Project Prometheus. But it extends far deeper as each area contains further sub-sections filled with participatory activities such as an Employer ID card creator and the Microsoft HTML 5-driven Training Centre where fans can discover whether they have what it takes to join the Prometheus mission, by undertaking a series of cognitive and physical "tests." There is also a "Discover New Worlds" feature enabling viewers to travel through space exploring Weyland's planetary colonies. But critically, the site invites visitors to register as "investors" in the company's project and thereby establishes a connection to the visitor's email box for future marketing communications (see Figure 6.1).[20]

A vast reservoir of mise-en-scène is detailed in the "Investor Information" section, which takes the form of an annual company report with a battery of tables, graphs, bar charts, pie charts, and statistics, mimicking its primary-world counterparts. The company's report is littered with acronyms, and badged with corporate logos and copyright statements to create what has been described as "a veneer of corporate logics and aesthetic officialdom."[21] Indeed, the site's dimensions exceed the computer screen and require

Figure 6.1 "Building Better Worlds" on weylandindustries.com.

scrolling to explore it in its entirety, adding to the sense of the scale of the fictional world.

Wolf suggests that one of the key features of world building is "timelines and chronologies [that] connect events together temporally, unifying them into a history."[22] In *Weylandindustries.com* the fictional world's temporal infrastructure is underpinned by a timeline mapping a period of eighty years from the birth of the company's Chief Executive Officer Sir Peter Weyland in 1990 to 2073 when the film begins, providing the back story to events that are taken up in the film. In effect, the timeline is a company biography: from the granting of a certificate of incorporation (the equivalent of a corporate birth) through key points in the "life" of the company including venture capital investments, buyouts, patent registrations, prototype manufacture, and even product recall notices. These elements are all described in prodigious detail that would far exceed the duration of the average site visit, which according to recent research is currently around just three minutes.[23]

The website provides a framework chronology for the film series too. As *Prometheus* is a prequel, chronologically Weyland Industries predates the Weyland-Utani company featured in previous *Alien* films. The website's timeline serves to create a sense of continuity across the film series by looking forward to the forthcoming release of *Prometheus*, as well as referring back in time to previous films. At one point, the timeline previews the "med pod"—an automated surgical station in which Dr. Elizabeth Shaw (Noomi Rapace) will perform an abortion on herself in *Prometheus*. Elsewhere on the timeline, reference is made to the invention of "hypersleep" and the Yutani corporation's mining activities that featured in previous *Alien* films. Features like these illustrate the narrative "work" undertaken by the *Weylandindustries.com* site to integrate the latest film into the *Alien* world.

There are other points on the timeline referring to tropes like "androids" and "terraforming" that are familiar to not only the *Alien* universe but the science fiction genre too. As Wolf argues, imaginary worlds may operate transmedially across the genre, as well as platforms, and, by so doing, the Weyland industries site incorporates the narrative threads from the different films, and effectively braids them together to create the "narrative fabric" of the *Alien* world.[24] This function is particularly apposite to a franchise like *Alien* where the order of the film productions does not correlate with the chronology of the narrative. For while *Prometheus* may be the latest film in the series, narratively speaking, it is a prequel and so must be consistent with the narrative future of the *Alien* canon.

As indicated earlier, *Weylandindustries.com* is not unique. Fictional corporations have become a widely used format for film marketing websites because, as Fox's Digital Creative Director Jeff Kelly explained, "you need to plant a flag in the ground" and in-movie corporate world websites fulfil this function.[25] From a commercial perspective the most obvious reason for the proliferation of these elaborate fictional world-corporation sites is that to compete in an increasingly crowded entertainment market, audiences cannot be taken for granted. Franchise films must win audience attention. This bears out Jonathan Hardy's observation that

> there is a correlation between levels of investment in promotions and popularity, measured by consumer spending, so that the greatest promotional effort is expended on event films and major brand franchises.[26]

The more modest marketing budgets of independent films produce scaled-down versions of these corporate worlds that may take the form of in-movie corporate advertisements located on *YouTube* such as the Mirando Corporation for *Okja* (Bong Joon-ho, 2017) or Lunar Industries for *Moon* (Duncan Jones, 2009).

The (Evil) Corporation Topos

Another way to account for why fictional corporate websites are so prevalent in film marketing is to regard them as topoi. Topoi are commonplace or formulaic themes often deployed for instrumental reasons in the marketing of film and other media.[27] Media archaeologist Errki Huhtamo explains how topoi are commandeered for marketing to provide advertisers with "tried and tested formulas" that can be used to introduce new products in a short space of time, embedding them within ways of thinking customers already know (whether they are aware of them or not).[28] However, Huhtamo cautions that while topoi may at first glance seem to be an innocuous cliché, it is their banality we need to be alert to, as it belies their discursive significance.[29]

Various theories have been put forward to explain why the fictional corporation has become such a central idea in twentieth-century culture. But with the demise and demonization of socialism and communism in the USSR, eastern Europe, and People's Republic of China, one of the most cogent reasons is that there are no other alternatives.[30] In short, capitalism is the way the world is.[31] Furthermore, many of these fictional corporations are depicted as inherently malign in their intent, as can be seen in Weyland Industries' ruthless disregard for its employees and its infamous executive order to preserve the alien creature at all costs but regard the ship's crew as expendable. Dan Hassler-Forest suggests that a storyworld's "spatiotemporal organization" is critical to understanding the ideological implications of the narrative that takes place within its purview.[32] So, while on the one hand *Weylandindustries.com* offers opportunities to explore the excitements of the corporate world, on the other the company is depicted as an evil and rapacious entity, and it is the tension between the two that makes the *Alien* world so enthralling.

Media Conventions

Transmedia marketing does not just encompass world building but invites viewer participation in the world of the film. Annual media conventions, known as "cons," are many things—trade show, collector's market, arts festival, and press junket—all rolled into one.[33] But the main reason cons are used by studios to launch film marketing campaigns is because they take place "at the intersection of fandom and media industries."[34] In her book on cons, Erin Hana draws on economist B. Joseph Pine II and business strategist James H. Gilmore's concept of the "experience economy" to comprehend the role of these events in marketing film. Pine and Gilmore propose that economic value does not just reside in goods and services but can be generated through "the staging of experiences,"[35] and these "experiences" are at their most fascinating when they seek, in Wolf's term, to "interlace" the primary and secondary worlds.[36]

At the 2011 WonderCon in Anaheim, California, Weyland Industries business cards were distributed to attendees featuring the company's contact details.[37] Dialing the number on the card met with a "caller busy" message, but, by return, a text was received containing a link to an "unboxing" film of Weyland's latest product—the David 8 android (Michael Fassbender)—thereby providing a film-related reward for the caller's interest in the forthcoming film.[38] In recent years "unboxing videos" have found considerable popularity online, in which a recording is made of the unwrapping of a new product from its packaging and uploading it to *YouTube*.[39] Hana explains how in the context of cons, audience experiences are created through the "construction of exclusivity and its subsequent undoing," and clearly this is what is happening here.[40] Attendees at the *Prometheus* event were treated to an exclusive first screening of the full length trailer and a live panel presentation by director Ridley Scott, writer Damon Lindelof, and cast members. While these experiences are designed to be exclusive to convention attendees, as can be seen in the repeated preface to all announcements "Only at WonderCon . . . ," the "live" event is streamed online, and attendees are encouraged to share their experiences as widely as possible on social media.[41]

The cultivation of a sense of exclusivity to incentivize what Jenkins calls the "spreadability" of word about a forthcoming film release through social media does, at first glance, seem to be something of a contradiction. But from a marketing point of view, the real value of the experience lies beyond the convention center. As a result, Hana argues that these events reframe fans as "part and parcel of the promotional paratext," and this is most clearly evident in the way hashtags are ritualistically signposted at the start of each event.[42] Cons recruit fans to act as volunteer campaigners to share, like, tag, and generally produce "buzz" online in the service of film marketing and promotion.[43] What this analysis indicates is that, by implication, fandom has come to encompass audiences who actively seek out and share promotional content, as well as consuming media and its merchandise.[44]

From Participation to Personalization

The mainstreaming of fandom in the service of marketing is further demonstrated in a strategy used in the *Alien: Covenant* campaign to communicate with audiences, which indicates a shift from participatory engagement to personalization. As a web destination, *Weylandindustries.com* hosted activities enabling fan participation. However, for *Alien: Covenant*, a Twitter campaign rewards retweets about the film with real-time personalized (and, critically, sharable) content, whereby the user's name is incorporated into trailers and crew badges in the week before the film's theatrical release.[45] The UK's Channel 4 TV broadcaster debuts a VOD (video on demand) that addresses viewers directly.[46] At the end of an *Alien* TV spot, an announcer calls out to the viewer, literally grabbing their attention by calling out their name.[47] This shift from addressing viewers, in general terms, as "investors" or "crew members" on the Weyland site, to named individual fans, reflects the move to a customizable, consumer-centered online experience, and demonstrates how highly fans are valued for their social media activity. In the context of such campaigns, it has been observed that participatory fan practices have become "difficult to distinguish from other forms of consumerism."[48]

As the campaign rolled out, it was not just fans who were targeted. The professional network *LinkedIn* was incorporated into the campaign to target "key influencers," that is to say, individuals who influence the opinions of others on the web.[49] By harvesting information from *LinkedIn* user profiles, personalized emails were sent to influencers inviting them to apply for positions in the Prometheus Project.[50] Harnessing the secondary fictional world to the primary world networks paid off in promotional terms, as journalists, like the writer for the business magazine site *Forbes.com*, allowed themselves to be co-opted into the film's promotional campaign when they wrote about their experiences.[51]

Experiential Marketing

"Bringing a fictional text to life" so that audiences can immerse themselves in the film's world is the principal aim of what has become known as "experiential marketing," closely followed by the secondary aim of presenting something to those audiences that they will want to share on social media as they are experiencing it.[52] To this end, one of the most prominent current trends is Virtual Reality (VR) that typically takes the form of a 360-degree computer-generated simulation of a real or imaginary environment, which enables a person, wearing either a special electronic helmet or sensor-equipped gloves, to interact in a seemingly real and physical way, and shows the effects of the interaction real time.[53] VR has become a familiar feature of franchise marketing campaigns from the *Apatosaurus VR experience* for *Jurassic World* (2015) to the *Jakku Spy VR experience* promoting *Star Wars: The Force Awakens* (J. J. Abrams, 2015). What these emergent technologies bring to campaigns is summed up on the *Star Wars* website, "Ever since 1977, we've only watched *Star Wars*, read *Star Wars*, or played *Star Wars*. Now we can step inside it."[54]

For *Alien: Covenant*'s marketing campaign, Fox studio collaborated with Scott's production company, RSA films, and the tech companies, Technicolor, AMD, and Dell, to develop a VR experience.[55] Titled *In Utero*, it tells its story

Figure 6.2 The *In Utero* VR experience tells its story from the perspective of the new *Alien* neomorph—from inception in its human host's bloodstream to the bloodbath of its "birth." © 20th Century Studios, UK.

from the perspective of the new *Alien* neomorph—from its inception in its human host's bloodstream to the bloodbath of its "birth" bursting out of its human host's torso (see Figure 6.2). Narratively speaking, the VR experience functions as what Wolf describes as a *paraquel*, in which the events that take place in the film's story are regarded from different points of view in the VR experience, but the key to the attraction is that it reprises the franchise's most iconic trope—the birth of the alien.[56]

While VR experiences claim to extend the film's story, in practice what they currently do most effectively is create novel spectacles providing a fore-taste of the forthcoming film. VR consists of static long shots, with little ed-iting and minimal movement, although the soundscape is important for navigation as it signals the shifting perspective as the user moves their head. However, because VR is an emerging technology, it is expensive, and like many of its counterparts, *In Utero* is just two minutes long. But part of what makes these experiential marketing activations feel so closely integrated with the film is their proximity to it. For *In Utero*, producers were able to use the same assets as the film, in terms of mise-en-scène, cast, and even the same digital doubles,[57] illustrating how, when film marketing is developed in close collaboration with the film, it can create an entertaining complementary experience.

"Characters Are the New Movie Stars"

One of the core ingredients of a successful film franchise is a familiar set of characters pitched into different scenarios, to the extent that an *LA Times* article declared that "characters are the new movie stars."[58] Rebooting franchises for new audiences can entail the reprise of older "legacy" characters, alongside the introduction of new characters to promote cross-generation appeal. In *Tron: Legacy* (2010), Jeff Bridges reprises the Kevin Flynn character, thirty years after the original *Tron* (1982), but Flynn's son, Sam (Garrett Hedlund), takes up the role of action hero.[59] So, while stars are often closely identified with franchise characters, the retention of the core characters is one of the main commercial obligations of the franchise. In the *Alien* films, action heroine Ellen Ripley (Sigourney Weaver) is a constant feature in the first four films, but when her role comes to an end, the feisty action heroine character-type persists with Elizabeth Shaw (Noomi Rapace) in *Prometheus* and Janet Daniels (Katherine Waterston) in *Alien: Covenant*.

The *Prometheus* marketing campaign introduced a roster of new characters through a series of short films. Sir Peter Weyland introduces himself in a fictional TED talk set in the year 2023 launched in the primary world at the TED2012 event complete with as-if-real speakers' "biographical" notes on the TED site (see Figure 6.3).[60] The *David 8* android is introduced in a product commercial outlining Weyland Industries' goal to "create artificial intelligence almost indistinguishable from mankind itself." The third

Figure 6.3 Sir Peter Weyland (Guy Pearce) opens his TED talk in 2023, "Allow me to introduce myself: my name is Peter Weyland. And if you'll indulge me, I'd like to *change* the world." *Prometheus* Viral © Twentieth Century Fox, 2019.

introductory film, titled *Quite Eye*, is Dr. Elizabeth Shaw in a video-call style film to Weyland Industries where she makes her pitch to join the Prometheus mission. The rationale in operation here is that each of these short films directed by Ridley Scott's son, Luke, introduces new characters to the franchise's fictional world, so that by the film's theatrical release, audiences can be familiar with these new characters, which, in screenwriting, is conventionally regarded as one of the first tasks of the film itself.[61]

The success of this strategy was confirmed by its subsequent application to *Alien: Covenant*, where Luke Scott created a second in-world advertisement, *Meet Walter* (also played by Michael Fassbender), about how the next-generation synthetics were manufactured by 3D printing their exoskeletons. *The Last Supper*, co-directed by Ridley and Luke Scott, was used to introduce the Covenant's crew, and nodded back to the dinner scene in the original *Alien* film. This short film was flanked by epistolary-style webcam transmissions home by the Covenant's crew to introduce each of the characters. The films were of varying length depending on the character's significance to the story and began the process of establishing their personalities. In an interview, Luke Scott explains that he regards contemporary film trailers as problematic because of their tendency to extract the best scenes from the film and preview these highlights so that by the time audiences see a film, there are no surprises left.[62] He regards the short films made for the *Alien* series as "pieces of a puzzle" and claims this is a new approach to trailers.[63]

Alienuniverse.com

The concept of the "universe" has become another central feature of franchise marketing in recent years, but it is not a new one. It originates in the Marvel comic universe created by Jack Kirby, Stan Lee, and others in the early 1960s, where different characters and events inhabit the same fictional world.[64] The concept gathered momentum with the launch of the *Marvel Cinematic Universe* (MCU) in 2008 that has gone on to become the most powerful franchise in contemporary Hollywood. The success of this model has seen film franchises eager to repeat this commercial success establish their own web-based worlds and universes, like *Starwars.com*, *Jurassicworld.com*, and *Wizardingworld.com*, to provide a locus for online marketing. When the *Alien* franchise graduated from *Weylandindustries.com* to *Alienuniverse.com*, the connotation was clearly one of commercial expansion.

As the franchise's web base for the *Alien: Covenant* campaign, *Alienuniverse.com* is the official *Alien* movies fan hub and invites visitors to "join the crew" and participate in special missions and contests, and to receive news updates about *Alien*-related events, merchandise, and promotions, including "making of" features that previously would have featured as extras on DVD or Blu-ray formats. The "Universe" site consists of a series of subsections—"Mainframe," "Transmissions" (news), "Alien Day" (April 26), "Films," "Communications," "Gear," and "Join." But, of particular interest to this chapter is the Mainframe section, which accommodates the transmedia narrative elements of the film's marketing, expanding the world of *Alien* firstly in the form of a digital animation series, and secondly, the fortieth-anniversary shorts.

The animation series is based not on the films, but the game, *Alien: Isolation* (2014, Creative Assembly/Feral Interactive), and takes place fifteen years after the events of the first *Alien* (1979). It tells its story from the perspective of Ripley's daughter, Amanda (Andrea Deck), but has a game-framed objective to find the Nostromo's flight recorder and the truth behind her mother's disappearance. In Wolf's world making terms, the animation series is located in the same fictional world, building on the original film's story as a sequel, and claiming fidelity with close and frequent reference to *Alien*'s diegesis.[65]

Fan Film Competitions

The fortieth-anniversary shorts were the outcome of a competition set up by Tongal in association with 20th Century Fox, inviting filmmakers to create *Alien*-inspired films to mark the film's anniversary. The brief was to create a wholly original story, five to nine minutes in length, with completely new characters but drawing on features that made the franchise so successful. In the event there were more than five hundred submissions. The six winners were each provided with a budget to produce a film and promotional materials. Studio ownership and management of its intellectual property were asserted at every stage of the process. The short films were titled in keeping with other elements of the franchise as *Alien: Containment* (Chris Reading, 2019), *Alien: Specimen* (Kelsey Taylor, 2019), *Alien: Night Shift* (Aidan Brezonick, 2019), *Alien: Ore* (The Spear Sisters, 2019), *Alien: Harvest* (Benjamin Howdeshell, 2019), and *Alien: Alone* (Noah Miller, 2019).

These shorts were then incorporated into *Covenant*'s marketing campaign, screened at both con events and online. Badged with 20th Century Fox and Tongal logos, the films clearly illustrate how studios draw on fan creativity to refresh the franchise.

Studio-run competitions have become a familiar feature of franchise marketing, such as the annual *Star Wars* Fan Film competition that began back in 2002, and Paramount Pictures' contest inviting participants to make their own videos in response to the question "Where were you when the monster hit?" for J. J. Abrams', *Cloverfield*.[66] As a result, fan "collaborations" with studios have been the subject of much critical commentary in recent years where these activities have been framed as co-creation,[67] participation, and fan communities,[68] but also criticized as unpaid labor[69] and even "industrial occupation."[70]

From a marketing perspective, what becomes evident on viewing the fortieth-anniversary shorts is that what makes these films competition winners is that they have effectively distilled the core elements of the *Alien* franchise. The Weyland logo is ubiquitous in signage on buildings and employee uniforms. Similarly, the industrial environment of colony factory greenhouses, mines, or stores is a recurrent factor, often lit by yellow flashing warning lights. Common to all is the blue-collar workplace culture preoccupied with shifts, rotations, bonuses, and time clocks, and the spacecraft depicted not as gleaming visions of the future like the USS Enterprise in *Star Trek* but as industrial workhorses—frigates, haulers, harvesters, and couriers ploughing back and forth across space. Kenneth Sloan's chapter in this anthology agrees that the franchise's core elements constitute a "powerful aesthetic," but he characterizes its repeated consumption in the film series as an experience of ever-diminishing returns.[71] By contrast, however, in *Film Remakes and Franchises*, Daniel Herbert argues that while recycling of a collection of tropes is "incredibly unoriginal," this is precisely the point.[72] To comprehend why *Alien* remains so popular, he suggests that a preoccupation with originality must be set aside because the secret of franchise's popularity lies in its films' intertextuality with each other.[73]

Online, fans hypothesize about the purpose of the anniversary shorts, possibly operating as talent incubators, a mechanism for story prospecting, or the filmic equivalents of paint-tester pots. But I would suggest that here we see filmmakers invited to engage not with the specific story of *Alien*, but with what has become the essential schema of its transmedia world. In their consideration of transmedial design in relation to computer games, Lisbeth

Krastrup and Susana Tosca describe how successful stories can be understood as

> *abstract content systems* from which a repertoire of fictional stories and
> characters can be actualized or derived across a variety of media forms.
> What characterizes a transmedia world is that the audience and the
> designers share a mental image of the "worldness"—a number of distin-
> guishing features of its universe.[74]

Likewise, the fan filmmakers draw upon the fictional world tropes of the
Alien films. As *Alien* moved from being a blockbuster film series to the
transmedia franchise it is today, its generation and regeneration draw on this
abstract content system, in the process increasingly blurring distinctions between marketing and what was formally known as "content."

In the *Alien* franchise, the "nested stories" that together make up the
fictional world include the films, the paratextual scenarios, the Weyland
Industries website world, the film franchise, the science fiction genre, and
finally the real "primary" world. The diagram in Figure 6.4 shows how these

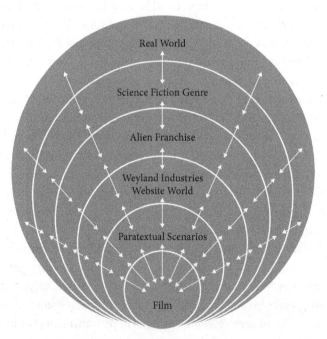

Real World

Science Fiction Genre

Alien Franchise

Weyland Industries
Website World

Paratextual Scenarios

Film

Figure 6.4 The nested narratives of a transmedia film franchise.

narratives can be understood to sit inside one another like Russian dolls. For the viewer, these layers of fictiveness are engaged with along "horizontal" vectors of memory of the transmedia experience of the franchise.[75] As Herbert argues, franchises are first and foremost "industrial intertexts,"[76] and it is by engaging with these layers of fictiveness that audiences make sense of the *Alien* world.

The Expanded Role of Alien's Online Marketing Campaigns

It has been observed that film theory is often "structured by the distance that it seeks to claim from the industrial and commercial,"[77] and clearly this tendency persists. Film scholarship can be disparaging of marketing and promotion with derisory remarks about "marketing *efforts*,"[78] "the *carpet-bombing* promotional strategy,"[79] or "a *deluge* of advertising and promotional materials."[80] Comments like these are more often than not based on distinctions drawn between creative and commercial content that laud the former but are dismissive of the latter, but consequently overlook the contribution of marketing and promotion to the contemporary film experience. Jonathan Gray made an intervention in this prevailing narrative when he reframed promotion as "paratext" in *Show Sold Separately: Promos, Spoilers and Other Media Paratexts* (2010).[81] Adopting the concept from the literary scholar Gerard Genette, he argued that media paratexts function as "thresholds" shaping expectations and framing interpretations, as well as creating anticipation for a forthcoming film.[82]

What this chapter illustrates is why is it significant for the *Alien* franchise to consider these paratextual techniques. For a franchise that has recently marked its fortieth anniversary, these strategies play an increasingly significant role in its maintenance, above and beyond promotion. As the franchise's narrative becomes more sprawling and its chronology becomes increasingly complex, for *Prometheus*, the promotional website functions as a base showing how the film narratives connect with one another. The film's website also acts as a hub for exposition, providing audiences with information about the franchise's fictional world such as the *Alien: Covenant* character cameos on *YouTube* to introduce new characters to the diegesis. In both instances, the film's paratexts take on aspects of storytelling that were formerly the preserve of the film itself.

Another reason why it is significant to consider these paratextual techniques is that in a fiercely competitive media entertainment landscape, *Alien*'s existing fan base may form the franchise's core audience, but the attention of new audiences cannot be assumed—it has to be won. The razzmatazz of media conventions, film trailer premieres, star appearances, and VR activations is presented as "exclusive" experiences for visitors but designed to provide material for hashtags, likes, shares, and posts to spread the word on social media platforms, which is where their real value lies. In short, these experiences effectively recruit convention attendees into the promotional effort.

The chapter went on to establish exactly how highly *Alien*'s fans are valued by promotional campaigns in the shift from a general participatory address to the personal interpellation techniques in order to garner the attention of a new generation of audiences. Fan creativity is harnessed through a studio-run film competition, and the winning short films are commandeered to contribute to the franchise's promotional campaign too. What makes *Alien* franchise marketing so compelling continues to be its close proximity to the film's production, making use of the cast, sets, and assets, and, as a consequence, one of the franchise's legacies is that its advertising is part of the picture.[83] The chapter concludes that *Alien*'s promotional campaign provides a vital life-support system for this aging franchise.

My sincere thanks to Jeff Kelly for his fascinating insights into franchise film marketing, and to Ed Cole for his reminiscences about the Alien "experience" at London's Trocadero in Trafalgar Square back in the 1990s.

Notes

1. Pamela McClintock, "$200 Million and Rising: Hollywood Struggles with Soaring Marketing Costs," July 31, 2014 (accessed September 30, 2020), https://www.hollywoodreporter.com/news/200-million-rising-hollywood-struggles-721818.
2. Susan Keselenko Coll, "20 Scary Minutes with the 'Alien,'" December 17, 1993 (accessed June 23, 2020), https://www.nytimes.com/1993/12/17/style/IHT-20-scary-minutes-with-the-alien.html.
3. "Alien War-26 Years of Terror," ScareTour (accessed June 23, 2020), https://www.scaretour.co.uk/alien-wars—-26-years-of-extraterrestrial-terror.html.
4. The *Internet Archive*'s site summary includes a pie chart mapping the websites' different features which indicates that in 1998 the *Alien: Resurrection* site consists of

around 75 percent text, in comparison with the 2012 *Prometheus*'s site made up of just over 30 percent text with far more graphic material.

5. Stephanie Argy, "Hot Summer Sites: Web Movie Promos Become Business as Usual," *Variety*, May 21, 1998 (accessed June 23, 2020), https://variety.com/1998/more/news/hot-summer-sites-1117471159/.

6. Ibid.

7. Ibid.

8. Barbara Klinger in Thomas Austin, *Hollywood, Hype and Audiences* (Manchester: Manchester University Press, 2002), 29–30.

9. Paul Grainge and Catherine Johnson, *Promotional Screen Industries* (London: Routledge, 2015), 164.

10. Henry Jenkins, "Three Reasons Why Pottermore Matters . . . " June 24, 2011 (accessed June 19, 2020), http://henryjenkins.org/blog/2011/06/three_reasons_why_pottermore_m.html.

11. Ralph Clare, *Fictions Inc. The Corporation in Postmodern Fiction, Film and Popular Culture* (New Brunswick: Rutgers University Press, 2014), 10.

12. Henry Jenkins, *Convergence Culture: Where Old and New Media Collide* (New York: New York University Press, 2006), 116.

13. Henry Jenkins, "The Revenge of the Origami Unicorn: Seven Principles of Transmedia Storytelling," December 12, 2009 (accessed November 12, 2017), http://henryjenkins.org/blog/2009/12/the_revenge_of_the_origami_uni.html.

14. Dan Hassler-Forest, *Science Fiction, Fantasy, and Politics: Transmedia World-Building Beyond Capitalism* (London: Rowman & Littlefield, 2016), 6.

15. Mark J. P. Wolf, *Building Imaginary Worlds: The Theory and History of Subcreation* (London: Routledge, 2012), 2–3.

16. Wolf, *Building Imaginary Worlds*, 23–24

17. Wolf, *Building Imaginary Worlds*, 25.

18. Henry Jenkins, "Building Imaginary Worlds: An interview with Mark J.P. Wolf (Part Two)," September 4, 2013 (accessed January 31, 2017), http://henryjenkins.org/blog/2013/09/building-imaginary-worlds-an-interview-with-mark-j-p-wolf-part-two.html.

19. "Prometheus Transmedia Campaign" *Behance* (accessed June 28, 2020), https://www.behance.net/gallery/14357945/Prometheus-Transmedia-Campaign.

20. Jeff Kelly, "Prometheus" (accessed July 15, 2020), https://www.jeffkellytoday.com/prometheus.

21. Sarah Atkinson, *Beyond the Screen: Emerging Cinema and Engaging Audiences* (London: Bloomsbury, 2014), 44.

22. Wolf, *Building Imaginary Worlds*, 165.

23. Dann Albright, "Benchmarking Average Session Duration: What It Means and How to Improve It," July 23, 2019 (accessed June 12, 2020), https://databox.com/average-session-duration-benchmark.

24. Wolf, *Building Imaginary Worlds*, 200.

25. Jeff Kelly, conversation with author via Zoom, July 15, 2020.

26. Jonathan Hardy, *Cross-Media Promotion* (New York: Peter Lang, 2010), 66.

27. Errki Huhtamo, "Dismantling the Fairy Engine: Media Archaeology as Topos Study," in *Media Archaeology: Approaches, Applications, and Implications*, ed. Errki Huhtamo and Jussi Parikka (Berkeley and Los Angeles: University of California Press, 2011), 38.

28. Ibid., 39.

29. Ibid., 37.

30. Richard D. Wolf, "Alternatives to Capitalism," *Critical Sociology* 39, no. 4.

31. Clare, *Fictions Inc.*, 16.

32. Hassler-Forest, *Science Fiction, Fantasy, and Politics*, 9.

33. Henry Jenkins, "Superpowered Fans: The Many Worlds of San Diego's Comic-Con," *Boom: A Journal of California* 2, no. 2 (2012), 23, https://doi.org/10.1525/boom.2012.2.2.22.

34. Erin Hana, *Only at Comic Con,* (New Brunswick, NJ: Rutgers University Press, 2019), 5.

35. B. Joseph Pine II and James H. Gilmore, *The Experience Economy,* (Boston: Harvard Business Review Press, 2011), ix.

36. Wolf, *Building Imaginary Worlds*, 167.

37. Alex Billington, "WonderCon Weyland Corp. Viral Cards Unlock a New Android Video," March 18, 2012 (accessed November 15, 2017), https://www.firstshowing.net/2012/wondercon-weyland-corp-viral-cards-unlock-a-new-android-video/.

38. Ibid.

39. Ibid.

40. Hana, *Only at Comic Con*, 4.

41. Ibid., 164.

42. Ibid., 95.

43. Ibid., 167.

44. Ibid.

45. John McCarthy, "How 20th Century Fox marketed *Alien: Covenant* with Personalised and Branded Content," May 15, 2017 (accessed March 10, 2020), https://www.thedrum.com/news/2017/05/15/how-20th-century-fox-marketed-alien-covenant-with-personalised-and-branded-content.

46. Ibid.

47. John McCarthy, "Behind All 4' New Personalised VOD Ads that Call Out the Name of Viewers," April 28, 2017 (accessed September 24, 2020), https://www.thedrum.com/news/2017/04/28/behind-all-4s-new-personalised-vod-ads-call-out-the-names-viewers.

48. Hassler-Forest, *Science Fiction, Fantasy, and Politics*, 14.

49. "Project Prometheus," *Ignition Interactive*, accessed November 16, 2017, http://ignitioncreative.com/work/detail/prometheus.

50. Ibid.

51. Michael Humphrey, "How Weyland Recruited Me for Prometheus, and Why They Chose Linked-In," May 29, 2012 (accessed November 26, 2017), https://www.forbes.com/sites/michaelhumphrey/2012/05/29/prometheus-what-weyland-knows-about-linkedin-and-post-social-value/#6c012322b0ec.

52. Hana, *Only at Comic Com*, 167–168.

53. "Virtual Reality," *The Free Dictionary* (accessed July 7, 2020), https://www.thefreedictionary.com/virtual+reality.

54. "Experience Star Wars Like Never Before in Jakku Spy," *Starwars.com* (accessed June 29, 2020), https://www.starwars.com/news/experience-star-wars-like-never-before-in-jakku-spy.

55. John Gaudiosi, "Alien: Covenant In Utero': Director on VR as a New Storytelling Platform," April 26, 2017 (accessed June 29, 2020), https://www.alistdaily.com/media/alien-covenant-utero-director-vr-new-storytelling-platform/.

56. Wolf, *Building Imaginary Worlds*, 210.

57. Gaudiosi, "Alien: Covenant In Utero.'"

58. Marc Bernardin, "The 25 Most Powerful Film Franchises in Hollywood ... and Why They Matter More than Movie Stars," June 17, 2016 (accessed April 16, 2020), https://www.latimes.com/entertainment/movies/la-ca-mn-25-most-powerful-franchises-20160524-snap-story.html.

59. Kim Walden, "Nostalgia for the Future: How TRON: Legacy's Paratextual Campaign Rebooted the Franchise," in *The Politics of Ephemeral Digital Media*, ed. Sara Pesce and Paolo Noto (London: Routledge, 2016), 100.

60. "Prometheus Transmedia Campaign," *Behance* (accessed June 28, 2020), https://www.behance.net/gallery/14357945/Prometheus-Transmedia-Campaign.

61. Syd Field, *Screenplay: The Foundations of Screenwriting* (New York: Bantam Dell, 2005), 61, 98; Robert McKee, *Story* (York: Methuen, 2014), 105.

62. Jenny Brewer, "Director Luke Scott, Ridley Scott's Son, on Reinventing the Movie Trailer for *Alien: Covenant*," May 12, 2017 (accessed June 24, 2020), https://www.itsnicethat.com/features/luke-scott-ridley-scotts-son-on-reinventing-the-movie-trailer-for-alien-covenant-120517.

63. Ibid.

64. Terence McSweeney, *Avengers Assemble: Critical Perspectives on the Marvel Cinematic Universe* (New York: Columbia University Press, 2018), 14.

65. Wolf, *Building Imaginary Worlds*, 205.

66. Emanuelle Wessels, "Where Were You When the Monster Hit? Media convergence, branded security citizenship, and the trans-media phenomenon of *Cloverfield*," *Convergence: The International Journal of Research into New Media Technologies* 17, no. 1 (2011), 69–83, https://journals-sagepub-com.ezproxy.herts.ac.uk/doi/pdf/10.1177/1354856510383362.

67. Henry Jenkins, Sam Ford, and Joshua Green, *Spreadable Media: Creating Value and Meaning in a Networked Culture* (New York: New York University Press), 182.

68. Mel Stanfill and Megan Condis, "Fandom and/as Labor" [editorial], in "Fandom and/as Labor," ed. Mel Stanfill and Megan Condis, special issue, *Transformative Works and Cultures* 15, https://doi.org/10.3983/twc.2014.0593.

69. Wessels, "Where Were You When the Monster Hit?," 70.

70. Derek Johnson, *Media Franchising: Creative License and Collaboration in the Culture Industries* (New York: New York University Press, 2013), 198–199.

71. Kenneth Sloan, "The Unescapable Labyrinth: Archetypal Retrogression and Aesthetic Rigidity in *Alien³*," in *Alien Legacies: The Evolution of the Franchise*, ed. Nathan Abrams and Gregory Frame (Oxford: Oxford University Press, 2023), 80.

72. Daniel Herbert, *Film Remakes and Franchises* (New Brunswick, NJ: Rutgers University Press, 2017), 1.

73. Ibid., 21.

74. Lisbeth Klastrup and Susana Tosca, "Transmedial Worlds-Rethinking Cyberworld Design," *2004 International Conference on Cyberworlds* Tokyo, Japan, November 18–20 (accessed June 30, 2020), https://www.researchgate.net/profile/Lisbeth_Klast rup/publication/4109310_Transmedial_worlds_-_Rethinking_cyberworld_design/ links/0912f512dddfe2e26f000000.pdf.

75. Colin Harvey, *Fantastic Transmedia: Narrative, Play and Memory ·across Science Fiction and Fantasy Storyworlds* (London: Palgrave Macmillan, 2015), 93.

76. Herbert, *Film Remakes and Franchises*, 23.

77. Matt Hills, "Star Wars in Fandom, Film Theory, and the Museum: The Cultural Status of the Cult Blockbuster," in *Movie Blockbusters*, ed. Julian Stringer (London: Routledge, 2003), 186.

78. Mark T. Decker, *Industrial Society and the Science Fiction Blockbuster: Social Critique in Films of Lucas, Scott and Cameron* (Jefferson, NC: McFarland, 2016), 103.

79. Geoff King and Tanya Krzywinska in Matt Hills, "*Star Wars* in Fandom, Film Theory, and the Museum: The Cultural Status of the Cult Blockbuster," in *Movie Blockbusters*, ed. Julian Stringer (London: Routledge, 2003), 181.

80. Herbert, *Film Remakes and Franchises*, 8–9.

81. Jonathan Gray, *Show Sold Separately* (New York: New York University Press, 2010).

82. Ibid., 25.

83. Jeff Gomez and Simon Pulman, "In Ridley Scott's 'Prometheus,' the Advertising Is Part of the Picture," March 23, 2012 (accessed November 17, 2016). https://adage. com/article/digitalnext/ridley-scott-s-prometheus-advertising-part-picture/233452.

7

"What the Hell Is That?"

A Transmedial Approach to Taxonomic Ambiguity and Horror Affect in the *Alien* Franchise

Zoé Wible

Since the release of Ridley Scott's *Alien* and its widespread success, the familiar shape of the titular monster has become a cultural icon, the status of which has been reinforced by the creation of a transmedia franchise centered around its mythos. Surveying the various iterations of the alien over time and across media reveals variations, ambiguities, and contradictions. The alien is eminently fluid, at the crossroads between biomechanical creature, reptilian lifeform, and genetically modified organism. Throughout the franchise, information is given about its lifecycle, physiology, level of intelligence, feeding, and hunting habits. Subsequent variations appear due to different roles in the "hive," different hosts for the parasitic larvae, or genetic tampering from humans. These changes can then be related to specific aesthetic strategies in a certain text, medium, or context of reception, but they also evidence a complex hierarchy among various media, authors, and genres, which also complicates the notion of the canon itself. The alien's mutations in different texts are realized aesthetically and narratologically, which in turn influences our understanding of its ontological nature and our affective response to it.

This chapter investigates the ways the alien species appears to us, acknowledging both the transmedial aspect of the creature and its medium-specific characteristics, especially as it relates to the perceptual-affective impact of the creature. While the franchise as a whole is characterized by its affiliation to the horror genre, the different texts do not aim to create the same specific affect, nor provide the same pleasures to the audience. To account for the subtle variations in the horrific apparitions of the alien, we need a more precise vocabulary for the aesthetic emotions the films' creative strategies aim to elicit. For this purpose, I will follow Julian Hanich's phenomenological analysis of cinematic fear, while adapting it to the transmedial nature of the

Zoé Wible, *"What the Hell Is That?"* In: *Alien Legacies.* Edited by: Nathan Abrams and Gregory Frame,
Oxford University Press. © Oxford University Press 2023. DOI: 10.1093/oso/9780197556023.003.0007

Alien franchise.[1] The perceptual-cognitive encounter the audience has with the alien can be linked to the medium-specific semiotic affordances, that lead to aesthetic strategies aiming to elicit precise affective responses.

A Transmedia Franchise

Cognitive narratology supports an analysis of the audience's progressive construction of the Fabula. Media consumption (watching a film, reading a novel) is a process that happens in duration. David Bordwell in *Narration in the Fiction Film* conceptualizes the audience as pro-actively making sense of the narrative as the plot unfolds.[2] The experience of narrative is based on hypothesis-making and inferences, and it mobilizes both general schemas and knowledge of the text's (and potential franchise's) internal norms. In the case of *Alien*, the perception and understanding of the creature by audiences are mediated and informed by the medium and the genre the creature evolves in. As Bordwell says, "different types of [texts] call forth different rules and procedures of sense-making."[3] The franchise appears to be, like the titular alien, a constantly evolving beast, which targets various audiences and impacts them in different ways. Indeed, not all texts in the franchise have the same popularity, reach, and critical acclaim. Some texts, like the comics or the video games (and the wealth of fan-generated, unofficial content) represent more of a niche targeted at long-standing fans of the franchise. This relative marginality can sometimes lead to more ambitious or daring creative choices, which merit attention in their own right. The breadth and range of the franchise mean that the understanding of the creature will not be the same for a casual viewer, or for a fan (who will probably have consumed a wider range of texts in more diverse media). Pamela Church Gibson already notes a certain "academic shunning" of *Alien³* and *Alien: Resurrection*, which she calls "pariah films."[4] The same can be said of the novels and comic books of the *Alien* franchise. One can suppose that this is due to the lower social status of comic books in general, and their (real or perceived) "pulpy" quality. This is a regrettable value judgment that causes long-lasting blind spots and adversely impacts our understanding of franchises and transmedia storyworlds. Thomas Leitch argues that "scholars should no longer engage in value-comparative judgements that persistently devalue adaptations into newer media."[5] While he specifically refers to film adaptations of classical novels, this hierarchy is reversed in the case of the *Alien* franchise, as the novels and comic books are less valued than the films (especially the original film directed by respected "auteur" Ridley Scott). The point still stands though: blanket value judgments regarding new media adaptations prevent us from considering rich primary sources and incredibly vivacious fan activities. It also prevents a thorough examination of transmedia franchises that accounts for transmedial and medium-specific aesthetic strategies, especially as they relate to transmedia storyworlds.

Colin Harvey in *Fantastic Transmedia* notes examples of transmedia franchises as early as the nineteenth century. The success of franchises such as *Star Wars* (1977–) and *Star Trek* (1966–) have contributed to the commercial viability of science-fiction franchises, and "science fiction and fantasy boast generic characteristics which make them particularly suited to storytelling across different media platforms."[6] Moreover, as Katarina O'Dette argues, the rise of digital media has increased the possibilities of creating storyworlds across multiple media and to provide diverse experiences.[7] These franchises tend to shift the focus from characters toward storyworlds themselves. These transmedia storyworlds are not only stories told through different media: they are made to be experienced together, and to reward audiences who invest time and resources into the storyworld by seeking out its various offerings. Changing the focus from single text(s) to the storyworld itself enables us to better account for the transmedial nature of the franchise. In the original quadrilogy of *Alien* films, Ellen Ripley (Sigourney Weaver) is the only recurrent character. On the contrary, the titular alien is a different individual (or group of individuals) in each film, with no transmission of knowledge or memory from one to the other, and the human cast in each film is usually ignorant about the alien (or at least, unaware of how dangerous it can be). Similarly, most of the other texts in the franchise feature different casts of characters. This reinforces the prevalence of the storyworld itself, as opposed to specific characters or settings.

As O'Dette highlights, using the example of J. K. Rowling's "Wizarding World" as a franchise that expands through more texts and media, the issue of canon is bound to become more and more problematic. She mobilizes Tolkien's notion of "inner consistency of reality"[8] to assert that "while many instances of inconsistencies are largely cosmetic and pedantic, some can cause fundamental confusion about how a storyworld operates."[9] The point is not to catalog or decry the various contradictions in the *Alien* storyworld, but to highlight how some of them can be correlated to various aesthetic and narrative uses in different media and genres.

The construction of the *Alien* franchise storyworld is made more complicated by the involvement of multiple authors (writers, directors), and the changes in ownership of the rights from Fox to Disney in 2019. Contrary to *Star Wars*, for which the studio has had a permanent official continuity consultant (Leland Chee) for a while, the *Alien* franchise has historically not made a concerted effort to provide continuity, until Fox hired Andrew E. Gaska in 2017 as a consultant. He authored canon bibles for the *Alien*, *Predator*, and *Planet of the Apes* franchises and is also one of the writers for *Alien: The Roleplaying game* (2020). Gaska explained that the usual approach of tossing out canon texts that contradict canon does not work for him.[10] Instead, he proposes another approach which he calls "barroom canon":

> These are stories overheard in a bar (or read in a comic, or played in a video game, or even posted on Facebook) that may or may not have some truth to them. This allows canon to have some flex in regards to including stories that otherwise could no longer count in a franchise's development.[11]

He introduces a Tier system, which corresponds to the centrality to canon and truth value of certain texts. Tier I includes core texts, Tier II texts that are "canon until the producer throws a curveball," and Tier III includes texts that mostly fit canon, with some minor problems that can be explained as myth or hearsay. Some entire texts are grouped under the heading "myths or legends," "stuff [that] should be thought of as tall-tales told in bars. The events may or may not have happened as described, but the locations exist."[12]

In the *Alien* franchise, canon seriality is made particularly problematic by the existence of prequels (*Prometheus* and *Alien: Covenant* both directed by Scott), which imply a different relation to temporality, and a crossover franchise (*Alien vs Predator* and *Alien vs Predator: Requiem*, hereafter "*AvP*"). There is a deep fracture between two (unequal) competing canons. The original quadrilogy came out between 1979 and 1997, each film set after the other. The *AvP* film franchise adapted the popular crossover comic book franchise, which presented an origin story for the alien that dates back to the pre-history of Earth. Five years after the *AvP* film franchise, Scott resumed his role as director for *Prometheus*, which presents a contradictory origin story. The film takes place in 2093, just a couple of decades before the events of *Alien*. In it, we learn that the alien was created by the genetic hybridization between alien races, and an unknown chemical compound nicknamed "black goo" by fans. This creation occurs within the diegetic time of the film, and not in Ancient times. This "retconning" changes the ontological nature of the aliens and invites very different interpretations of them. In this case, neither diegetic nor intertextual linear chronology is respected. *Prometheus*, and later

Alien: Covenant, is in direct contradiction with the *AvP* franchise. This incompatibility has been resolved by kicking the *AvP* franchise out of the official canon, which reasserts Scott's authorial control over the franchise, and the hierarchical value judgments between media at play in canon disputes.[13]

This example highlights the distinction between two types of canon: imaginative and logical. Imaginative storyworlds can present conflicting alternate realities, without any single one having any more claim to be the "real" one, for example in long-running comics. Conversely, texts set in a logical storyworld cannot admit inconsistencies. New texts must adhere to previously established canon, and inconsistencies have to be resolved. The ejection of the *AvP* films from the main *Alien* canon actualizes this resolution. The *Alien* prequels directed by Scott take precedent, therefore the canon origin story for the alien is that of the "black goo" established in *Prometheus*. Nonetheless, several critics and fans have noted that the most recent film, *Alien: Covenant*, somewhat retcons "every non-Scott directed *Alien* movie out of mythology, and doesn't exactly fit like a glove even with the 1979 original and *Prometheus*," to quote David Crow for *DenOfGeek*.[14] *Covenant* ignores the expansions of the alien's lifecycle introduced by James Cameron's *Aliens*, in particular erasing the need for an alien "Queen" to lay eggs. Crow notes several other inconsistencies (for example the alien's gestation period), which cannot be attributed to a change in author. The entire franchise presents a problematic canon that tends to prioritize the storyworld over specific characters and settings, constantly re-negotiating the alien's characteristics to suit different types of aesthetic visions. The canon itself appears riddled with conflicts among several agents, including the various producers and writers (legal rights owners) as well as various fan communities, which routinely disagree about canon.

This approach to canon is also mirrored in academia. Claudio Pires Franco suggests replacing the notion of "fidelity" to canon (and its associated hierarchy and value judgment) with that of "brand consistency," which "embraces medium-specificity and [. . .] the multifaceted influences of intertextuality and extratextuality."[15] Pires Franco sees tone and mood as central to brand consistency, rather than specific characters, narrative structures, or format, which are determined "partly by affinities between narrative genres and game genres, and partly by audience consideration."[16] The changes in the alien's ontological nature and its aesthetic uses could be explained by the desire to maintain a consistent brand identity based on general horror affects. Specific horror affects created (suggested or direct horror, shock, and dread) vary depending on the medium and the text. An overview of the *Alien* franchise has to acknowledge the general transmedial affective aim of horror while paying attention to the specific affects created in singular texts. Our affective reaction to the alien creature(s), as cued in by the texts, is, therefore, key to the apprehension of the franchise's brand consistency across media.

In "Media, mythology and morphogenesis: *Aliens^{TM}*," Karin Littau uses the alien to discuss intertextuality and intermediality; she sees it as an example of evolutionary adaptation in the diegesis and outside of it, a figure that becomes "transmedially available and realizable, i.e. available and realizable across media borders."[17] She focuses on diversification and hybridization, and the fact that the alien "appears variously as male/female, alien/human, alien/animal, organic/inorganic hybrid," and relates this diversification and hybridity to intermedial adaptation.[18] Littau defines intermediality as a mirror image of intertextuality: all texts bear echoes of other texts, and all texts in a specific medium bear echoes of modes of representation of other media. In the case of the alien, its presentation in one text mobilizes memory of its presentation in others (intertextuality), but it also owes to the way it appears to us in other media.

According to Mary-Laure Ryan, various media present different spatio-temporal extensions and "semiotic affordances" that mobilize our perceptual and cognitive functions differently.[19] The type of encounter the audience has with a character is mediated by the medium being used, the technological apparatus that connects the alien's body with the audience's human body. For example, the alien in the films is a moving image that mobilizes our sight and hearing, while the alien in the novels is presented to us via descriptions. This means that films are better equipped to produce certain effects, such as shock, surprise, or horror, by playing with timing, for example. It also means that visual media are better equipped to create a mental image in the audience than, say, a novel. There is no strict determinism though: specific texts are influenced by artistic and generic choices, and social or industrial practices around various media (which shape the utilization of media technologies). The intermedial aspect of the alien is crucial to its realization in the franchise: due to the predominance of the films, all other products rely on the visual image the audience already has. There is the assumption of familiarity with the appearance of the alien's life forms, and therefore description is sparser than it otherwise would have been if the novels had been someone's first encounter with the franchise. Angela Ndalianis suggests a relationship between intertextuality and seriality: "the serial logic of contemporary media is reliant on a rampant self-reflexivity: each addition to the serial whole is reliant on an intertextual awareness of serial predecessors."[20]

The official texts comprise films, novels, graphic novels, and comic book series, audiobooks and audiodramas, board games, roleplaying games, and video games on multiple platforms. They interact with the filmic franchise and with each other in a complex web of influence and adaptation.[21] Various texts problematize not only the notion of the medium, but also the distinction made by Henry Jenkins between adaptation, "which reproduces the original narrative with minimum changes into a new medium and is essentially redundant to the original work, and extension, which expands our understanding of the original by introducing new elements into the fiction."[22] All non-visual texts in the *Alien* storyworld are still imbued with the intermedial nature of the franchise. For example, in the novel, *Alien: Earth Hive* (1992), Steve Perry introduces the alien via an "audiovisual presentation" that characters see. The novel directly reproduces "excerpts from the script," including directions such as "fade in" or "musical sting." The alien itself is not described at all, simply referred to as "an alien" (chapter 5).[23]

The first literary texts to be published in the *Alien* franchise were novelizations of the movies, by Alan Dean Foster, which makes them adaptation, even though they often expand on the films. For example, the novelization of the first film is based on the original shooting script and also makes use of unused or cut material.[24] Similarly, several other literary texts bear the echoes of the production context of the original films. The most extreme examples are the comic series by Dark Horse and the audiodrama *Alien III*, which both adapt the unused script written by William Gibson for the third film.[25] They, therefore, occupy the same space as Fincher's *Alien³* in the continuity (as evidenced by the titles), but they exist as competing stories: Hicks and Newt are still alive in *Alien III*, but dead in *Alien³*. Gibson also confirmed the artificial nature of the alien, as characters note that its genetic material seems to have been engineered for ease of manipulation. The genetic material is also able to "infect" humans via spore-like particles, causing them to mutate into a hybrid xenomorph. These ideas seemed to have influenced the writing of subsequent films, more specifically *Alien Resurrection* and *Alien: Covenant*. Looking at the non-filmic texts in the franchise shows a complex cross-pollination of ideas between texts from various media, rather than a strict adaptation hierarchy. Concepts or ideas from less known and less popular texts (including unofficial fan products) can resurface in the most visible texts of the franchise (the films). An overview of the alien in the transmedial franchise can show us how the primacy of the filmic medium is negotiated and sometimes challenged by other texts.

Xenomorph(s) on Film

The alien is originally a filmic creature. Film is a visual-kinetic medium: it involves moving images. The spectator encounters the alien through the medium's specific perceptual-cognitive extension. Julian Hanich analyzes the way the "pathic" quality of sight and sound is particularly important when discussing film, and especially horror film: it is impossible to disconnect the perception of the film's text from our bodily, affective response to it.[26] Hanich quotes W. J. T. Mitchell, whose phrasing is particularly apposite to a discussion of the alien: he speaks of cinema as providing a "living image" or "the image-as-organism," and he calls images "ghostly semblances" or "pseudo-life-forms."[27] The visual and aural quality of the alien in films impact and affect us directly, dictated by pre-production choices (creature design, special effects), and filmic techniques (cinematography, mise-en-scène).

In the first four films, even if the creature evolves and changes, the overall storyworld remains based on a logical serial canon: the films follow each other chronologically, each one adding information about the creature without directly contradicting previously established facts. The creature appears mysterious and fluid: according to star Sigourney Weaver, "the alien would constantly evolve. Giger's alien was the perfect creature for [the films]. But it has to evolve accordingly, become something you don't expect."[28] The alien takes different forms, as evidenced in the graph below (Figure 7.1), for which I have used the terminology favored by fans and critics.

It appears briefly in each form, in a limited number of scenes, which contributes to the feeling of an evasive, ever-changing creature. It adopts distinct forms (egg, "facehugger," "chestburster," and finally adult), metamorphosing from one to the other off-screen before (literally) bursting into view. The appearances of the creature are late, few and far between, usually favoring short shots, fast editing, with the body of the alien often appearing in small fragments. Apart from the chestburster scene, none of the alien's attacks are graphically shown on screen. This horror strategy can be summed up by what Hanich names the "cinema of invisibility," in which "the viewer compensates the visual lack with mental visualization."[29] More specifically, *Alien* often relies on dread (anxious anticipation) and suggested horror (which causes fear by inviting us to imagine the violence of the monster).

This mystery covers the very ontological nature of the alien: what kind of creature is it? Kelly Hurley considers the alien to exemplify an alternative species logic:

THE CREATURE'S VARIOUS FORMS IN ALIEN (1979)

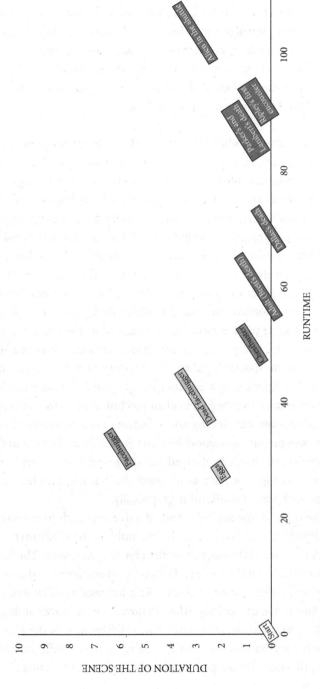

Figure 7.1 The creature's various forms in *Alien* (1979).

In its confusion of tentatively recognizable forms it resembles nothing at all. The adult Alien is even more unplaceable with taxonomies of natural history: a living organism composed of materials that should be inimical to organic life (cells made of "polarized silicon" and "molecular acid for blood"). Vaguely humanoid in forms (at times, since the flexible body collapses and contorts in unexpected ways), the adult alien also resembles a reptile, an insect, and a full exoskeleton stripped of flesh.[30]

She also notes that the alien straddles the boundaries between organic and inorganic, and thus "constitutes a collapsing of multiple and incompatible morphic possibilities into one amorphous embodiment—a logic of 'identity' that serves as an alternative, or possibly an ontological challenge, to a human one predicated on a body that's a discrete, bounded and stable unit."[31] The alien not only changes bodily forms, it also invades and transforms the human host by injecting it with the "facehugger," literally breaching the human body on its way in and on its way out. The characters themselves struggle to identify or categorize the creature: Kane describes "organic life," and Dallas "some form of organism," to which Ripley answers: "I need a clear definition." This request is never answered, and as the death toll rises, the characters devolve into profanity ("tough motherfucker," "son of a bitch").

This alternative species logic and the mystery as to its precise characteristics enable additions in subsequent films (Figure 7.2), which can be linked to two main factors. Firstly, practical and technical improvements in special effects enable more convincing and effective visual representations of the alien (for example, animatronics and CGI). Secondly, as the creature's form is already known, the mystery of dread and suggested horror is replaced by direct horror and a greater reliance on spectacle. Namely, the creature is more visible, moves faster, and kills more graphically.

This evolution of the aesthetic and affective approach to the alien is also paired with other narrative additions that build on the alien's mythos. As the film series goes on, it introduces new alien forms (The Queen, The Newborn), new information on its lifecycle and behavior (eusociality), and new forms of hybridity (with a dog or ox in *Alien³*, with humans in *Alien Resurrection*). The last film of the quadrilogy, *Alien Resurrection* embraces ambiguity and hybridity to an unprecedented level. Church Gibson sees the film as more transgressive and innovative than it usually receives credit for, welcoming readings influenced by the post-modernist approach of Donna Haraway or Sadie Plant:

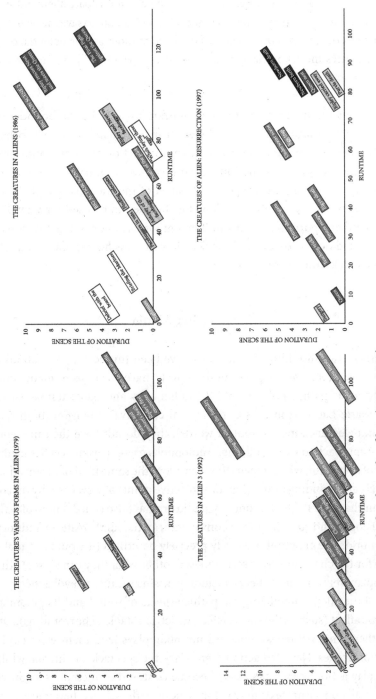

Figure 7.2 The creatures in the first four *Alien* films (1979–1997).

The ending of this film, where a six-foot woman who is part-alien and a small female android bond together, socially and sexually, to save the planet from destruction, could seem almost designed to showcase the potential of the alliances and acknowledgments advocated in [Haraway's] "A Manifesto for Cyborgs."[32]

Throughout the quadrilogy, the alien appears to straddle the boundaries between mechanical and organic, between mammalian and insect forms, and between genders, and in turn invites us to question our assumptions regarding the fixity of these notions when it comes to humans. The horrors of fluidity and ambiguity are part and parcel of the franchise's appeal and its brand consistency. They also allow for the alien to be used for very different aesthetic purposes, cueing in different forms of horror (such as direct or suggested horror, dread, and shock). How can this horror brand consistency be carried on into other media?

Alien in Other Media

The *Alien* franchise film novelizations have been turned into audiobooks, while several of the original tie-in novels have also been made into audiodramas with a full cast. While audiobooks and audiodramas share what Marie-Laure Ryan calls a "perceptual-cognitive" extension (both rely on aural elements, mostly spoken words), they do not have the same epistemic approach to worldbuilding. Audiobooks present events via the mediation of a narrator, which means they can adopt the same kind of focalization a novel can, including omniscient or subjective points of view (usually that of human characters). On the contrary, audio dramas (also called "audio plays") use dialogue and soundframe to convey information and create an auditory storyworld. The creatures are rarely precisely described (it would not make sense for the characters to describe to each other what they can all see). The audioplays rely on sound effects, including hissing sounds, to evoke the presence of the aliens, mobilizing the pathic aspects of sound and its potential somatic affect (such as the startle effect, which is a staple of horror films). On the other hand, neither audiobooks nor audioplays lend themselves easily to action scenes. Narrated action scenes lack the spectacle of cinema, while audioplay action scenes can easily become confused or messy. As a consequence, all non-visual texts tend to focus more on the science-fictional aspect of the franchise, playing on mystery and epistemophilia and relying on our scientific and taxonomical curiosity. For example, Alan Dean Foster's novelization for *Alien* includes lengthier scenes in which the crew discuss what they can know about the creature, led by Ash's scientific knowledge. This can be related to Noël Carroll's analysis of the specific type of epistemophilia elicited by horror monsters, which "arouse interest and attention through being putatively inexplicable or highly unusual vis-à-vis our standing cultural categories, thereby instilling a desire to learn and know more about them."[33] This quote is particularly appropriate for this alien and its resistance to taxonomical categories, as I have shown earlier.

A similar shift in affect and genre can be seen in the *Alien* comic books. Almost contemporarily to *Alien*, a graphic novel adaptation was released: *Alien: The Illustrated Story* (hereafter "*TIS*").[34] Nicolas Labarre presents a close comparison between the original film by Scott and its comic adaptation, noting that the comic "seeks to emulate the perceived continuity of cinema rather than the necessary discontinuity of the comic page."[35] For example, the chestburster scene escapes the traditional grid structure, projecting blood splatters onto the whole page. The chestburster itself appears more detailed and nimbler than the film version and its head is duplicated several times to signify movement, an example of what Neil Cohn calls "polymorphic panels."[36] Labarre sees this technique as an imitation of the effect of cinematic movement:

> The creature appears to break panel boundaries, to run over the fold and eventually to leave the scene altogether through the edge of the right-hand page. The effect of surprise is effective, through the change of scale of the panel, the change of color scheme (the two pages are literally drenched in red) and the appearance of a shock to the very system of the comic.

I would disagree, in that I do not believe that shock is possible in comics, and definitely not to the same extent as in cinema. As Thierry Groensteen explains, comics present a "dechronologized mode" of representation: readers are presented with two pages at the same time, and their attention does not necessarily follow the chronological or sequential arrangements of panels.[37] Labarre acknowledges this fact, saying that these moments call attention to the "constraints inherent to the construction of this type of shock effects in comics," and that these affective strategies are "highly constrained [...] by the medium." The affective impact of these comic pages cannot elicit proper pathic and somatic shock at all. On the contrary, the chestburster scene provides a different affect: the reader is free to linger on the creature's form and examine it at will, which feeds more into scopophilic and epistemophilic pleasures. Labarre compares the alien to a butterfly pinned on a page. I would push this metaphor further and compare it to a pinned spider, whose potentially dangerous and disgusting form is immobilized and preserved, submitted to our examination. The comic format offers a new way to look at the alien. One might even say that the comic manages to evoke the alien's speed and sliminess in a way that the special effects of the film did not quite manage (limited as they were by puppetry technology).

Labarre's analysis of medium specificity leads him to his main argument about generic hybridity: "The identification of [. . .] differences in the context of a work which emphasizes its faithfulness to the original movie suggests the existence of a medium-specific negotiation of genre affiliation."[38] Labarre considers that the alien itself embodies the generic hybridity of the franchise: "At the intersection of science fiction and horror, and belonging to both genres, is the monster/alien."[39] Its adaptability and hybridity are realized through changes in the balance between the various poles (human/insect/reptile, organic/inorganic, male/female). The main example given by Labarre is the fact that the comic presents a full image of the alien's face on the inside front cover. This sets the story in the horror genre, as opposed to the film, which has a definite "point of inflexion"[40] at around the hour mark with the chestburster scene, switching from the dominant genre of science-fiction into horror. This inside front cover representing the alien does not spoil the surprise of the alien's form, but rather teases its promised appearance to readers who had already watched the film. As such, this peritextual choice is not merely a generic change, but also an intertextual and intermedial one. While Labarre focuses on the shift in the balance of generic elements, I would add that the affective impact also shifts, while remaining under the broader umbrella of "horror." This example shows once again the need for precise vocabulary when discussing horror affect, which is why phenomenological studies such as Hanich's prove particularly valuable to the study of horror transmedia franchises.

The semiotic affordances of a medium are not the only things that can influence genre and affect: industrial and reception contexts also play a part. In the case of the *Alien* franchise, this is the most obvious with the licensed comic books published by Dark Horse. Kerry Gough presents a thorough and insightful exploration of these comics, praising their "breadth and scale," considering them "far reaching in aims and outlooks," while still negotiating the influence of the two films released at the time the comics came out.[41] The relative "indie" status of Dark Horse and the generous terms of the licensing agreement allowed the series to explore new dramatic possibilities, and significantly expand the worldbuilding. I will take for example the *Aliens* series published since 1988, intended as a direct sequel to Cameron's *Aliens* (featuring its main characters).[42] They introduce additional information about the alien's species, for example, the existence of a literal "hive mind" (allowing the individuals to communicate with each other, but also to "infest" some humans with nightmares and visions), competing hives (with color-coded aliens), and "royal jelly," a substance produced by the aliens that gives humans superhuman abilities and acts like a psychotropic drug. These additions to the lore provide sustained dramatic interest and open various storytelling possibilities for a medium that cannot rely on direct affective techniques favored by horror films (such as startle effect, or the "pathic" quality of sight and sound mentioned above when discussing the films). On the other hand, unburdened by filmic budget restrictions, the comics are free to explore ambitious storylines that would have been difficult and costly to show on film: for example, the comics show the Earth overrun by aliens.

Gough also notes the affinities between the style of the pencil-and-ink illustrations by Mark A. Nelson and H. R. Giger's vision for the xenomorph, which hark back to the visual art origins of the creature. Several editorial choices also position these comics closer to Scott's original aesthetic vision, despite being titled after Cameron's film. As editor Randy Stradley acknowledged, the comic book form is more suited to the "tension and mood" of the former rather than the "full-tilt" action of the latter.[43] This also means that the first few issues of the *Aliens* comic take a different approach to the creature than *TIS*: the creature is revealed later, and more progressively. It lurks in the background and corners of the panels, often cropped and ill-lit. This is a move away from the scopophilia of *TIS*, and a return to the aesthetic of invisibility of the original film. As the *Aliens* comics series progresses, this approach shifts, and starts to indulge in the more gory, graphic aspects of the creature's attacks, proving once again the flexibility of both the creature and the medium. The *Aliens* comic book series presents a symbiosis between the two original films in terms of aesthetic and narrative uses for the creature. Comparing the *Aliens* comics to *TIS* also highlights the absence of mediatic determinism: both texts approach the creature in different ways and negotiate their relationship with the flagship films differently. They reflect different editorial, aesthetic, and intermedial/intertextual choices.

Similar choices had to be made in the licensed video games in the *Alien* franchise. Official games cover the most popular genres: beat-em-ups, arcades, and first-person shooters. The only common point between these games is the presence of one (or more) of the titular aliens. They offer a good opportunity to compare the alien's aesthetic and narrative uses in a different medium, but also in various sub-genres of said medium: the procedural possibilities encoded within the gameplay allow very different types of encounters between the alien and the player.

Matthew Weise and Henry Jenkins analyzed the affective impact of the first-person shooter game *Aliens vs Predator 2*, which is based on Cameron's *Aliens*.[44] While the film relies on para-social camaraderie to create an emotional response, the game relies on ego-centric affect: the procedural design places us in the shoes of a colonial marine who has to master the tools (machine gun, motion detector) and techniques ("short controlled bursts") as the Marines in the film. The aliens are still fast and deadly, but the player can assert their dominance over them. The narrative elements are limited, and the games favor not only the pathic aspect of sight and sound but also kinetic affect. The bodily affect caused by the creatures (shock, horror, terror) is combined with the neuromuscular feedback loop inherent to video gaming. In other words, the player cannot give in (or turn away from) the shock, but on the contrary has to react to it by activating the controls to survive and progress in the game.

Brandan Keogh and Darshana Jayemanne make a similar assessment of most alien shooters: "Alien-adapted first-person shooter videogames consist of acquiring and eliminating multiple targets, rather than desperately avoiding the petrifying gaze of one invincible monster."[45] They mobilize Barbara Creed's analysis of Scott's *Alien*, in which she compares the creature to Medusa: looking at the alien causes it to look back, with deadly consequences.[46] On the contrary, shooters demand the player keeps looking. Keogh and Jayemanne contrast this approach to that of *Alien: Isolation*, in which the alien (and its narrative and aesthetic uses) more closely resemble that of Scott's film:

> The most powerful element of *Isolation* is players' encounters with the alien itself. The creature that stalks the halls of Sevastopol cannot be defeated nor can it be easily predicted. [. . .] Looking at the alien becomes a game of hoping that the alien doesn't ever look at you. In this way the game recreates the affect of *Alien* within the blockbuster first-person space, and it achieves this in part by stripping out the "shooter."[47]

It might also be interesting to note that *Isolation* supports Virtual Reality, which further reinforces the pathic and kinetic affect of the game by merging the body of the character to that of the player. This raises questions of identification and embodiment: playing an *Alien* video game, the player almost becomes a cyborg, using their own body aided by technological apparatus to mediate the encounter with the alien. All of the games reuse and refer to the film franchise, but the alien's behavior and the way the player encounters it (as encoded by the gameplay and the creature's AI) differ drastically.

Conclusion

The alien undergoes multiple metamorphoses over the course of the various texts, both literally and meta-narratively: not only is it metamorphic by nature, it is also put to different uses by the creators of the texts it inhabits. There seems to be a connection between the perceptual-cognitive extension of a medium, the affective goals of a genre, and the categorization of the alien species. In this chapter, I have paid closer attention to the ways lesser-known texts of the franchise negotiate transmedial adaptation by positioning themselves relative to the flagship film(s), maintaining brand consistency while adapting horror aesthetic strategies. This shows the usefulness of precise phenomenological vocabulary to account for medium- and genre-specific ways to create what is broadly categorized as a "horror" affect.

At the center of this negotiation are the mystery and suggested horror affect of Scott's masterpiece, which sets the overall tone for the franchise. This general affect is then built upon and modified by subsequent texts, in particular Cameron's *Aliens*, which takes an action-oriented approach favoring spectacle, direct horror, and shock. It is interesting to note that different texts in the same medium can choose to align themselves with the aesthetic strategies of the former or the latter, which shows the flexibility and adaptability of both the media and the creature itself: the examples I have given of comics and video games show that these media can lend themselves to either strategy. Just like the xenomorph resists biological determinism, the various texts of the franchise resist medium determinism, and strict logics of adaptation and seriality in favor of a looser canon. A similar approach could be used to analyze other transmedia franchises in the horror genre, especially those centering an imaginary creature.

Notes

1. Julian Hanich, *Cinematic Emotion in Horror Films and Thrillers: The Aesthetic Paradox of Pleasurable Fear* (New York: Routledge, 2011).
2. David Bordwell, *Narration in the Fiction Film* (New York: Routledge, 2013).

3. Ibid., 150.

4. Pamela Church Gibson, ""You've Been in My Life So Long I Can't Remember Anything Else": Into the Labyrinth with Ripley and the Alien," in *Keyframes: Popular Cinema and Cultural Studies*, ed. Amy Villarejo and Matthew Tinkcom (New York: Routledge, 2003), 55.

5. Thomas Leitch, "Adaptation Studies at a Crossroads," *Adaptation* 1, no. 1 (2008), 63–77.

6. Colin B. Harvey, *Fantastic Transmedia* (London: Palgrave Macmillan, 2015), 1.

7. Katarina O'Dette, "Chasing Canon in J. K. Rowling's Wizarding World: Towards a Poetics of Reception of Transmedia Storyworlds," *Fantastika Journal* 2, no. 1 (2018), 81–94.

8. John Ronald Reuel Tolkien, *On Fairy-stories* (Oxford: Oxford University Press, 1947), 47.

9. O'Dette, "Canon," 85.

10. Andrew E. Gaska, "Defining Canon in an Alien World," roguereviewer.wordpress. com. https://roguereviewer.wordpress.com/2020/10/12/defining-canon-in-an-alien-world/ (accessed November 2020).

11. Ibid.

12. Ibid.

13. For example, the *Alien* Anthology Wiki page explains that the AvP series is no longer canon: https://alienanthology.fandom.com/wiki/Alien_Universe_Timeline (accessed November 2, 2020).

14. David Crow, "How Alien Covenant Retcons James Cameron's Aliens and More," May 1, 2018, DenOfGeek, https://www.denofgeek.com/movies/how-alien-covenant-retc ons-james-cameron-s-aliens-and-more/ (accessed November 2, 2020).

15. Carlos Pires Franco, "The Muddle Earth Journey: Brand Consistency and Cross-Media Intertextuality in Game Adaptation," in *Storytelling in the Media Convergence Age*, ed. Roberta E. Pearson and Anthony N. Smith (London: Palgrave Macmillan, 2015), 40–53.

16. Franco, "The Muddle Earth Journey," 45.

17. Karin Littau, "Media, Mythology and Morphogenesis: *Aliens*™," *Convergence* 17, no. 1 (2011), 28.

18. Ibid., 30.

19. Marie-Laure Ryan, "Toward a Definition of Narrative," in *The Cambridge Companion to Narrative*, ed. David Herman (Cambridge: Cambridge University Press, 2007), 22–35.

20. Angela Ndalianis, *Neo-baroque Aesthetics and Contemporary Entertainment* (Cambridge, MA: MIT Press, 2004), 72.

21. For example, several comics have been adapted into novels, and several novels have been adapted into audiobooks and audioplays.

22. Henry Jenkins, "Transmedia Storytelling and Entertainment: An Annotated Syllabus," *Continuum* 24, no. 6 (2010), 945.

23. Steve Perry, *Aliens: Earth Hive* (London: Bantam Books, 1992), included in *Aliens: Omnibus*, Titan Books, 2016.

24. Alan Dean Foster, *Alien: The Official Movie Novelization* (New York: Warner Books, 1979), included in *The Complete Alien Omnibus* (London: Sphere, 1993)

25. *Alien 3: The Unproduced Screenplay*, written and drawn by Johnnie Christmas, based on the screenplay by William Gibson (Dark Horse Comics, 2018–2019). Five-issue comics series; *Alien III*, directed by Dirk Maggs, starring Michael Biehn and Lance Henriksen (Audible Studios, 2019). Audiodrama.

26. Hanich, *Cinematic Emotion*, 90.

27. Ibid., 91.

28. Andrew Abbott, Russell Leve, *Alien: Evolution*, documentary produced by Nobles Gate for 20th Century Fox Home Entertainment, 2001, in *Alien Quadrilogy* DVD boxset, 2003.

29. Hanich, *Cinematic Emotion*, 104.

30. Kelly Hurley, "Reading Like an Alien: Posthuman Identity in Ridley Scott's *Alien* and David Cronenberg's *Rabid*," *Posthuman Bodies* (1995), 219.

31. Ibid., 220.

32. Church. "You've Been in My Life So Long," 53.

33. Noël Carroll, *The Philosophy of Horror or Paradoxes of the Heart* (New York: Routledge, 1990), 182.

34. *Alien: The Illustrated Story*, written by Archie Goodwin and drawn by Walter Simonson (Heavy Metal, 1979), graphic novel.

35. Nicolas Labarre, "*Alien* as a Comic Book: Adaptation and Genre Shifting," *Extrapolation* 55, no. 1 (2014), 91.

36. Neil Cohn, "The Limits of Time and Transitions: Challenges to Theories of Sequential Image Comprehension," *Studies in Comics* 1, no. 1 (2001), 127–147.

37. Thierry Groensteen, *The System of Comics* (Jackson: University Press of Mississippi, 2007), 146.

38. Labarre, "Alien," 77.

39. Ibid., 81.

40. Labarre uses Rick Altman's term to refer to moments in a story where the balance of genres switches.

41. Kerry Gough, "Translation Creativity and Alien Econ(c)omics: From Hollywood Blockbuster to Dark Horse Comic Book," in *Film and Comic Books*, ed. Ian Gorden, Mark Jancovich, and Matthew P. McAllister (Jackson: University Press of Mississippi, 2007), 55.

42. *Aliens*, written by Mark Verheiden and drawn by Mark A. Nelson. Dark Horse Comics, 1988–1989, comic book series.

43. Randy Stradley, "Bug Hunt," Editorial Response, letter column appearing in *Aliens #4* (Milwaukee: Dark Horse Comics, March 1989).

44. Matthew Weise and Henry Jenkins, "Short Controlled Bursts: Affect and Aliens," *Cinema Journal* 48, no. 3 (2009), 111–116.

45. Brendan Keogh and Darshana Jayemanne, "'Game Over, Man. Game Over': Looking at the Alien in Film and Videogames," *Arts* 7, no. 3 (2020), 43.

46. Barbara Creed, *The Monstrous-Feminine: Film, Feminism, Psychoanalysis* (New York: Routledge, 1993).

47. Keogh and Jayemanne, "Game Over," 11.

8

From Personal Files to Blueprints

Exploring the *Alien* Universe through Epistolary Paratexts

Tonguç Ibrahim Sezen

One of the extras on the 2010 *Alien Anthology Blu-ray Collection* was a special feature called *Weyland-Yutani Inquest: Nostromo Dossiers*. It was a collection of corporate documents containing detailed chronological records of the past professional lives of the crew of the Nostromo, and individual performance statistics and remarks written by unnamed company officials. Originally barely visible set decorations in the background of one of the earlier scenes of *Aliens* (1986), these crew profiles were part of James Cameron's script at least since the 1983 preliminary treatment[1] and were also mentioned in the official novelization of the film.[2] Establishing the mood of the scene by linking *Alien* (1979) and *Aliens*, these profiles were diegetic documents holding information on characters, whom Cameron described in an interview as existing in a vacuum, without a past or a life beyond *Alien*.[3] The profiles shed new light on these characters and made suggestions on why they may have acted in certain ways: Kane (John Hurt) was an idealist, Lambert (Veronica Cartwright) was a transwoman, and Dallas (Tom Skerritt) had a failed military career. By revealing that Ripley (Sigourney Weaver) had an unauthorized pregnancy, the documents also established the background of her relationship with Newt (Carrie Henn) in *Aliens*. Within these personal histories, the profiles also offered glimpses of the economic, political, and technological aspects of the *Alien* universe: the United Kingdom was a socialist state, Luna and Mars were long colonized hubs, and high-speed terrafoil racing was a popular motorsport. Some of this information was taken from obscure details on costumes and props used in *Alien*,[4] forming a continuation of worldbuilding elements across the two films. Most importantly though, these profiles were reflecting Cameron's vision for the world of *Aliens* by

Tonguç Ibrahim Sezen, *From Personal Files to Blueprints* In: *Alien Legacies*. Edited by: Nathan Abrams and Gregory Frame, Oxford University Press. © Oxford University Press 2023. DOI: 10.1093/oso/9780197556023.003.0008 revealing Weyland-Yutani's cold-hearted policies through their form and style as corporate documents: personal statistics and evaluations dictated how each crewmember should be treated to ensure subordination and company profit, and transfer details disclosed how they were put together hastily as a group of expendable misfits.

The company profiles of the Nostromo crew were diegetic documents previously inaccessible to audiences, only disclosed by becoming digital paratexts. Their style and presentation ascribed them a unique artistic pseudo-factual claim of being documents originating in the *Alien* universe.[5] They revealed new aspects and extended the audiences' understanding of the fictional world not only through the information they introduced, but also through their form, which imitated authentic, non-fictional documents with a unique intra-diegetic perspective. Similar publications, both collections of on-screen documents and original productions claiming to be texts from the fictional future of the films, have been in circulation at least since the late 1980s across media. They fulfilled various functions throughout the transmedial evolution of the *Alien* franchise (see Wible in this collection for more on this subject). Finding their roots in stories, design, and worldbuilding elements of the series, they studied, expanded, promoted, and curated the *Alien* universe in unique ways as technical guides, field manuals, diaries, and even children's books. This chapter explores these largely overlooked publications, which we will call epistolary paratexts—ancillary reference material accompanying narrative urtexts while claiming to be authentic documents originating in imaginary worlds—and their evolution and use within the *Alien* franchise as it grew as a transmedia text.

At the Threshold of Text and Fiction

Epistolary paratexts are products of the evolution of transmedia paratextuality,[6] and the aesthetics of verisimilitude,[7] which blur the line between reality and fiction in cross-media and transmedia practices. Usually written and designed to look like scientific reports, field manuals, and other factual reference publications, epistolary paratexts aim to systematically organize data on fictional worlds originally communicated through other narrative texts. While they usually retell or reorganize data, they may also introduce new information to build up coherence, establish a backstory, or propose an outcome. Masquerading as if they were written by characters inhabiting fictional worlds, they may also reinforce personal perspectives or institutional positions and policies.

Proposed by Gérard Genette[8] to describe a textual threshold introducing or commenting on literary works, the concept of a paratext refers to elements such as titles, notes, publicity materials, and their fictional simulations supposedly written by fictional authors. Adopted by transmedia scholars,[9] it has since been reframed and expanded to encompass a wide range of officially sanctioned and fan-made phenomena across media including trailers, tie-in comics, making-of publications, and wikis that not only present but also have the potential to extend and enrich transmedia texts. According to Jason Mittell, one of the ways paratexts can help audiences make sense of complex transmedia texts is orientation.[10] Focusing on fan-made maps, lists, and other types of entries on wikis, Mittell argues that orienting practices reside outside the diegetic storyworlds and aim to create a correct and singular account of complex narrative material by looking at them from a distance.[11] Mark J. P. Wolf lists official orienting paratexts such as atlases among paratextual publications contributing to the worldbuilding of transmedia texts by usually revealing less important diegetic material obscured in the background.[12] Discussing fictional geographies, Gerard Hynes too argues that fictional maps as paratexts form a threshold around narratives, but not as part of the diegetic world itself.[13] Yet despite functioning like orienting paratexts, due to their pseudo-factual narrative style resembling epistolary fiction[14] or fictional films of the found footage genre,[15] epistolary paratexts are intra-diegetic elements. Their form and style contribute to fictional worlds as much as the information they curate or ideas they introduce.

Precursors of epistolary paratexts can be traced back to the late nineteenth-century New Romance adventure novels. According to Michael T. Saler, the inclusion of supposedly authentic documents like archaeological illustrations and maps as well as fictional simulations of footnotes and appendices contributed to the transformation of literary imaginary worlds into cohesively structured, empirically detailed, and logically based "virtual realities" for readers.[16] Since then, epistolary paratexts evolved and changed with the media while keeping their core properties. Creating an almost symbiotic relationship between the visual and verbal contents, J. R. R. Tolkien's use of maps of the Middle-Earth, including the epistolary paratextual Thror's map, set a new standard for fantasy literature.[17] In the late 1950s, children's magazines like the *Eagle* popularized the publication of meticulously labeled technical diagrams of fictional vehicles.[18] In the mid-1960s, *Doctor Who* writer Terry Nation published a series of books marketed as authentic Dalek chronicles, containing chapters imitating multiple scholarly apparatus such as technical illustrations, maps, and dictionaries.[19] Throughout the 1970s, fans codified and elaborated *Star Trek*'s fictional world through blueprints which led to the publication of official reference books claiming to be twenty-third-century Starfleet manuals.[20] In the 1980s, many story-driven digital games came with physical props, or "feelies," materializing storyworld entities such as newspapers and letters to intensify players' imaginative immersion.[21] From the late 1990s onward, online dramas and alternate reality games utilized diegetic online presences of fictional characters with increasing complexity and allowed real-world audiences to interact with fictional worlds through constructs existing on both.[22] Finally, following contemporary multimodal novels adapting the aesthetics of verisimilitude in the print form by imitating catalogs or scrapbooks,[23] the 2010s saw a rise in the publication of pseudo-factual guide books from major franchises like *Star Wars*,[24] supposedly compiled or altered by fictional characters.

Positioning themselves at the threshold of both text and fiction, epistolary paratexts combine the object-oriented materiality of extra-diegetic reference publications like making-of-books, with the make-believe of fictional narratives while at the same time rejecting being one. As tie-in products, they target audiences Bob Rehak describes as reference-[25] and design-oriented fans, who are interested in production design and worldbuilding elements of a franchise as much as its stories. Using factual, technical, and scientific language, these texts contribute to the recognition of fictional worlds, particularly the ones created for fantasy and science-fiction texts, as functional, plausible, and consistent realities by these fans. The *Alien* franchise, with its thought-provoking design aesthetics blending cinematic realism with the uncanny[26] and transmedial hybridization under diverse creative directions,[27] was an almost natural testbed for epistolary paratexts and over the years utilized them to reach and satisfy its fans.

Experimentations in Transmedia Seriality

As an early case of mutually beneficial economic collaboration between the comics and film industries, the acquisition of the *Alien* comic rights by Dark Horse Comics in the late 1980s led to the production of praised translations of filmic reality into the comic book format.[28] Dark Horse's *Alien* run also provided a platform for experimentation with epistolary paratexts, which started with the eight-page comic *Aliens: Theory of Alien Propagation* (hereafter *ToAP*).[29] Promoted as a " 'side bar' story taking the readers inside the mind of an Alien Queen,"[30] *ToAP* was a tie-in to the limited comic series *Aliens: Outbreak*,[31] which was a sequel to *Aliens*. Later included in the collected editions of *Outbreak*, *ToAP* was not the only epistolary section in the storyline narrating concepts and events through documents to lend seriousness to fiction.[32] Excerpts from various fictional sources, including a 2057 book "*The Evolution of Television*" by Emmett Webster and an internal memorandum of the multinational conglomerate Bionational, were inserted into the comic through captions. These sections were integral parts of the storyline, providing context or moving the narrative forward. Bearing resemblance to documentary graphic novels based on factual documents, materializing the physically absent in the comic form,[33] *ToAP* on the other hand was in many ways a standalone mockumentary comic elaborating on an epistolary paratextual document that only existed in the quotes in its captions.

Presented as an excerpt from a confidential report written by Dr. Waidslaw Orona, a civilian advisor to the Colonial Marine Corps and one of the main characters of *Outbreak*, the script of the comic imitated the tone and style of an academic essay about the titular creatures. As an epistolary paratext, it explored the alien-hive concept introduced in *Aliens* instead of the idea of the aliens being bioengineered creatures hinted at in *Alien* that would later be further explored in its prequels. The text started with a series of hypotheses on the lifecycle of the aliens and their homeworld, including a process of hive separation, cannibalism among aliens, and possible natural predators. Orona then continued with remarks on how the creatures may have spread to other star systems and turned into alpha predators themselves. The essay concluded with a comparative analysis of the survival instincts of the aliens and humans based on earlier encounters seen in films. The documentary imagery in *ToAP* was combined with the script in an additive manner,[34] amplifying and elaborating the concepts in it: the visuals showed the natural habitat of the aliens to the readers for the first time, offered a scenario based on Orona's vague remarks in which a spacefaring reptilian captured an egg and became its victim, and illustrated the events of the films from the aliens' perspective. Building upon the readers' architextual knowledge of the franchise and reaffirming the specificities of previous *Alien* texts, or by enforcing what Nicolas Labarre calls the intermedial generic convergence in comic book adaptations,[35] each section visually repeated and interpreted key elements of the alien reproduction cycle seen in the movies within new settings (see Martens in this collection for more on the intertextual understanding of the *Alien* franchise). Various intra-diegetic hypotheses presented in *ToAP* as a supposed scientific essay on the other hand were evidence-based thought experiments on the narrative possibilities emerging from these core elements. Intentionally or incidentally, some of these speculations were later portrayed in other *Alien* media, such as hive separation in Dark Horse's *Aliens: Genocide*[36] miniseries and cannibalism in *Alien Resurrection* (Jean-Pierre Jeunet, 1997). In this regard, as a mockumentary comic, *ToAP* had been instrumental to the construction and promotion of a loosely tied *Alien* comic book continuity running parallel to the films and other *Alien* transmedia, reflecting the serial[37] aspects of the franchise's transmedia economics at the time, or how its imaginary world spread across media platforms, without forming a cohesive narrative continuity system.

In 1992 Dark Horse published *Cyberantics*.[38] Promoted as the annotated edition of a previous illustrated children's book on ant socio-biology, supposedly written by the cyberneticist Stanislaw Mayakovsky, it was an epistolary paratext of the Dark Horse's *Aliens: Harvest*[39] miniseries. *Harvest* was a heist story set in a future shaped by the events of *Outbreak*, in which multinationals were harvesting secretions from aliens for medicinal and recreational applications. The comic starts with the recruitment of Mayakovsky, a brilliant scientist diagnosed with terminal cancer, by an experienced thief to steal "royal jelly" from an alien nest on a remote planet. Based on his earlier research on the exploration of ant colonies using synthetic ants, Mayakovsky builds a synthetic alien named Norbert to infiltrate the hive. The story then takes an unexpected turn when they encounter other humans on the planet. As a child-friendly account of Mayakovsky's studies on ants, the core narrative of *Cyberantics*, the content of the unannotated first edition, tells the story of the synthetic ant A7, or Ari. Armed with artificial pheromones, heightened senses, and even a microlaser, Ari explores multiple nests, meets various insects, befriends some, and by making autonomous decisions plays a vital role in the survival of an ant colony. As the inspiration behind the heist plan, this imaginary 2172 edition of *Cyberantics* gets quoted several times in *Harvest*, establishing parallels between Ari's and Norbert's experiences and Mayakovsky's theories on artificial intelligence. Ari also plays the role of a silent observer and a sole survivor in the story of *Harvest*. The synthetic ant's unexpected discovery years later on a space freighter supposedly becomes the inspiration for the publication of the annotated edition.

Absent of any direct reference to the *Alien* franchise in its design and script, the annotated edition of *Cyberantics* looks and reads like a standalone children's book on biological and robotic ants. The annotations "added" by Jerry Prosser (the actual author of *Harvest* and *Cyberantics*), who claims to be a student of Mayakovsky, quote real-world scientific books on ant biology and computing, as well as fictitious documents on synthetic research supposedly written by Mayakovsky in the late twenty-second century. The long afterword by Prosser also summarizes the life, achievements, and troubles of the scientist up until his disappearance, providing insights into his character and his theories on artificial intelligence without mentioning the aliens at all. According to Sid Sondergard, as a tool of meta-structural meaning creation, these annotations help "to illustrate the scientific principles and references to information theory originally encoded"[40] by Mayakovsky in the imaginary first edition. As fictional paratexts, they are also the main apparatuses giving the book its epistolary paratextual characteristics, establishing strong links to the comics continuity.

Reading *Harvest* and *Cyberantics* together deepens readers' understanding of concepts, settings, and characters in both stories and contributes to the plausibility of the franchise's fictional world by exposing similarities and differences between ants and aliens as insectoid species and by providing multiple perspectives on the functioning of cybernetic brains. Nevertheless, both texts can also be read, enjoyed, and analyzed on their own without acknowledging the existence of the other. While this is a common feat for narrative urtexts like *Harvest*, it is unusual for an epistolary paratext like *Cyberantics*, which, thanks to its self-presentation as a children's book, can be read as a text unrelated to the *Alien* franchise. This rare feature shows how the balance between epistolarity and paratextuality in epistolary paratexts can be fluid. Form and style play an important role in the meaning creation of epistolary paratexts. The strongly epistolary *Cyberantics* fulfills the literary functions of the genre it imitates, so much so that these functions overshadow its connection to and reliance on narrative urtexts to create meaning. In this regard, appropriating *Cyberantics* as a postmodern alternative to established textual practices of formal science education, consciously emphasizing its own artificiality, education scholar Noel Gough argues that the book "raises many questions about the conduct of scientific research, the nature of human, animal and artificial intelligence, the social organisation of scientific labour and the reconstruction of scientific knowledge for public consumption."[41] Gough's approach disregards the epistolary paratextual aura of *Cyberantics* and leaves the meanings emerging out of the book's claim of being the product of a specific time and space in an imaginary future defined by the *Alien* franchise in general and by *Harvest* specifically unaddressed. His reading exposes how conceptual layers embedded to the annotated text as identified by Sondergard may permit alternate, partial readings beyond the interdependencies of paratextuality because of its strong epistolarity. In this regard, *Cyberantics* even today remains a unique book in the history of the *Alien* franchise. No other *Alien* epistolary paratext would push the limits of transmedial seriality of the franchise that far again. Instead, they would follow to a more sequential[42] approach in later decades, seeking and promoting a continuity between and across media.

Evidence-Based Speculations

Following the success of *Alien* comics in the United States, in the early 1990s Dark Horse established its international branch to take advantage of the demand in the European markets.[43] In line with the common overseas comics syndication practices in the United Kingdom at the time,[44] instead of simply reissuing comics in their original form, Dark Horse International incorporated them into the monthly *Aliens Magazine*, reprinting serialized versions of several titles in each issue and featuring additional exclusive content such as news articles, interviews, and the regular *Technical Readout* section. Written by Lee Brimmicombe-Wood in an in-universe style and covering various scientific and technological aspects of the fictional world of *Alien* films, *Technical Readout* was a reference-oriented episodic epistolary paratext originating in fan practices. According to a 2007 interview,[45] Brimmicombe-Wood wrote a series of fan essays inspired by *Aliens* years before the *Aliens Magazine*. Then, in the search for new material as a writer, he polished them to become the first *Technical Readout* content. With positive feedback from fans, Dark Horse proposed to turn the section into a comic miniseries, but the project got dropped when Dark Horse International was closed.[46] Brimmicombe-Wood took the idea to Boxtree Publishing, which could only provide a license for *Aliens*, and thus the edited and extended

Technical Readout content was released as *Aliens: Colonial Marines Technical Manual*[47] (hereafter *CMTM*) in 1995.

CMTM was a guide describing the history, organization, and tactics of Colonial Marine Corps, supposedly written by unknown authors appointed by the Corps after the events of *Aliens*. Utilizing a technical writing style supported by technical diagrams,[48] the book imitated the form of an internal document. It combined institutional and technological data and imagery with personal accounts of servicemen and commanders. While recounting *Aliens* in its last chapter, the book's focus was on providing a detailed, realistic, but also engaging description of the film's world beyond the screen. Besides explaining the working principles of the military machinery seen in *Aliens*, Brimmicombe-Wood also introduced a plausible organizational structure for interstellar military operations, technical and tactical data on new arms and equipment, as well as new vehicles inspired by the design of the film which would arguably be needed by the Colonial Marine Corps if it were an operational military force.

Speculating on what it would take to make props, models, and set pieces to actually function, the book filled in gaps in various world infrastructures. Thus, it contributed to what Wolf calls the "completeness" of a fictional world, or "to the degree to which the world contains explanations and details covering all the various aspects of its characters' experiences, as well as background details which together suggest a feasible, practical world."[49] So much so, *CMTM* was mentioned alongside *Aliens* in an unclassified military operational research study[50] as an example of extensive level research conducted on future military technologies in speculative fiction that had the potential to inform and educate armed personnel on tactical developments based on new technologies. Nevertheless, the book also reflected the critical position of *Aliens* toward the military[51] through multiple personal accounts quoted in the text. These quotes reflected a dichotomy between an official gung-ho position praising military technology and the might of the Corps, and one hinting at corruption, mismanagement, and even war crimes. On the humorous side, the book also quoted several rumors on the events of *Aliens* among lower-ranking soldiers, which ranged from brief hearsays to tall tales filled with exaggerations, reflecting the secrecy and corruption within the Corps. This corruption becomes even more evident in the last chapter mainly consisting of logs of exchanges between Weyland-Yutani executives and scientists who review the events of the film and cold-heartedly discuss profitable follow-up strategies.

Recounting his research for the book, Brimmicombe-Wood describes[52] how he had studied the film and production documents intensively, interviewed actors, visited prop houses, and collaborated with the organizers of the *Alien War* attraction in London for costumed photoshoots. Despite being a licensed endeavor, Brimmicombe-Wood's research on the film and its paratexts resemble what Mittell[53] calls forensic fandom, approaching *Aliens* as a drillable text to understand the complexity of its story and its telling. Leading to the creation of wikis and other online platforms to share findings and discuss future possibilities, fan forensics is a part of the contemporary *Alien* fandom as well. Multiple wikis and so-called lore channels on YouTube aim to present a total summary of the world of the *Alien* franchise by compiling and organizing data from various sources. Describing such forensic texts as evidence-based paratexts, compiling and (re-)presenting existing information, John Quinn argues that they enrich "the intellectual property of the Alien cinematic universe, rather than specifically creating new works of fan fiction that modify or advance the Alien concept."[54]

Yet, *CMTM* was not only a curated text but had its roots in evidence-based fan speculation as well. In this regard, it was a product of what Rehak calls design-oriented blueprint culture, "taking materials offered by official production sources and elaborating on them to fill in gaps, explain contradictions, and connect dots, building stable, consistent frameworks from the inevitably partial and fragmentary pieces doled out by the media industry."[55] Seeking out a fine balance between a curated retelling of and elaboration on the concepts introduced in the film, Brimmicombe-Wood took a twofold approach. To present perspectives and hypotheses on the alien species without reaching strict conclusions and risking contradictions with future installments,[56] he utilized creative apparatuses such as observations and quotes. These allowed him to introduce new ideas on the nature of creatures as speculations that can be falsified by future *Alien* media. But when it came to military organization and technology, areas with relative importance in terms of the franchise's general themes, he offered a wide range of new concepts as factual data. Describing the technological aspects of the imaginary future of *Aliens*, much like *Star Trek* epistolary paratexts of the past, *CMTM* designed with fiction and imagined, as Julian Bleecker suggested, a "different kind of world by outlining the contours, rendering the artifacts as story props, then using them to imagine new possibilities."[57] The book described convincingly how *Aliens'* futuristic military-industrial complex worked, by properly extrapolating contemporary military tradition, resembling the way Andrew May argued convincing science fiction should approach scientific methodology.[58] By doing so, *CMTM* contributed to the worldbuilding of the *Alien* franchise without contradicting its hybrid reality. It became a core source material on the *Alien* universe's military technology and culture, as evidenced by the borrowing of its concepts and ideas by games like *Aliens versus Predator*[59] (1999), *Aliens versus Predator: Extinction*[60] (2003), and *Aliens: Colonial Marines*[61] (2013).

Indexical Transmedia and Constructive Curation

In the years following the publication of *CMTM*, the production of *Alien* epistolary-paratexts stagnated. The epistolary paratexts published in this period were rare tie-ins to *Alien* transmedia, such as promotional mocku-mentary comics[62] and intra-diegetic databases attached to video games.[63] These were written as what Mittell calls "what is" transmedia texts, seeking "to extend the fiction canonically, explaining the universe with coordinated precision and hopefully expanding viewers' understanding and apprecia-tion of the storyworld."[64] But without a strict policy on the canonicity of li-censed *Alien* products,[65] they were, in many ways, apocryphal transmedia extensions, similar to "what if" transmedia texts, which according to Mittell multiply "the possibilities of [fiction] into the realm of hypothetical varia-tions and transmutations."[66] Starting with the 2010s though, new types of epistolary paratexts started to emerge as part of the attempts to construct a consistent, sequential *Alien* storyworld across media. Accompanying *Alien* prequels, they followed industry trends in film promotion and object-oriented transmedia publication (see Walden in this collection for more on online marketing campaigns of *Alien* prequels).

In 2012, the *Alien* prequel *Prometheus* was preceded by a month-long marketing campaign bearing resemblance to alternate reality games (ARGs). Utilized in film promotion since the early 2000s, ARGs are com-plex narrative-driven transmedia treasure hunts built around the princi-ples of ubiquitous computing.[67] Components of ARGs are intra-diegetic and appear as authentic online content. According to Palmer and Petroski, ARGs function as "a transmedia storytelling device that blurs the lines be-tween the real world and the game world."[68] In this regard, they are ludic online epistolary narratives. Built around "a veneer of corporate logics and aesthetic officialdom,"[69] the *Prometheus* campaign utilized a series of corporate websites providing detailed information on Weyland Corporation. Online epistolary videos such as Peter Weyland's (Guy Pearce) 2023 TED Talk, advertisements for David-8 (Michael Fassbender) model synthetics, and communication logs featuring Dr. Elizabeth Shaw (Noomi Rapace) introduced these key characters and their core motivations.[70] Initially linked through ludic activities positioning players as corporate employees,[71] most of these epistolary documents became accessible to wider audiences as the campaign proceeded, and later were collected in Blu-ray releases of the film, along with new epistolary paratextual documents such as the intra-diegetic personal archives of Peter Weyland. Instead of telling a coherent side story, the campaign constructed the corporate and technological backdrop of the film and subtly linked it to the *Alien* franchise. The products section of the Weyland Industries website, for example, provided descriptions of tools which would play a key role in the film, and technologies like the Power Loader, which would become staples of the *Alien* universe's future. According to Anne Zeiser, the *Prometheus* campaign "blended the story's fictional universe with the audience's real-world [. . .], heightened the mystery around the film with a drip-feed of in-universe content, [. . .] and, it blended the story and its promotion into a single storytelling enterprise."[72] The ARG inspired campaign resembled "indexical storytelling" in video games where the narrative discovery revolves around the investigation of various kinds of documents spread to the game world.[73] The indexical transmedia approach of the *Prometheus* campaign revolved around the investigation of epistolary paratexts spread to the web instead, in line with Henry Jenkins's conceptualization of transmedia texts inviting audiences to construct a fictional reality from fragments.[74]

The 2017 sequel to *Prometheus*, *Covenant* would be marketed by a similar but less ludic campaign. Online video transmissions of the crew of the colony ship Covenant,[75] focused more on character introduction than worldbuilding. Even the advertisements for the new Walter (Michael Fassbender) model synthetics were designed to emphasize the androids' differences from the David-8 model.[76] Sponsored by the semiconductor company AMD, these promotions presented the construction of the Walter series with a poetic yet plausible industrial realism. According to Herlander Elias and Flávio Almeida, these advertisements were using "the story world and the hype of this new movie to tell the audience a story that is not in the movie and at the same time [mixing] fantasy [...] with reality,"[77] which arguably provided these epistolary paratexts with an even higher level of pseudo-factual credibility.

The release of its epistolary paratexts continued after the theatrical run of the *Covenant*. They acted as indexical transmedia components moving the plot of the film forward. The 2018 book *David's Drawings*[78] collected dozens of drawings briefly seen in the film. Like *Nostromo Dossiers*, they were previously inaccessible diegetic documents inviting the readers to an exploration of the synthetic David's activities during his isolation between the two films. Revealing the details of his gruesome experiments on Dr. Shaw, these drawings were worldbuilding documents imitating the records of a scientific study reflecting David's thought processes. Released as an extra in the *Covenant* Blu-ray, the epistolary paratextual short film *Advent* (Matthew Thorne, 2017) took the form of a transmission sent by David to Weyland-Yutani after the events of the film. In it, David summarizes his previous experiments and actions, then reveals his plans, and finally challenges the company. Acting as a sequel, *Advent* sets the ground for not only possible future feature films but also for the official short *David's Lab: Last Signs of Life* (2019), in which Weyland-Yutani tracks the rogue synthetic.

Throughout the 2010s, attempts towards a coordinated transmedial expansion of the *Alien* franchise also led to the publication of epistolary paratextual books trying to construct a cohesive history and a continuous universe. Coinciding with the emergence of similarly functioning fan productions such as online "lore" and "explored" videos,[79] these books were curating and linking the events of multiple *Alien* films and occasionally other *Alien* media. The 2014 *Alien: The Weyland-Yutani Report*[80] by S. D. Perry presented itself as a confidential document describing the agenda of the corporation. It tried to establish a plausible corporate history by linking the events of the films. The book also contained personal profiles and annotated technical drawings. Treating the aliens as a resource, the report presented concepts for weaponizing the creatures as well. A multimodal book, it came with a series of replica documents which aimed to strengthen the report's authenticity, including the memoir of Robert Morse (Danny Webb), the sole survivor of Fiorina 161 from *Alien³*, which was mentioned in the official novelization of *Alien Resurrection*.[81] Claiming to be a practical combat guide for the Colonial Marine Corps, the 2017 *Alien: Augmented Reality Survival*

Manual[82] by Owen Williams had a similar structure to *Weyland-Yutani Report*. In addition to summaries, personal profiles, and technical data, the book also contained tactical instructions based on the military encounters depicted in the films, albeit not as detailed as *CMTM*. The book also used the artwork of and made references to technologies, creatures, and events of the 2013 video game *Aliens: Colonial Marines*, which was advertised by 20th Century Fox as a canonical story linking *Aliens* and *Alien*[3].[83] Finally, the 2019 *Alien: The Blueprints*[84] by Graham J. Langridge was a collection of detailed blueprints of major spacecraft, vehicles, and structures from the films, accompanied by technical notes explaining their workings. Building upon sets photography and production art, these blueprints were artistic speculations on the series' design history.

All three books utilized apparatuses like quotes and retellings in varying levels to differentiate observation-based "hard facts" from speculations to prevent future inconsistencies. This seems to be influenced by factors besides the creative decisions of the authors. Perry[85] describes how her writing process had been monitored by multiple stakeholders and she was directed not to explore certain themes reserved for future films, but also to refer to specific tie-in titles for promotional purposes. Calling his work a "weird line between writing a companion to the films and actually writing in-universe fiction,"[86] Williams explains how the content of his book was influenced by the app development. Langridge[87] describes how his yearlong fan work had led to the publication of his book, and his creative process was shaped by design archaeological research and a desire for realism and consistency. A common aspect among all authors was their collaboration with fan communities and various degrees of reliance on fan theories and content, reflecting the importance of fandom in keeping track of complex fictional universes of long-running transmedia franchises. In this regard, instead of competing with fan-made referential paratexts, these epistolary paratexts seem to offer fans validation and new speculative perspectives emerging out of their pseudo-factual forms.

Conclusion

Since the beginning of the transformation of Ridley Scott's 1979 film into a media franchise, epistolary paratexts have been part of *Alien*. They contributed to its construction by fulfilling various functions and were shaped by its transformations. Early epistolary paratexts methodologically investigated the franchise's narrative possibilities, expanded it with detailed and plausible speculations, used form and style to explore institutional ideologies, and exposed how properly imitating factual writing can contribute to other fields of inquiry. They were providing new perspectives to fans who had few alternatives. The release of *Prometheus* marks a turning point between these experimental and highly focused epistolary paratexts and later coordinated, brand-oriented, industrial titles. Some prequel-era epistolary paratexts were utilized as components of indexical narratives contributing to the films' stories and worldbuilding synchronously. Others acted as curatorial texts weaving previous titles together as a continuous canonical transmedia narrative, highlighting selected parts of a decades-old corpus. They drew inspiration from fan products and through corporate posture and technical speculation inspired them at the same time. As intra-diegetic non-fictional documents, epistolary paratexts offered unique perspectives as companion pieces to established and ongoing narratives of the franchise in both periods. The changes in their style reflected the changes in the franchise's size and direction. With the future of the *Alien* franchise in flux after the recent acquisition of 20th Century Fox by Disney,[88] epistolary paratexts may become instrumental again in its reshaping under new management, as platforms for speculation, curation, and promotion.

Notes

1. Jonathan W. Rinzler, *The Making of Aliens* (London: Titan Books, 2020).
2. Alan Dean Foster, *Aliens: The Official Movie Novelization* (London: Titan Books, 2014), ebook, chap. 1.
3. Victor Wells, "Aliens: An Out of This World Communication with Director James Cameron," in *James Cameron: Interviews*, ed. Brent Dunham (Jackson: University Press of Mississippi, 2012), 19–22.
4. Jeffrey Walker, *The Authorized Portfolio of Crew Insignias from The United States Commercial Spaceship Nostromo* (Los Angeles: The Thinking Cap Company, 1980).
5. Nicholas Paige, "Pseudofactuality," in *Narrative Factuality—A Handbook*, ed. Monika Fludernik and Marie-Laure Ryan (Berlin: De Gruyter, 2020), 593–600.

6. Matt Hills, "Transmedia Paratexts: Informational, Commercial, Diegetic, and Auratic Circulation," in *The Routledge Companion to Transmedia Studies*, ed. Matthew Freeman and Renira Rampazzo Gambarato (London: Routledge, 2019), 289–296.

7. C. Dena, "Transmedia Practice: Theorising the Practice of Expressing a Fictional World across Distinct Media and Environments" (PhD diss., University of Sydney, 2009).

8. Genette, Gérard, *Paratexts: Thresholds of Interpretation* (Cambridge: Cambridge University Press, 1997).

9. Raul Rodriguez Ferrandiz, "Paratextual Activity: Updating the Genettian Approach within the Transmedia Turn," *Communication & Society* 30, no. 1 (2017), 165–182.

10. Jason Mittell, *Complex TV: The Poetics of Contemporary Television Storytelling* (New York: NYU Press: 2015), ebook.

11. Ibid.

12. Mark J. P. Wolf, "Appendix: Types of World-Building," in *World-Builders on World-Building, an Exploration of Subcreation*, ed. Mark J. P. Wolf (London: Routledge, 2020), Google Play Books, appendix.

13. Gerard Hynes, "Geography and Maps" in *The Routledge Companion to Imaginary Worlds*, ed. Mark J. P. Wolf (New York: Routledge, 2018), ebook, chap. 13.

14. Maria Löschnigg and Rebekka Schuh, "Epistolarity. Theoretical and Generic Preliminaries," in *The Epistolary Renaissance: A Critical Approach to Contemporary Letter Narratives in Anglophone Fiction*, ed. Maria Löschnigg and Rebekka Schuh (Berlin: De Gruyter, 2018), 15–44.

15. Alexandra Heller-Nicholas, *Found Footage Horror Films: Fear and the Appearance of Reality* (Jefferson: McFarland, 2014), ebook.

16. Michael T. Saler, *As If: Modern Enchantment and the Literary Prehistory of Virtual Reality* (New York: Oxford University Press, 2012).

17. Sally Bushell, "Paratext or Imagetext? Interpreting the Gictional Map," *Word and Image* 32, no. 2 (2016), 181–194.

18. Stuart Sillars, *Visualisation in Popular Fiction 1860–1960: Graphic Narratives, Fictional Images* (New York: Routledge: 1995).

19. Alwyn W. Turner, *The Man Who Invented the Daleks: The Strange Worlds of Terry Nation* (London: Aurum Press, 2011).

20. Bob Rehak, *More Than Meets the Eye: Special Effects and the Fantastic Transmedia Franchise* (New York: New York University Press, 2018).

21. Veli-Matti Karhulahti, "Feelies: The Lost Art of Immersing the Narrative" (conference paper, DiGRA Nordic '12: International DiGRA Nordic Conference, University of Tampare, Tampare, June 5–8, 2012)

22. Hank Blumenthal, "Storyscape: A New Medium of Media" (PhD diss., Georgia Institute of Technology, 2016).

23. Alison Gibbons, "Reading S. Across Media: Transmedia Storyworlds, Multimodal Fiction, and Real Readers," *Narrative* 25, no. 3 (2017), 321–341.

24. Daniel Wallace, *The Jedi Path: A Manual for Students of the Force* (Bellevue: Becker&Mayer, 2011).

25. Bob Rehak, "Transmedia Space Battles: Reference Materials and Miniatures Wargames in 1970s *Star Trek* Fandom," *Science Fiction Film & Television* 9, no. 3 (2016), 325–345.

26. Caetlin Benson-Allott, "Dreadful Architecture: Zones of Horror in Alien and Lee Bontecou's Wall Sculptures," *Journal of Visual Culture* 14, no. 3 (2015), 267–278.

27. Martin Flanagan, "The Alien Series and Generic Hybridity," in *Alien Identities: Exploring Differences in Film and Fiction*, ed. Deborah Cartmell, I.Q. Hunter, Heidi Kaye, and Imelda Whelehan (London: Pluto Press, 1999), 156–171.

28. Kerry Gough, "Translation Creativity and Alien Econ(c)omics. From Hollywood Blockbuster to Dark Horse Comic Book," in *Film and Comic Books*, ed. Ian Gordon, Mark Jancovich and Matthew P. McAllister (Jackson: University Press of Mississippi, 2007), 37–63.

29. Mark Verheiden and Mark A. Nelson, "Alien," *Dark Horse Presents*, Now 01, 1988, 1–8.

30. "Dark Horse Presents #24," *Dark Horse Comics*, NA (accessed May 17, 2020), https://www.darkhorse.com/Comics/91-156/Dark-Horse-Presents-24

31. Mark Verheiden, *Aliens: Outbreak* (Milwaukie: Dark Horse, 1988–1989).

32. David Herman, Manfred Jahn, and Marie-Laure Ryan, ed., *Routledge Encyclopedia of Narrative Theory* (London: Routledge, 2005), s.v. "Epistolary Novel."

33. Hillary L Chute, *Disaster Drawn: Visual Witness, Comics, and Documentary Form* (Cambridge: Harvard University Press, 2016).

34. Scott McCloud, *Understanding Comics: The Invisible Art* (New York: Harper Colins, 1993).

35. Nicolas Labarre, *Understanding Genres in Comics* (London: Palgrave Macmillan, 2020).

36. Mike Richardson and John Arcudi, *Aliens: Genocide* (Milwaukee: Dark Horse, 1991–1992).

37. William Proctor, "Transmedia Comics: Seriality, Sequentiality and the Shifting Economies of Franchise Licensing," in *The Routledge Companion to Transmedia Studies*, ed. Matthew Freeman and Renira Rampazzo Gambarato (London: Routledge, 2019), 52–61.

38. Jerry Prosser, *Cyberantics* (Milwaukee: Dark Horse, 1992).

39. Jerry Prosser, *Aliens: Harvest* (Milwaukee: Dark Horse, 1992).

40. Sid Sondergard, "The Unconscious Structured Like a Comic Book: (Re)constructive Psychology and Matt Howarth's Bugtown Mythos," *Semiotics* NA (1992), 288–299.

41. Noel Gough, "RhizomANTically Becoming-Cyborg: Performing Posthuman Pedagogies," *Educational Philosophy and Theory* 36, no. 3 (2004), 258.

42. Proctor, "Transmedia Comics: Seriality, Sequentiality and the Shifting Economies of Franchise Licensing."

43. "Aliens Magazine: Highlights from the Dark Horse International Publication," *Alien Archives*, March 23, 2019 (accessed May 10, 2020), https://alien-archives.com/2019/03/23/aliens-magazine-highlights-from-the-dark-horse-international-publication/.

44. Phillip Vaughan, interviewed by Dez Skinn, "No Cricket Strips Here!," *Studies in Comics* 8, no. 1 (2017), 85–102.

45. Lee Brimmicombe-Woods, interviewed by NA, "Lee Brimmicombe-Woods, Author, CMTM," Alien Experience, May 4, 2007 (accessed May 10, 2020), https://web.archive.

org/web/20100917072054/http://alienexperience.com/index.php?option=com_cont
ent&view=article&id=86:lee-brimmicombe-woods-author-cmtm&catid=36:intervi
ews&Itemid=50.

46. Brimmicombe-Woods, interview.

47. Lee Brimmicombe-Woods, *Aliens: Colonial Marines Technical Manual* (London: Boxtree Ltd., 1995).

48. Gerald J. Alred, Walter E. Oliu, and Charles T. Brusaw, *The Handbook of Technical Writing, Eleventh Edition* (Boston: Bedford/St. Martin's, 2015).

49. Mark J. P. Wolf, *Building Imaginary Worlds: The Theory and History of Subcreation* (New York: Routledge, 2012).

50. Ian M. Mitchell, "Shaping Things to Come: Combat Scenarios for Planning" (conference paper, The 13th International Symposium on Military Operational Research, The Royal Military Collage of Science, Shrivenham, September 3–6, 1996).

51. Tanine Allison, "How to Recognize a War Movie: The Contemporary Science-Fiction Blockbuster as Military Recruitment Film," in *A Companion to the War Film*, ed. Douglas A. Cunningham and John C. Nelson (Chichester: John Wiley & Sons, 2016) 253–270.

52. Brimmicombe-Woods, interview.

53. Jason Mittell, "Forensic Fandom and the Drillable Text," in Spreadable Media: Creating Value and Meaning in a Networked Culture, ed. Henry Jenkins, Sam Ford, and Joshua Green (New York: NYU Press, 2013), web-exclusive essay (accessed June 5, 2020), http://spreadablemedia.org/essays/mittell/#.W4cZUvZFwYw.

54. John Quinn, "Beyond the Space Jockey: YouTube, Morphogenetic Paratexts and the Alien Universe," *Cinephile* 14, no. 1 (2020), 34–39.

55. Rehak, *More Than Meets the Eye*, 29.

56. Brimmicombe-Woods, interview.

57. Julian Bleecker, "Design Fiction: From Props to Prototypes" (conference paper, 6th Swiss Design Network Conference, Institute for Research in Art and Design HGK, Basel, October 28–30, 2010).

58. Andrew May, *Fake Physics: Spoofs, Hoaxes and Fictitious Science* (Berlin: Springer, 2019).

59. *Aliens versus Predator* (Rebellion, Fox Interactive, 1999), video game.

60. *Aliens versus Predator: Extinction* (EA Games, Fox Interactive, 2003), video game.

61. *Aliens: Colonial Marines* (Gearbox, SEGA, 2013) video game.

62. John Arcudi, *Free Comic Book Day: Aliens/Predator* (Milwaukie: Dark Horse: 2009).

63. *Aliens versus Predator: Extinction Bestiary* (EA Games, Fox Interactive, 2003), information database.

64. Mittell, *Complex TV*, chap 9.

65. Rüdiger Heinze, "Alien Adapted (Again and Again): Fictional Universes between Difference and Repetition," in *Adaptation in the Age of Media Convergence*, ed. Johannes Fehrle and Werner Schäfke-Zell (Amsterdam: Amsterdam University Press, 2019), 159–174.

66. Mittell, *Complex TV*, chap 9.

67. Sarah Arkinson, *Beyond the Screen: Emerging Cinema and Engaging Audiences* (New York: Bloomsbury, 2015).
68. Charles Palmer and Andy Petroski, *Alternate Reality Games: Gamification for Performance* (Boca Raton: CRC Press, 2016).
69. Sarah Arkinson, *Beyond the Screen*, 44.
70. Nicole Gabriel, Bogna Kazur, and Kai Matuszkiewicz, "Reconsidering Transmedia(l) Worlds," in *Convergence Culture Reconsidered*, ed. Claudia Georgi and Brigitte Johanna Glaser (Göttüngen: Universitätsverlag Göttingen, 2015), 163–194.
71. Anne Zeiser, "Prometheus: Blending Fictional and Real Worlds," Transmedia Marketing, NA (accessed June 14, 2020), https://s3-eu-west-1.amazonaws.com/s3-euw1-ap-pe-ws4-cws-documents.ri-prod/9780415716116/PrometheusCaseStudyFI NAL.pdf.
72. Anne Zeiser, "Prometheus," 7.
73. Clara Fernández-Vara, "Game Spaces Speak Volumes: Indexical Storytelling" (conference paper, DiGRA International Conference: Think Design Play, Utrecht School of the Arts, Hilversum, September 14–17, 2011).
74. Henry Jenkins, "Revenge of the Origami Unicorn: The Remaining Four Principles of Transmedia Storytelling," *Confessions of an Aca-Fan*, December 12, 2009 (accessed July 11, 2020), http://henryjenkins.org/blog/2009/12/revenge_of_the_origami_unic orn.html.
75. "Crew Message: Daniels," 20th Century Studios UK, April 20, 2017 (accessed July 11, 2020), https://www.youtube.com/watch?v=njj1R4mh5PM.
76. Chris Eyerman, "Meet Walter," Chris Eyerman Personal Website, NA, accessed July 11, 2020, http://chriseyerman.com/work/meet-walter/.
77. Herlander Elias and Flávio Almeida, "Narrative-Verse: On Transmedia, Narrative and Digital Media Audiences," *Communication Studies* 27, no. 2 (2018), 3–16.
78. Dane Hallett and Matt Hatton, *Alien: Covenant—David's Drawings* (London: Titan Books, 2018).
79. Quinn, "Beyond the Space Jockey: YouTube, Morphogenetic Paratexts and the Alien Universe."
80. Stephani D. Perry, *Alien: The Weyland-Yutani Report* (San Rafael: Insight Editions, 2014).
81. Ann Carol Crispin, *Alien Resurrection: The Official Movie Novelization* (London: Titan Books, 2015).
82. Owen Williams, *Alien: Augmented Reality Survival Manual* (New York: Harper Design, 2017).
83. James Fleury and Stephen Mamber, "The (Im)perfect Organism: Dissecting the *Alien* Media Franchise," in *The Franchise Era: Managing Media in the Digital Economy*, ed. James Fleury, Bryan Hikari Hartzheim, and Stephen Mamber (Edinburgh: Edinburgh University Press, 2019), 31–51.
84. Graham J. Langridge, *Alien: The Blueprints* (London: Titan Books, 2019).
85. Stephani D. Perry, "Reply #379," *Alien: The Weyland-Yutani Report* (AvPGalaxy Forums), September 06, 2014 (accessed July 8, 2020), https://www.avpgalaxy.net/forum/index.php?topic=49493.msg1981127#msg1981127.

86. Owen Williams, interviewed by Andrew Jamieson "Geekzine Q&A: Owen WIlliams," *Geekzine UK*, February 14, 2018 (accessed May 10, 2020), http://www.geekzine. co.uk/2018/02/geekzine-qa-owen-williams/?LMCL=fUGVUc.

87. Langridge, *Alien: The Blueprints*.

88. Matt McGloin, "Aliens, Predator Movies Likely from Disney with New Marvel Comics Titles," *Cosmic Book News*, July 3, 2020 (accessed July 11, 2020), https://cos micbook.news/aliens-predator-marvel-comics.

9

"Must Be a Chick Thing"

Ripley, the *Alien* Franchise and the Female Gothic

Frances A. Kamm

In his 1979 review, Vincent Canby calls *Alien* a "Gothic set in space," noting that there is something "old-fashioned" about the film: "There was once a time when this sort of thing was set in an old dark house, on a moor, in a thunderstorm. Being trendy, Mr. Scott and his associates have sent it up in space."[1] In this chapter, I will reflect upon the implications of describing the film as "Gothic," arguing that the franchise engages with the traditions of the Female Gothic, specifically. The Female Gothic is typically defined by stories in which a central female protagonist is imperiled within isolated locations, usually because of a villainous male figure and/or patriarchal structures more broadly. *Alien* evokes this narrative patterning as the film comes to center on Ripley as the heroine, resisting the sexualized threat of the xenomorph in conjunction with the exploitative nature of the Company. The decision to interpret the film as a Female Gothic is not arbitrary: indeed, Female Gothic stories enjoyed a resurgence in the 1970s, during *Alien*'s production and release. This is not to claim that *Alien*'s filmmakers were consciously referencing the Female Gothic but, rather, to highlight how the two are historical contemporaries: as shall be seen, Canby's description of the film parallels the increased visibility of Female Gothic motifs and themes evident in other stories with a comparable focus on a woman's perception and experience.

Furthermore, I will show how these Female Gothic tropes continue to appear within the film's larger franchise, following Ripley's appearances in *Aliens* (1986), *Alien³* (1992), and *Alien Resurrection* (1997).[2] Indeed, when analyzing the franchise through the lens of the Female Gothic, it is fascinating to see how these four films—produced within varying historical contexts, with different filmmakers and diverse narrative set-ups—can be brought into a new dialogue, with the Female Gothic functioning as an intertextual and

Frances A. Kamm, *"Must Be a Chick Thing"* In: *Alien Legacies.* Edited by: Nathan Abrams and Gregory Frame, Oxford University Press. © Oxford University Press 2023. DOI: 10.1093/oso/9780197556023.003.0009 transmedial structuring element. To trace these links, the following is divided into three sections. First, I outline some defining features of the Female Gothic, emphasizing the historical contextualization between this enduring tradition and the emergence of *Alien* in the 1970s. Next, I highlight how Gothic figures have coincided with transmedia storytelling and argue that the Female Gothic can be conceptualized within this trend, and Ripley's continued presence within the franchise's "Quadrilogy" is an excellent case study for this purpose. The final section analyses the films themselves, focusing on three main tropes reoccurring in the franchise: isolated space(s), (secret) male threats, validating female experience. The final sub-section—return of the repressed (m)others—offers some concluding remarks.[3]

Revisiting the *Alien* franchise via the Female Gothic will provide another way of considering these films together, illuminating both the continued cultural currency of the Female Gothic tradition, and Ripley as a screen icon.

The Female Gothic

The *Alien* films have elsewhere been described as "Gothic": *Alien* as an "old dark house in space,"[4]; *Aliens* as a Gothic science-fiction,[5] and the franchise's films owing "much to the Gothic for their effects and narratives."[6] That Canby should call *Alien* "Gothic" at the time of its release is especially significant. Contemporaneous to *Alien* was the popularity of a particular type of Gothic story that focused on a woman's experience of traumatic events in remote locations. In 1973, Joanna Russ called this fiction "Modern Gothics": paperbacks emerging in the 1960s from publishers like Ace Books and authors such as Phyllis A. Witney. Russ's overview of the genre's "elements" are evocative of Canby's observations: "To a large, lonely, usually brooding *House* (always named) comes a *Heroine* who is young, orphaned, unloved, and lonely. . . . The House is set in exotic, vivid and/or isolated *Country*."[7] Alongside the combination of "Heroine" and "Old Dark House," Russ outlines tropes like the "Super-Male" and a "Buried Ominous Secret" the Heroine uncovers, revealing "immoral and usually criminal activity."[8] The latter also forms a key inspiration for Angela Carter's *The Bloody Chamber*: a 1979 feminist re-telling of fairy-tales published the same year as *Alien*'s release. The titular story re-imagines "Bluebeard," an important pre-text for the Gothic stories Russ describes: "Bluebeard" is about a woman who defies her husband's command by unlocking his secret chamber to which she has been given a key. Upon doing so she discovers the murdered bodies of his previous wives—women who, presumably, also committed this transgressive act. Four years later another feminist author, Margaret Atwood, published her own re-telling of the tale in "Bluebeard's Egg."[9]

The Gothic-inspired narrative patterning and imagery evident in these literary works was not new to the 1960s and 1970s: in fact, at the same time the Gothic was enjoying this resurgence in popular culture, scholars were beginning to re-assess an earlier literary trend that provides a crucial predecessor for these "Modern Gothics" and, by extension, Carter's and Atwood's work.[10] This trend or genre is the Female Gothic. The Female Gothic is a term coined by Ellen Moers in 1976 to identify a specific trend in literature that focuses on "the work that women writers have done in the literary mode that, since the eighteenth century, we have called the Gothic."[11] For Moers, the work of Ann Radcliffe and Mary Shelley are key examples. Shelley is famous for her seminal Gothic text *Frankenstein; or, The Modern Prometheus* (1818), but, Moers argues, the novel is also an example of the *Female* Gothic. Moers writes that despite the novel not having a main female protagonist, *Frankenstein* still embodies female concerns. Moers calls *Frankenstein* a "birth myth" that engages with its real-life author's traumatic experiences of pregnancy and motherhood: "Death and birth were thus hideously intermixed in the life of Mary Shelley as in Frankenstein's 'workshop of filthy creation.'"[12] Therefore even though Shelley's work does not follow the narrative patterning identified by Russ, *Frankenstein* evokes key gendered themes, including one that can be argued to be at the heart of Female Gothic narratives: motherhood.[13]

Prior to Shelley was Ann Radcliffe, whose novels more directly mirror the conventions Russ would identify in paperbacks two centuries later. Radcliffe's Female Gothic stories concern "a young woman who is simultaneously persecuted victim and courageous heroine." This heroine is a woman "who moves, who acts, who copes with vicissitude and adventure,"[14] which includes the navigation of challenging terrain—in both literal and figurative terms. Sandra M. Gilbert and Susan Gubar—again in 1979—build on Moers's methodology to trace these tropes into the nineteenth century, similarly aiming to analyze a "neglected" history of women's writing, with Charlotte Bronte's *Jane Eyre* (1847) a key text. Like Moers, Gilbert and Gubar read these female authors and their characters as emblems of a "female impulse to struggle free from social and literary confinement."[15] It is for these reasons that the Female Gothic concerns itself with gender politics:

[It] is the heroine's experiences which become the focus of attention, and her experiences are represented as a journey leading towards the assumption of some kind of agency and power in the patriarchal world.[16]

That the Female Gothic (re)emerges in literary fiction and academic discourse in the 1970s is, perhaps, unsurprising: stories about a woman struggling against patriarchal forces, told from her point of view, bears much radical potential in a world seeking reproductive rights and other significant reforms for the lives of women within Radical Feminism and Second-Wave movements. The Female Gothic heroine is, after all, a transgressive figure: she has narrative agency, her perception of events is privileged, and her investigation invariably challenges oppressive patriarchal forces that seek to control and remove her political, societal, and even bodily autonomy. For these 1970s feminist scholars, the Female Gothic is "a subversive genre which expressed women's fears and fantasies, their protests against the conditions of patriarchy."[17]

Such a context is equally significant to Ripley in *Alien*. Ripley "engages the audience as a representative of the women's movement, and particularly its Second Wave struggle for affirmation during the period of the film's production in the late 1970s," with the film tracing the "radicalization" of Ripley in response to "the patriarchal nature of the Company's plans."[18] This is not to say that Ripley was, then, an inherently "feminist" woman: Ripley's "radicalization" only takes place when her "explicit trust in the hierarchical assumptions of the organization and an investment in the micro-society of the ship" is broken.[19] Similarly, the Female Gothic heroine is not without criticism when it comes to her progressive potential: "Whether female Gothic should be seen as radical or conservative has been an issue of particular concern."[20] Russ, for example, is skeptical that the 1970s paperbacks ever break free of "a middle-class" belief in the feminine mystique.[21]

Whether the Female Gothic is, ultimately, progressive is beyond the scope of the present investigation.[22] The analysis below will, however, demonstrate how Ripley is continually reinvented as an imperiled woman under conditions that are reminiscent of those Female Gothic narratives as they appeared in the eighteenth and nineteenth centuries, and in their re-emergence in the 1970s; in consequence, the franchise engages with feminist issues concerning female experience in patriarchal worlds.

Intertextual and Transmedia Gothic

The Gothic, in general, "remains a notoriously difficult field to define."[23] It is "a set of often-linked elements rather than a fixed genre," but even as the Gothic has evolved from its literary beginnings into diverse mediums, it continually recalls its own "earlier forms."[24] A good example of this is the Gothic's on-screen translation where distinct figures have coalesced in a "variety of guises," including "1930s vampires, Jekylls and Hydes, Frankensteins and monsters."[25] *Frankenstein* demonstrates how the Gothic engages with intertextual and transmedia practices in this way, as a text that "is ceaselessly rewritten, reproduced, refilmed and redesigned."[26] *Frankenstein* has a complex "transmedia afterlife" that engages with diverse discourses that can "radically reposition it in relation to both to culture and media." Such is the strength of this "afterlife," that audiences of *Frankenstein*'s transmedia translations do not require a familiarity with the "pretext"—that is, Shelley's novel—in order to engage with such adaptations, nor does a transmedia afterlife need to explicitly reference it.[27] *Frankenstein*'s "mythos" is thus indicative of the way Gothic stories "emerge as a recognizable milieu for transmedia storytelling."[28]

The Female Gothic, too, has a diverse "transmedia afterlife" that, like *Frankenstein*, arguably solidified in the translation of such stories to the screen. The Female Gothic enters film history with the 1940s Hollywood Gothic films, which include *Rebecca* (1940), *Gaslight* (1944), *The Spiral Staircase* (1946), and *Secret Beyond the Door* (1947). Such films place a consistent emphasis on the central heroine, who is imperiled in some way within a threatening environment, and she must navigate this space (while often fighting for her life) in order to face and dispel hidden secrets and terrors. This type of Gothic narrative is later disseminated in a variety of forms, including an important connection to horror—particularly the 1970s "Final Girl"—as well as a more self-conscious reviving of the archetype with the "neo-Gothics" at the turn of the century.[29] A major difference between the afterlives of the Female Gothic and, say, *Frankenstein*, is that the Female Gothic does not have a single "pre-text." Beyond Radcliffe and Shelley, some of the 1940s films are adaptations of other sources (such as *Rebecca*), while older tales—particularly, as highlighted above, Bluebeard—helped establish the tradition's key generic tropes too.[30]

This lack of an individual ancestor does not, however, negate the ability to contextualize the Female Gothic in transmedial terms: as noted, knowledge of a pre-text is not requisite to this process. Robert Stam's notion of "intertextual dialogism" also helps to trace the afterlives of the Female Gothic. For Stam, adaptations engage in an "ongoing dialogical process," forming "an intersection of textual surfaces," which exceeds far beyond the notion of an "original":

> All texts are tissues of anonymous formulae, variations on those formulae, conscious and unconscious quotations, and conflations and inversions of other texts. In the broadest sense, intertextual dialogism refers to the infinite and open-ended possibilities generated by all the discursive practices of a culture.[31]

Stam's approach is suited to analyzing the malleability of the Female Gothic tradition, which is loose enough to embrace "infinite and open-ended possibilities," but defined enough that the "formulae" can still be identified: indeed, the distinct set of motifs Moers helps to identify in coining the phrase "Female Gothic" function as a form of pre-text through which one can begin to trace the "quotations" and "conflations" within the *Alien* franchise. Finally, Stam's conceptualization reminds us that such a process is a dialogue: as a franchise, the later *Alien* films inevitably reference the earlier incarnations of the story, further underlining specific intertextual references to the Female Gothic.

Isolated Space(s)

As Canby's review of *Alien* reminds us, Female Gothic stories begin in suitably remote locations—and what could be more remote than space? *Alien* opens in darkness, some rays of light giving shape to a silhouetted planet, the blackness surrounding it punctuated by stars. Russ notes that in Female Gothic narratives the Old Dark House is always named; in *Alien* a vessel floating in the gloom of space is revealed as *Nostromo*. An edit reveals the interior of the ship, a mobile camera roaming around the empty corridors (Figure 9.1). Corridors are liminal spaces, the connective tissue of buildings bridging the delicate divide between the public and the private; outside and inside. These are boundaries that the xenomorph's attack will explicitly breach, and it is within these corridors that we will later view Ripley navigating the last vestiges of a home rendered inhospitable; like other Female Gothic stories,

Figure 9.1 The "Old Dark House" of the Nostromo (*Alien*, 1979; Twentieth Century Fox).

the security and safety of the domestic is violently disrupted, dramatizing the conflict Freud finds in the etymology of the word *unheimliche* (or the Uncanny): the homely made strange.[32]

The other films place a similar early emphasis on isolated locations that juxtapose commercial functionality with domesticity. *Aliens* opens with Ripley's escape shuttle center-frame in darkness; inside, an inquisitive mobile camera reveals Ripley in hypersleep. Later the film re-introduces LV-426—now a colony—with a panning camera detailing an alien-looking terrain, partially obscured by dust whipped up by howling winds. Again, this place is named—a sign says "Hadleys Hope"—before the camera rises to reveal a vast industrial complex dominating the horizon. Inside two colonists discuss a "ma and pa" crew out investigating unexplored co-ordinates, walking down corridors dominated by metal grating and pipes, until their conversation is interrupted by children playing near another sign: "Weyland-Yutani Corp: 'Building Better Worlds.' "

Inclement weather is emphasized again in *Alien³*. In the Theatrical Version, Fury 161's inmates squint into the darkness of the crashed pod, raising their voices against the rain and wind outside. The treacherous conditions are underlined by one of the men: "Hey Frank can we hurry this up? It's going to be 40 below in 5 minutes!" In the Assembly Cut, the extreme weather is further contextualized: waves crash against a deserted beach, lined with enormous cranes. Chains and hooks sway and clank in the breeze. Their echoing sound suggests the place has long been deserted, until the lone figure of Clemens walks through the fog. The *Alien* franchise finds its home in the wilderness: the derelict ship; the abandoned colony; the forgotten prison; the illicit military ship.

Alien Resurrection again emphasizes the isolated location but plays with expectations of size. The Special Edition opens on an extreme close-up of fierce jaws suggesting the ferociousness of the xenomorph. The camera pulls back to reveal, instead, an insect that is then unceremoniously crushed beneath a human finger. The camera continues its backward track to eventually reveal the bug's killer in a pod, which constitutes a tiny fraction of the vast ship. This opening also evokes the Female Gothic's trope of locked or hidden spaces within the remote Old Dark House. After the scale of USM *Auriga* is established, an edit shows a darkened doorway guarded by two soldiers. The camera, as though given privileged access, is permitted to pass through this door into a small laboratory, until it finds a pre-pubescent female figure suspended within a giant tube.

The film establishes how dangerous secrets are kept within hidden spaces, the transgression of which has deadly consequences. Kane's exploration of the derelict spaceship established this trope in *Alien*; the invasion is inverted again when the creature conceals itself within Ripley's escape shuttle, a tactic repeated in the sequels. The discovery or breaching of a space concealed somewhere within the labyrinth of the Old Dark House functions as a turning point across the franchise: in *Aliens* it is the discovery of the Alien Queen's nest; in *Alien³* it is the failed attempt to keep the creature contained within the toxic waste dump and leadworks; in *Alien Resurrection* it is clone Ripley's trauma of investigating what is behind the door mysteriously labelled "1–7."

(Secret) Male Threats

Frustrated by Aaron's refusal to disobey the Company's orders in *Alien³*, Ripley resolves to find the xenomorph which she states is "down there, in the basement." Aaron points out "this whole place is a basement," and Ripley laughs to herself before noting: "It's a metaphor." Her comment is, first, another poignant reminder of the importance of location to Female Gothic narratives, as the above analysis underlines. The physical space enables the heroine's imperilment: the remoteness removes the chance of rescue, while the interior structures harbor unknown dangers. The franchise consistently anchors the action around an impossible and unknowable geography: in

Aliens there is the failure to explain how the xenomorphs can be in the room on the motion-tracker; in *Alien Resurrection* the remaining survivors have to contend with flooding; *Alien* and *Aliens* both find Ripley working against the clock before the self-detonation explodes.

The metaphoric potential of Ripley's "basement" comment extends further: basements are hidden places, access to which is infrequent or prohibited. The basement itself is not scary: rather it is what this space conceals and—importantly—*who* put it there that becomes the real threat. The analogy evokes Bluebeard. As mentioned earlier, this fairytale forms another pre-text for the Female Gothic, with the heroine's transgression into a forbidden secret space at the story's core. The secret unlocked by the heroine in Bluebeard is the reality of an oppressive and fatal patriarchy. One could argue the same applies in the *Alien* franchise: the snapping jaws of the xenomorph or the smothering of a facehugger are an immediate threat to the body, but these pale in comparison to the unrelenting ruthlessness and oppression enforced by overwhelmingly patriarchal forces. The franchise's narratives see these powers continually attempt to conceal their own natures—to lock the secret of the real threat in the "basement"—and yet Ripley's transgressions within these stories see her continually expose these structures; to bring the darkness within the basement into the light.

This male threat can take various forms. Despite an egalitarian façade, *Alien* exposes a patriarchal world: Parker disgusts Lambert by making a joke about "eating something else," while pictures of naked women adorn the walls during Ash's (notably sexual) attack on Ripley. Ripley struggles to garner the respect owed to her by her rank, and what "at first appears to be merely annoying instances of misogyny" actually turns out "to be an underlining ideology of the micro-society and its intentional suppression of one woman's independence."[33]

In *Aliens*, Ripley recounts her story to an unsympathetic, and predominately male, Company board. The only two women around the table—including the one who patronizes Ripley—are coded as masculine, wearing the same tailored suits and ties (Figure 9.2). Ximena Gallardo C. and C. Jason Smith argue this macho culture is echoed in the female marines Ferro and Vasquez, who are "women who have betrayed their sex to join the male circle."[34] This is signaled particularly with Vasquez's hard-bodied appearance, as she performatively flexes her muscles and weaponry. The aligning of power with an aggressive masculine sexuality is even more overt in *Alien Resurrection*, where the female members of the *Betty* are denied entry into

Figure 9.2 Masculinized women in the Company's patriarchal world (*Aliens*, 1986; Twentieth Century Fox).

the "male circle" entirely as sexual difference is entrenched. Elgyn sexualizes Hillard as a "woman all strapped up in a chair like that" while piloting the ship, and Call is confronted with Vriess's sexual advances. Elgyn's meeting with Perez frames military and criminal power in misogynistic terms: Call is discussed as "a little girl playing pirates" who is "severely fuckable." Johner immediately sexualizes Ripley upon seeing her: "If you don't wanna play basketball I know some other indoor sports."

Alien 3 explicitly reframes this conduct as part of larger systems of oppression which Other women and perpetuate rape culture: Ripley is represented as the mysterious female body to be feared, explored, and punished. The Theatrical Version of the film evokes the Ripley in hypersleep at the beginning of *Aliens* but extends her vulnerability: a high-angled, medium-long shot displays her unconscious body laid out, dressed only in her underwear. Close-ups of hands belonging to an unseen man (later established as Clemens) touch her flesh, removing her clothing and cleaning the dirt from her neck. Ripley is not just a person in need of medical assistance: she is a *female* body in peril. The Assembly Cut makes the distinction overt with the additional scene of Clemens bringing Ripley into the complex as some of the inmates wash: they look on with horror and amazement at the sight of her (evidently) female form.

Soon after the dynamics of Fury 161's patriarchal structures are revealed: they are anchored in religion and the capitalist penal system, respectively. Dillon's first sermon encourages spiritual discipline while Andrews's "rumor control" speech enforces logic and reason. Both worldviews are defined as male, meaning "female" is cast as the opposite: undisciplined, illogical, and irrational. Ripley's mere presence is an unacceptable threat—what Dillon calls a "violation" of the men's harmony. When Ripley regains consciousness, her possession of a female body is constantly reinforced: she gets out of bed, naked, and Clemens suggests she dresses "given the nature of our indigenous population"; Andrews orders Ripley not to "parade around," even blaming her for a prisoner's apparent accidental death in a fan ("It's what happens when one of these numb sons of bitches walks around with a hard on"); Dillon rejects Ripley's gratitude for his eulogy by reminding her he is a "murderer and rapist of women"; Murphy and Frank, notably while preparing a cow for butchering, discuss their sexual virility ("treat a queen like a whore, and a whore like a queen—you can't go wrong").

This sexist language—all too often dismissed by society as harmless "banter"—is exposed as an integral part of rape culture in the scene when a group of inmates attempt to rape Ripley. Her sexual difference is violently reinscribed, and her Otherness inextricably linked to her possession of female genitalia. And yet this difference is also a construct: as Gallardo C. and Smith highlight, for the most part Ripley *looks* like the others, with her shaven head and baggy clothing. Indeed, her sexual difference is introduced mainly via Andrews's rhetoric, highlighting how "'woman' in *Alien³* is a patriarchal construction of mythical proportions."[35] Either way, the men's masculinity in *Alien³* needs to be defined through the subjugation of the female. A Female Gothic story is anchored in this dynamic: isolation or imprisonment, murder (committed or suspected), and sexual assault (actual or threatened) feature in Bluebeard, the Radcliffean narratives and the Modern Gothics to varying degrees because these stories render their heroines vulnerable to a distinctly male threat.

This threat is embodied in what Russ calls the "Super-Male," the love interest or husband of the Gothic heroine. Interestingly, alongside the depiction of murderers and rapists of women, *Alien³* further mobilizes motifs from the Female Gothic by coding Clemens as the enigmatic "Super-Male." Clemens is the first person Ripley interacts with on regaining consciousness in a scene reminiscent of Ripley's introduction to Burke in *Aliens*, thereby casting Clemens in a suspicious light by association. Clemens is a man of mystery: he avoids Ripley's questions about his past, including his tattoo. His suspicious behavior is underlined by the film's stylistic choices: when Ripley returns to the crashed pod looking for clues, her investigation is intercut with a moving shot tracking its way around the craft. Strings build on the score as the camera moves closer, suggesting an imminent attack; they crescendo as Ripley, shocked, looks up: an edit reveals a low-angled shot of Clemens towering over her. Russ writes that the Super-Male creates anxiety for the heroine concerning "whether he (1) loves her, (2) hates her, (3) is using her, or (4) is trying to kill her."[36] It is fitting that the franchise should make Ripley's only sexual partner a figure who aligns with this level of ambiguity. The irony is that, even as Clemens is exonerated from the four charges listed above, he is still a murderer.

The scene when Clemens divulges this information—and Ripley solves the mystery behind the man—plays with the dynamics between the threat of death and sexual assault that infuses the whole film. Clemens asks Ripley if she "still trusts him," and she offers her arm for injection in response, a silent affirmation of her sympathy and understanding. Clemens is framed again from a low angle, emphasizing his ability to help or harm her body with the "cocktail" he prepared. The shot echoes the earlier predatory camerawork, a reminder of former suspicions. Such distrust is expelled twice: first through Clemens's emotional recounting of his past, and then via a violent interruption by a real killer, as Clemens is grabbed and murdered by the xenomorph moments later. The creature punctures Clemens's skull and, after salivating against Ripley's terrified face, disappears into the ceiling, dragging the doctor's body with it.

The attempted rape, the mysterious Clemens, and the xenomorph's attack bring together what is at the heart of the franchise's horror: the fear of rape. *Alien* established this with the violent pregnancy and birthing Kane is forced to endure, betraying a particularly patriarchal fear—the fear of being feminine:

> The male body is repositioned to correspond to the female body: the male mouth becomes the vagina, his chest the womb. The dichotomy male/female is broken down, as all humanity is female (a womb) in the face of the Alien.[37]

The xenomorph, then, reinforces core themes of the Female Gothic. The sexualized nature of the aliens' *modus operandi* reinforces the patriarchal dimensions of this danger because it is coveted by the sinister systems of control in the metaphoric "basement." Burke, (human) Bishop and Wren are men who believe they can control the xenomorph's—and Ripley's—body for their own advancement. The xenomorph is both victim to, and an emblem for, the Company's ruthless ambitions; an "externalized representation of the dehumanizing force of the Company," making the latter "the nastiest rapist of all."[38] Thus, Ripley's fight for survival is, in the short term, against an alien; in the long term, it is the patriarchal threats continually seeking to exploit her.

Validating Female Experience

In Female Gothic narratives we do not just observe the heroine imperiled. We must experience these fears from her perspective. *Alien* positions Ripley as the main protagonist—albeit subtly at first—via specific stylistic choices. Ripley's discovery that the SOS transmission is a warning is depicted through tight framing: her concerned face is juxtaposed with Ash, who she soon acknowledges she does not trust—a revelation that arouses viewer suspicion too. Later, Ash examines the facehugger alone in the lab and a moving camera approaches; Ripley enters the shot, thereby aligning this previous movement with her own. During Dallas's fatal exploration of the air ducts, Ripley is framed in a repeated close-up, and she is placed in the foreground when taking command of the ship as a result of his death.

Such narrative and visual agency is emphasized near the end when— echoing the film's opening—the corridors are shown again; this time the mobile framing is anchored to Ripley, mimicking her frantic running and even utilizing point-of-view shots. A similar style is used in *Aliens* when Ripley searches for Newt and finds the Alien Queen's lair. *Alien³* and *Alien Resurrection* are careful to privilege Ripley in close-ups, even to the extent that her face—framed head on—threatens to meet our gaze: this is seen in the moment she confirms her trust in Clemens, and in her anxious look at door "1–7" (Figure 9.3). Ripley's perspective is doubly underlined by the franchise's emphasis on dreams: sleep is how we are introduced to Ripley in all four films, and her promise to Newt that it is "safe" to dream again signals her triumph in *Aliens*. The fact the film opens with a dream sequence—a nightmare that she possesses a chestburster, a fear that will manifest in the next two films—emphasizes how Ripley's perception, including her subconscious, mediate our experience of events.

This shared hierarchy of knowledge ensures we align with Ripley, sharing her frustrations when her observations are frequently dismissed. In *Alien*

Figure 9.3 Ripley threatens to meet our gaze (*Alien Resurrection*, 1997; Twentieth Century Fox).

Ripley is ignored when she correctly ascertains the crew are not in "our system"; Ash disobeys her direct order by allowing Kane back on-board; Dallas dismisses her suspicions concerning Ash. Hindsight proves Ripley correct in these instances, but this is not needed in *Aliens*: we *know* what she describes to the unreceptive board is true. The Company renders Ripley's story unreliable by casting doubt on her sanity: "psych evals" are a condition of her downgraded employment. Burke manipulatively uses these tests to convince Ripley to return to LV-426—thereby quietly ignoring how the danger she warned about is confirmed.

Diane Waldman writes that Female Gothic narratives test the heroine's perception and will either validate or invalidate her experience in the end.[39] The *Alien* franchise modifies this trope: Ripley is always validated by the narrative; she is often invalidated by male structures seeking control. This is enabled by evoking a gendered stereotype associated with Female Gothic heroines: hysteria. The marines in *Aliens* smirk at Ripley's emotional recounting of her traumatic experiences: Ripley is the real alien, a "Snow White" in their macho world. Andrews in *Alien³* challenges Ripley's story: "You expect me to accept this at *your* word?"—Ripley's "word," of course, is invalid as a woman's. The idea that women are hysterical, or even insane, is signaled in the film's association of Ripley with Golic; a comparison established within the mess hall (Figure 9.4). This—significantly, domestic—location is marked as a transgressive site across the franchise: it is where Kane's chest explodes; Parker makes his sexist jokes; Ripley struggles for control; and where Ash attacks her. In *Aliens* it is the place of another android outing with Bishop; in *Alien Resurrection* it becomes the podium for another woman—Call—to plead for help against the military's corruption.

Figure 9.4 The mess hall becomes a transgressive site with Ripley's "violating" presence (*Alien 3*, 1992; Twentieth Century Fox).

In *Alien 3*, Ripley's entry into the mess hall is the "violation" Dillon warns about. In the Assembly Cut, prior to Ripley's arrival, Dillon chastises two inmates for rejecting "crazy" Golic. It is in this space that Golic shall later be found, covered in blood, following his colleagues' murder by the creature. After this he is—like Ripley—confined to the infirmary. Ripley's attempt to validate Golic's story of a "dragon" only reinforces the connection between them for Andrews: both are "stark raving mad," threats to his masculine order of control and logic. Ripley is only too aware of this judgment: when Clemens asks Ripley to tell him her story she refuses, reasoning that he will call her "crazy." Ripley trespasses into the male domain once more: Ripley's frantic running is intercut with Andrews's "rumor control" in the mess hall, before she bursts in, warning, "It's here!" This female hysteria and lies are too much for Andrews ("Stop this raving at once!"). Ripley, however, is always right, and her validation in this instance is quick and unforgiving: the creature immediately grabs and kills the Superintendent.

Return of the Repressed (M)others

Ripley's physical isolation in a patriarchal world, which places her in danger and seeks to control her by invalidating her perception of such peril, is what makes Ripley a Female Gothic heroine. The development of her character across the franchise reinforces these tropes, and, by *Alien Resurrection*,

Ripley's experiences have strengthened her survival skills. Indeed, Wren is right to be concerned that the Ripley clone has "memories": knowledge is power, as the bride in Bluebeard, or Emily in *The Mysteries of Udolpho* (1794), and Ripley's uncovering of the Company's betrayal in *Alien* all demonstrate. The Ripley of the final film is therefore a "return of the repressed" doubled: a return with Ripley's doppelgänger, and a self-conscious—and knowing—return to the previous films. This final film's "intertextual dialogism" becomes almost parodic ("Hey Ripley, I heard you, like, ran into these things before?"). This appeal to pastiche highlights why Botting characterizes the film in terms of "post"—post-modern, post-feminist, and post-human:

> The principal figures of identification may be female in appearance or feminine in terms of association, convention or typical emotional characteristics: a female human-alien hybrid, an android in feminine form, an alien who gives birth. But they are certainly not human.[40]

The heroine's transformation into a clone/hybrid, and a new heroine in Call as an android, means "structures collapse and meanings are confounded" between human/alien/android, and Botting concludes the film is therefore "post-Gothic." One wonders, then, whether the Female Gothic is similarly diluted as an intertextual, structuring element by the franchise's end. It is true that *Alien Resurrection* is different, particularly in its depiction of Ripley: the under-stated courage and calm of her former incarnations contrast the clone, who now appropriates the sexual aggression previously displayed by others ("Who do I have to fuck to get off this boat?"). Yet reading this film as part of the Female Gothic's "afterlives" reinforces the significance of this labelling. Far from being (in Botting's words) "redundant," the film returns us back to the term's beginnings with Moers in the 1970s.

As discussed earlier, Moers interprets *Frankenstein*—a key Female Gothic text—as an allegory for motherhood. This reading complements Claire Kahane's analysis of Female Gothics—incorporating Radcliffe's novels and Russ's "Modern Gothics"—which also emphasizes motherhood:

> What I see repeatedly locked into the forbidden center of the Gothic which draws me inward is the spectral presence of a dead-undead mother, archaic and all-encompassing, a ghost signifying the problematics of femininity which the heroine must confront.[41]

Alien Resurrection brings together Moers's and Kahane's ideas because the film is another Frankenstein story, but this time a re-enactment *explicitly* rooted in questions of motherhood, and its exploitation by patriarchal forces. The Theatrical Version's opening underlines the connection: extreme close-ups of the failed Ripley specimens immediately frame events with a Frankensteinian twist. Ripley's bodily integrity—which she fought to protect in the previous films—is now deconstructed, along with conventional ideas about creating life. Ripley is now the product of patriarchal, military, and scientific endeavors: *à la* Victor Frankenstein, men make life without women. And yet giving birth in *Alien Resurrection* is an exclusively female prerogative, upon which this patriarchy is still apparently reliant. Ripley's introduction is evocative of the previous films—her unconscious state reminiscent of the hypersleep in *Alien* and *Aliens*; her examination on a table like *Alien³*— except now she is immediately exploited and Othered as the scientists perform a perverse caesarean section.

Alien Resurrection, paradoxically, reinforces gendered boundaries even as it appears to erase them, as the alien/artificial woman is defined and judged by reproductive capabilities, or lack thereof: Ripley's ability to be "the monster's mother"; the Alien Queen's birthing of the "Newborn"; Call's rejection from the group for being a "toaster" suddenly renders her "severely (un)fuckable." Indeed, female reproduction is placed on a pedestal that fundamentally redefines what Ash termed the "perfect organism": Gediman now calls the Alien Queen "perfect" because she has a "female reproductive system." Such judgments are not restricted to the megalomaniac scientists: Call considers her android body "disgusting," a self-abjection clearly linked to her perceived "lack" of a "proper" (female) body. This is not to claim female bodies are suddenly powerful here: bodies are essentialized by their reproductive potential and even those which achieve "motherhood" are merely "meat by-products." *Alien Resurrection* therefore continues the trend of patriarchal oppression which Others the female, except now such control has found a renewed measure of success via a monstrous form of imposed motherhood: female agency is finally removed.

Motherhood has always been a central theme in the franchise: the *Nostromo*'s controlling "Mother" in *Alien*; Ripley's daughter, Newt and the Alien Queen in *Aliens*;[42] and Ripley's self-sacrifice against her "pregnancy" in *Alien³*. These connections are further discussed by Rose and Zitzelsberger in the following chapter in this collection, where motherhood as a site of "gender negotiation" is again re-defined through a consideration of the prequels within the larger franchise. Not only does motherhood signal another way in which the franchise intertextually incorporates the Female Gothic, but the manner in which it does so opens up further avenues for interpretation. Moers argues the horror of *Frankenstein* resides less in the creature's unnatural "birth," but in what comes next: "the trauma of the afterbirth."[43] *Alien Resurrection* follows a similar pattern: Ripley's imperilment is renewed by the consequences of an unnatural creation. This "afterbirth" scenario hypothesizes what happens when the systems of oppression present in the earlier films succeed: when the real threat in a Female Gothic story comes out of the "basement," and the heroine is trapped, controlled, raped, or murdered. As such it seems premature to call the film "post-Gothic": while it does create a story that is very much like a post-script—an alternative afterword to *Frankenstein* as a pre-text, as well as an "afterlife" or "afterbirth" of the typical Female Gothic narrative—it does so not to move away from this tradition but to reinforce it. *Alien Resurrection* continues the pattern established across the franchise, which I am characterizing here in terms of the Female Gothic: heroines are imperiled by patriarchal forces as a result of their gender identity (biological or otherwise), but they will always fight back. And—if they're Ripley—one way or another, they'll win.

Notes

1. Vincent Canby, "*Alien* Brings Chills from the Far Galaxy: A Gothic Set in Space," *The New York Times*, May 25, 1979.
2. My analysis concentrates on the franchise's "Quadrilogy" films to maintain focus; however, there is scope to extend the ideas within the franchise more widely.
3. My analysis uses the Theatrical Version of *Alien* and the Special Edition of *Aliens*. For *Alien³* and *Alien Resurrection* it is noted, where relevant, which version is referenced.
4. Roger Luckhurst, *Alien* (London: BFI, 2014), 8.
5. Frances A. Kamm, "The Gothic in Space: Genre, Motherhood, and *Aliens* (1986)," in *Gothic Heroines on Screen: Representation, Interpretation, and Feminist Enquiry*, ed. Tamar Jeffers McDonald and Frances A. Kamm (London and New York: Routledge, 2019).
6. Lauren Fitzgerald, "(In)alienable Rights: Property, Feminism, and the Female Body from Ann Radcliffe to the *Alien* Films," *Romanticism and Science Fictions* 21 (February 2001). Fitzgerald's fascinating work reads *Alien* with Radcliffe via "proprietary claims." This chapter also seeks a comparison, but here Radcliffe forms part of a wider lineage.

7. Joanna Russ, "Somebody's Trying to Kill Me—and I Think It's My Husband: The Modern Gothic," *Journal of Popular Culture* 6, no. 4 (Spring 1973), 667–668.

8. Russ, "Somebody's Trying to Kill Me," 669.

9. The inclusion of the egg in Atwood's story, along with the question "what will come out of it?," provides another coincidence with the story of *Alien*.

10. Russ links the Modern Gothics to precursors like Daphne du Maurier rather than Radcliffe. However, as shall be seen, Moers's conceptualization broadens this history.

11. Ellen Moers, *Literary Women* (New York: Doubleday, 1976), 90.

12. Moers, *Literary Women*, 96.

13. Claire Kahane, "The Gothic Mirror," in *The (M)other Tongue: Essays in Feminist Psychoanalytical Interpretation*, ed. Shirley Nelson Garner, Claire Kahane, and Madelon Sprengnether (Ithaca and London: Cornell University Press, 1985).

14. Moers, *Literary Women*, 126.

15. Sandra M. Gilbert and Susan Gubar, *The Madwoman in the Attic: The Woman Writer and the Nineteenth-Century Literary Imagination* (New Haven, CT: Yale University Press, 1979).

16. David Punter and Glennis Byron, *The Gothic* (Oxford: Blackwell, 2004), 279.

17. Punter and Byron, *The Gothic*, 280.

18. George Moore, "The *Alien* Feminist," in *Meanings of Ripley: The* Alien *Quadrilogy & Gender*, ed. Elizabeth Graham (Newcastle-upon-Tyne: Cambridge Scholars Publishing, 2010), 12–13.

19. Moore, "The *Alien* Feminist," 16.

20. Punter and Byron, *The Gothic*, 280.

21. Russ, "Somebody's Trying to Kill Me," 671.

22. I explore some of these concerns elsewhere in my chapter on *Aliens*: Kamm, "The Gothic in Space."

23. Punter and Byron, *The Gothic*, xviii.

24. Jerrold E. Hogle, "Introduction: Modernity and the Proliferation of the Gothic," in *The Cambridge Companion to the Modern Gothic*, ed. Jerrold E. Hogle (Cambridge: Cambridge University Press, 2014), 3.

25. Fred Botting, *Gothic* (London and New York: Routledge, 2005), 9.

26. Paul O'Flinn, "Production and Reproduction: The Case of *Frankenstein*," *Literature and History* 9, no. 2 (Fall 1983), 194.

27. Francesca Saggini and Anna Enrichetta Soccio, ed., *Transmedia Creatures: Frankenstein's Afterlives* (Lewisburg: Bucknell University Press, 2019).

28. Jason Whittaker, "The Media of Madness: Gothic Transmedia and the Cthulhu Mythos," in *TransGorthic in Literature and Culture*, ed. Jolene Zigarovich (New York and Oxford: Routledge, 2017), 179–198.

29. See: Frances A. Kamm and Tamar Jeffers McDonald, ed., "Gothic Feminisms," special issue of *Revenant* 4 (2019); Helen Hanson, *Hollywood Heroines: Women in Film Noir and the Female Gothic Film* (London: I. B. Tauris, 2007).

30. See: Maria Tatar, *Secrets Beyond the Door: The Story of Bluebeard and His Wives* (London: I. B. Tauris, 2009).

31. Robert Stam, "Beyond Fidelity: The Dialogics of Adaptation," in *Film Adaptation*, ed. James Naremore (London: The Athlone Press), 64.

32. Sigmund Freud, "The Uncanny," in *The Uncanny* (London: Penguin, [1919] 2003).

33. Moore, "The *Alien* Feminist," 16.

34. Ximena Gallardo C. and C. Jason Smith, *Alien Woman: The Making of Lt. Ellen Ripley* (New York and London: Continuum, 2004), 87.

35. Gallardo C. and Smith, *Alien Woman*, 139.

36. Russ, "Somebody's Trying to Kill Me," 668.

37. Gallardo C. and Smith, *Alien Woman*, 42.

38. Ibid., 150.

39. Diane Waldman, "'At Last I Can Tell It to Someone!' Feminine Point of View and Subjectivity in the Gothic Romance Film of the 1940s," *Cinema Journal* 23, no. 2 (1984), 29–40.

40. Fred Botting, *Gothic Romanced: Consumption, Gender and Technology in Contemporary Fictions* (London and New York: Routledge, 2008), 174.

41. Kahane, "The Gothic Mirror," 336.

42. I discuss *Aliens* as a Gothic film and its connection to motherhood in greater depth in Kamm, "The Gothic in Space."

43. Moers, *Literary Women*, 93.

10

Making the Mother

Pro/Creation and Female Agency in the *Alien* Series

Jonathan A. Rose and Florian Zitzelsberger

What makes a mother? Ellen Ripley (Sigourney Weaver), the heroine of the original *Alien* quadrilogy, has continuously prompted readings that re-evaluate femaleness and femininity. Often focusing on the feminist impetus of the films, *Alien* scholarship has equally questioned gendered notions of motherhood.[1] Based on Barbara Creed's reading of *Alien* (1979) as "a complex representation of the monstrous-feminine in terms of the maternal as perceived within a patriarchal ideology,"[2] our chapter considers the representations of motherhood in the latest additions to the *Alien* film series—*Prometheus* (2012) and *Alien: Covenant* (2017)—in connection with *Alien*[3] (1992) and *Alien Resurrection* (1997). This juxtaposition between sequels and prequels allows us to take into account the temporal implications of serialization on representation. Among others, we thereby draw on Susan Yunis and Tammy Ostrander's explorations of the horrors of motherhood as represented in *Aliens* (1986),[3] and Catherine Constable's analysis of "Ripley's [. . .] relation to the alien queen in *Aliens* and *Alien: Resurrection*,"[4] which changes in an effort to eliminate the dichotomies between human and Alien established in the first two films by Ripley's "becoming the monster's mother."[5]

Stephen Scobie highlights the essentiality of mothers for the narrative in the first three films, positing that "motherhood is not only a thematic motif but also structural one,"[6] a line of inquiry that our chapter continues by exploring the representations of motherhood in connection with the films' seriality. Our consideration of motherhood across the series hence acknowledges the complexities of (multiple) origins in serialized narratives. As such, the very structure of the *Alien* series, with the addition of prequels turning previous speculations about the Alien threat—as the other, "born" into our world—on their head, reflects back on the thematic engagement

Jonathan A. Rose and Florian Zitzelsberger, *Making the Mother* In: *Alien Legacies*. Edited by: Nathan Abrams and Gregory Frame, Oxford University Press. © Oxford University Press 2023. DOI: 10.1093/oso/9780197556023.003.0010 with motherhood. The prequels provide us with sobering answers concerning the origin of the Aliens as human creations of the second degree, which allows for readings of motherhood beyond the monstrous-feminine as a thematic anchor of the original series.

At first glance, Ripley appears to be the only character engaged in maternally coded kinship relations, respectively taking on the role of mother for her cat, Jonesy, in *Alien* and the child Newt (Carrie Henn) in *Aliens*.[7] Especially in the latter relationship, which is realized "as an image of generational continuity"[8] and has been read as an instance of "adoption,"[9] Ripley displays what could be considered genuinely maternal behavior based on the emotional bond between Newt and herself. Apart from this social display of motherhood, being a mother in a biological sense—being pregnant and giving birth—is integral to the discourse of motherhood in the *Alien* series, which challenges essentialist notions of gender because being a mother no longer correlates with "her" biological sex. Every single body, indiscriminate of gender, can become pregnant and serve as host and, thus, biological "mother" of alien offspring. Kane's (John Hurt) "pregnancy" in the first *Alien* film was considered "the ultimate outrage" by Amy Taubin, because "a *man* could be impregnated,"[10] showing the series' logical disjunction of motherhood and gendered notions of procreation. While the first alien pregnancy is rightfully considered outrageous, monstrous even, this cannot be attributed to the fact that men are the carriers of the alien offspring. Although masculinity is not commonly associated with pregnancy or motherhood in general, the true atrocity of this pregnancy lies in the lack of consent, the denied control over one's own body. This, together with the inevitable and necessarily fatal process of birth, proves to be the real horror—a horror that becomes all the more intelligible by its divorce from its usual gendered space. As Ronald Cruz contends, "the way it goes against what is considered normal anatomy and function in biological species"—that is, the fact that, in this universe, anyone can become pregnant—"is indeed biological horror."[11] The here implied "fundamental change in gender role" at the heart of the first alien impregnation lies in this divorce of motherhood from its biological limitations, emphasizing the universality of the trauma of being "orally raped and impregnated by aliens,"[12] which always also entails the host's, that is, the mother's, death during birth.

In this chapter, we explore how motherhood is rendered the site of gender negotiation in the original *Alien* series and its prequels. By focusing on procreation and creation as the films' central discursive paradigms, we show that mothers in the *Alien* series are as much *creators* of alien lifeforms as they are *creations* of an abusive system based on asymmetrically expressed gender and power relations. We might, then, rephrase the opening question, asking: *Who* makes a mother?

The following will contrast the progressions from *Alien³* to *Alien Resurrection* as well as from *Prometheus* to *Alien: Covenant* and expand on the thematic differences between these film pairs. Starting with the original *Alien* series and its representation of (maternally or female-coded) procreation, we then turn to the prequels, in which male-coded creation—as motherhood without mothering—takes center stage. Reading the two film pairs together allows for a more detailed assessment of the series' stance on motherhood and pro/creation as well as their relation to gender. Exploring the films' seriality through the lens of kinship or familial relations, we subsequently argue that the mechanics of serialization at play—with the film pairs themselves constituting sequels while the second pair also functions as a prequel in the overall trajectory of the series—are used to retroactively infuse the original series with female agency. Offering readings inflected by feminist and queer theory as well as post-human thought and focusing on later installments of the series, we hope not only to enrich scholarship on the *Alien* series, particularly the prequels that have not yet received much attention, and its engagement of gender and motherhood, but also to add to an ongoing debate about maternality beyond the binary and cis-femaleness.

Becoming the Mother's Mother: *Alien*'s Sequels and Prequels as Serial Relatives

We would like to begin our discussion of the prequels as additions to and potential correctives for discourses of motherhood in the *Alien* series with the assertion that the relationship between prequels and their core texts is both (metaphorically) familial and (temporally) queer. Prequels can be contextualized within the framework of seriality, as expansions of a pre-existing textual complex. Jason Mittell, in his discussion of television and transmedia storytelling, frames such means of serialization and continuation via the image of the mothership as an entity that conditions various assemblages.[13] In a narrow sense, the original *Alien* film can be described as a mothership—which it quite literally is with the Nostromo's computer called

"Mother"—whereas both sequels and prequels would latch onto this original installment of the series similar to transmedia extensions to the Alienverse such as the *Alien* comics or the video game *Alien: Isolation* (2014). Yet, the difference between sequels and prequels affects how the series as a whole is conceived both structurally and thematically. While familiarity might not be a prerequisite to watch and enjoy *Prometheus* or *Covenant*, their relationship to the first four *Alien* films substantiates an understanding of the latter as a coherent whole rather than dispersed segments.[14] The close connection between the films, which each present the next part in Ripley's fight against the alien threat, supports reading the original *Alien* quadrilogy as "one extended work."[15] If the quadrilogy as mothership lays the foundation for its prequels and other expansions, including entire crossover series such as *Alien vs. Predator* (2004, 2007), then questions arise about the distinctiveness of the prequels and their work on the *Alien* series as a whole.

While both sequels and prequels are means of serializing content, the "prequel is presented as a familial relation, parenthetically included like some form of close-yet-undesirable sibling, cousin, aunt or uncle."[16] Ben Davies here pointedly highlights the common practice of subsuming prequels under the sequel as an umbrella term. Yet the use of family imagery, together with Mittell's aptly named concept of the mothership, might also help rehabilitate the prequel as a form of serialization that is unique in the ways it adds to a textual core. The recognition of a series *as* a series, in the sense that its parts necessarily belong together, depends on familiarity. This familiarity is then also *familial* in the sense that it constitutes the effect of repetition (of characters, story arcs, motifs) and as such hinges on the *reproduction* of elements pertaining to the mothership. The difference between sequels and prequels is thus a question of temporality as much as ontology: in contrast to the sequel, which continues and can be located in the future, the prequel paradoxically combines a temporal leap *backward* with a genealogical dependency on and familiarity with a story that logically succeeds the prequel itself, which would presuppose a narrative teleology that is *forward*-looking. In other words, while the sequel can be regarded as the daughter of an initial installment, following and continuing the family line, the prequel complicates this relationship by simultaneously functioning as offspring of a mothership and becoming the mother itself. In the case of the *Alien* series, which features both sequels and prequels, the different simultaneous temporalities at play in the films' serialization make the "close-yet-undesirable" relative at once daughter and the mother's mother. While it is possible to regard the prequels as "additional extra,"[17] as paratextual, their unique position as following after the quadrilogy but logically constituting a before that contains vital information about the alien threat points toward a reading that treats the prequels as "distinctive and valuable contributions to the whole."[18]

We want to illustrate this with an example from the series. Both Ripley in *Alien*[3] and Elizabeth Shaw (Noomi Rapace) in *Prometheus* are about to become alien mothers and strive to end their pregnancies, instances that can be read as abortion scenes: Ripley kills herself to destroy the alien, and Shaw has a self-administered C-section. While *Alien*[3] "sanctifies [. . .] Ripley's death [by] representing it as a form of Christ's self-sacrifice on behalf of humanity,"[19] Shaw in *Prometheus* unknowingly puts humanity at risk in order to save herself. The alternative of surgically removing the alien parasite and thereby saving the mother's life, which is offered to Ripley by Bishop (Lance Henriksen), is chosen by Shaw on her own accord as she uses the technology of the Prometheus to conduct an abortion. The whole sequence is presented as an exclusively female experience, featuring point-of-view shots and close-up shots of Shaw's face, in contrast with the original series, where anyone can become a victim of an alien pregnancy. The depiction of Ripley's abortion speaks to the audience on a rather universal level: shot from a distance and in slow motion, Ripley emerges and perishes as a sublime figure, as a savior who dies for the sins of the human race. This image is rendered even more meaningful with the added information from the prequels: the aliens are indeed human creations of the second degree. Taken together, the scenes suggest some of the most fundamental differences between the two characters and are symptomatic of the tension between the films' diverging thematic focuses. While Shaw's C-section scene is loaded with biological connotations, Ripley's death scene elicits a religious context; while Shaw rejects the idea of motherhood, Ripley embraces it. As she leaps into the molten lead, the Alien Queen inside of Ripley ruptures her chest. The highly anticipated alien birth culminates in the series' arguably most genuine imagery of motherhood when Ripley presses the neonatal alien against her chest, signifying her taking on a maternal role and emphasizing the bond between them—a bond deepened in the sequel's alien-human hybrid Ripley. While Ripley's sacrifice in *Alien*[3] results in the death of mother and child, she accepts her own death so long as it means the end of the alien as well. The scene centering Shaw can therefore be seen as part of Ripley's legacy, but only to a limited extent since Shaw can remove the alien but cannot destroy it in the process.

Regarded as iterations within a serialized form, the two scenes show several continuities, but also updates, in terms of central themes, imagery, and their negotiation of gendered notions of agency, which seems plausible given about twenty years of technological and social advancement that separate the two films. A progressivist and simplified reading of the prequel films as sequels would focus on such continuations in *Prometheus* that work with material from the original *Alien* series and update it. However, such a reading inevitably constitutes an anachronism within the Alienverse since the prequels simultaneously look forward, in the sense that they are created after the original series and incorporate technological innovations and updates in views on gender, and backward, in the sense that they are set before the original series.

Returning to our initial thoughts on serialization, the temporally liminal character of prequels as simultaneously directed forward and backward brings to the fore the relationship between content and form as well as the disparities that arise from our comparison of the abortion scenes. While Ripley's pregnancy in $Alien^3$ potentially establishes a family line in terms of both the representation of motherhood and a continuation of this line in another installment of the series, both seem to be ruptured by her death. However, as we will show in the following section, by providing a sequel with *Resurrection* that brings Ripley back to life (albeit in a non-human form), the series manages to maintain the line that will eventually lead to Shaw's pregnancy and abortion in *Prometheus*. The promise of establishing familial bonds within and across narratives is both broken in Shaw's survival and failure to kill the alien and kept by the fact that the event eventually leads to Ripley's death in $Alien^3$. In other words, even though Shaw can cut the family line on the level of content, the mechanics of serialization continue it in two ways: *Covenant* offers a sequel to the events of *Prometheus*, and since both films function as prequels to the original series, the line they carry forward from their predecessor is logically (and non-chronologically) projected backward and will turn out to inform the very first installment, the 1979 *Alien*.

Serialization in the *Alien* series with its combination of sequels and prequels thus reveals a circular logic where progression is inevitably bound to regression, where motherhood eventually not only loses its biological connotations but also its linear reproductive logic. If the desire of the family is "the reproduction of its line,"[20] as Sara Ahmed suggests, and if this reproduction is undesired or cannot be afforded by Ripley and Shaw, then reading the *Alien* series along the nexus of motherhood and serialization provides insight into how familial bonds are forged on a textual and medial level. And as we will show, the relationship between sequels and prequels and their different approaches to heteronormative reproducibility become a productive site for queer and feminist interventions into previous readings of the series. The following sections will therefore follow the trajectory outlined here by comparing the transition from *Alien³* to *Resurrection* with that from *Prometheus* to *Covenant*—as sequels—and by contrasting them via the relation of the latter pair to the original series, functioning as prequels.

The Mother Making: Procreation in *Alien³* and *Resurrection*

While the first two *Alien* films explore motherhood according to its social function, foregrounding the act of mothering and the responsibility for those under one's care, *Alien³* and *Resurrection* move procreation from its position as an alien threat to the heart of the films. Motherhood becomes increasingly focused on its biological dimensions and at the same time more entangled with the aliens, from Ripley's involuntary pregnancy in *Alien³* to the alien-human offspring conceived in the hybridization effect of Ripley's cloning in *Resurrection*. What started as a straightforward opposition between humans and aliens, with a clear villain to be eradicated, develops into a more complex construct without any straight, or binary, answers to questions of good and evil or self and other.

Motherhood in the biological sense, connected to procreation, is overtly expressed in Ripley's alien pregnancy. This shift away from social motherhood is underlined by the first (offscreen) sexual encounter in the *Alien* series. While in *Aliens* Ripley and Hicks (Michael Biehn) may have shared a heterosexually coded interest in each other, Ripley expresses her sexuality by propositioning Clemens (Charles Dance) in *Alien³*. The first female alien pregnancy is preceded by sexual intercourse, a notion picked up again in *Prometheus*. Furthermore, in its setting on Fury 161, an all-male former prison colony, Ripley is repeatedly framed as a representation of reproduction and procreation; at the same time, she is perceived as "a violation of the harmony." The men on Fury 161 follow a religious cult and have "taken a vow of celibacy [which] also includes women." This first verbal reaction to the announcement that the survivor of the EEV pod is a woman shows not only the threat Ripley's arrival presents to the community but also that women are reduced to and made sense of in their procreative capacity. This approach toward women is continuously revisited throughout the film. Golic (Paul McGann), for example, asks Ripley whether she is married, then tells her that she "should get married [and] have kids" because she is a "pretty girl." Finally, the human Bishop tries to convince Ripley to let the Company "take care" of her and the alien fetus by appealing to her future motherhood: "You can still have a life. Children."

Throughout the film, the woman as an outsider on Fury 161 can therefore only become intelligible in her function as a mother based on a heteronormative logic, which is also mirrored in the use of rather archaic rhetoric, reducing women to their biological capacities. As a subject, which, like all others, "only comes into intelligibility through the matrix of gender"[21] and in the absence of any kind of diversity of female embodiment, Ripley can only be made sense of in her (potential) relations and in a heterosexual and procreative function, namely as wife or mother. Thus, "the discursive practice [. . .] simultaneously ontologizes and fixes that gendered matrix in its place";[22] or, as Ahmed puts it, societal "orientations [. . .] shape what becomes socially as well as bodily given."[23] It makes sense in this case that Ripley's arrival on Fury 161 causes "ripples in the water." Furthermore, this focus on procreation has already been present in its pronounced absence; by its very negation, it takes primacy in the logic of the community of men. The fact that they cannot procreate gets inscribed as law in their religious cult, thus performing and institutionalizing this inability. Their rejection of Ripley and what she represents to them also becomes visible in the use of the term "mother" as an expletive: "What does this *fucking beast* want? Is this *mother* going to try for us all?" As Scobie has posited for the first film, *Alien³* too presents "a very *male* fantasy; that is, a male fear of the mystery and unknown of women's power."[24]

In an attempt to remedy the absence of procreation, the community on Fury 161 makes sense of its relationships through kinship-inspired terminology. The men are brothers to each other; Ripley is symbolically included in this family and referred to as a sister. Ripley, too, understands her connection to the alien as a kinship relation, realizing that she has involuntarily become "part of the family." This signifies a move toward alien intelligibility, which is mirrored in the alien point-of-view shots included at the end of the

film: for the first time, viewers get to experience the world from an alien perspective. It is precisely Ripley's status as the mother to a future Alien Queen
that allows her to kill the alien, which recognizes her as one of its own kind
and spares her life. While in *Alien³* Ripley is, foremost, a figurative alien in
the sense that her presence on Fury 161 is almost as disruptive as the simultaneous arrival of the alien, clone Ripley in *Resurrection* displays several alien
behaviors, unsettling the humans around her, who also realize and comment
on this connection: Johner (Ron Perlman), for example, refers to the aliens
as Ripley's "brothers and sisters," whereas Call (Winona Ryder) expresses
her confusion when Ripley kills one of the aliens, claiming that this is "like
killing your own kind." Ripley's reply that the alien was in her way can be read
as an affirmation of both her humanity and alien-ness, as proof of her hybrid
status, which is difficult to categorize in the human-alien dichotomy underlying the *Alien* films.

The human-alien kinship ultimately rejected in *Alien³* by Ripley's death
becomes all the more explicit in *Resurrection*. The clone and alien-human
hybrid Ripley repeatedly establishes her relationship to the aliens, calling the
Alien Queen her baby and herself its mother. The alien carefully carrying
Ripley to the Queen's nest suggests a similar feeling of connectedness on
the part of the aliens. Ripley truly seems to have become part of the family;
her statement in *Alien³* thus functions as a performative in the Austinian
sense: she *becomes* part of the family because she *says* that she is part of the
family. According to Judith Butler, the performative always includes the
"reiteration of a norm or set of norms"[25] and is best understood in terms of
citationality, in this case, that of heteronormative kinship relations.

The films themselves perform this citationality through the increasing hybridization of human and alien. In the attempt to make sense of the alien
and of its connections to the humans, the films invariably fall back on a heterosexual logic, which, in turn, gets queered by its unruly citation, with the
resignification "expos[ing] the norm itself."[26] The cross-hybridization hinted
at in *Alien³* is further explicated in *Resurrection*. The Queen, after an initial
cycle of egg-laying, develops a "human reproductive system." Citing human
birth in an act of resignification, "Ripley's gift to [the Queen]" is the gift of
intelligibility. The massive belly or exterior uterus is a grotesque adaptation,
an exaggeration of human birth similar to the chest-bursting alien births
seen previously. The described cross-hybridization results in a creature with
the combined features of both Ripley and the Queen. A child born of two
mothers, the Newborn nevertheless makes an immediate choice between

its procreators, at the same time as their reactions to it are at odds with this choice. The Queen, after screaming in pain as the Newborn emerged from its womb, makes soft, cooing noises when its child approaches, only to be killed with a forceful blow to the head. Ripley, when faced with the Newborn, avoids eye contact, obviously afraid of the creature, which, in turn, displays signs of an immediate bond to her, making soft noises and licking her face, prompting Gediman (Brad Dourif) to exclaim: "your beautiful, beautiful little baby. Look, it thinks you're its mother." Ripley's feelings toward the creature remain ambiguous, even if she displays motherly or caring behaviors toward the Newborn. For example, she caresses and soothes it but does so to cut her hand on its teeth, flinging her acid blood onto the cargo hold's window and consequently creating the hole that will eventually kill her child. Ripley shows some regret about having to kill her offspring, whispering "I'm sorry" to the distressed Newborn as it is sucked into space. This death is a reference back to Ripley's encounters with the aliens in the first two films. Contrary to the swift expulsion from a spaceship in earlier iterations of this scene, the Newborn dies a slow and painful death, which appears to be equally painful to its mother, Ripley. The growing bond with the aliens, or "collapse [of] the boundaries between human and nonhuman,"[27] is thus also apparent in the difficulties attached to ousting that which can no longer be solely regarded as other. The complex web of social and biological kinship relations Ripley is engaged in throughout the original *Alien* series peaks in her relationship to the Newborn: it is because she is a mother that she can effectively kill it.

The Mother Made: Creation in *Prometheus* and *Covenant*

While *Resurrection*, like *Alien³*, focuses on procreation, it is creation-based procreation resulting from genetic engineering and cloning within a controlled scientific rather than a "natural" environment. As such, by blending the two concepts, *Resurrection* provides a bridge between the procreation-focused original series and the prequels, whose theme revolves around creation. In *Resurrection* already, the human as genetic engineer responsible for the alien-human hybrid becomes a creator, foreshadowing the events of *Prometheus* and *Covenant*, at the same time as David's (Michael Fassbender) assessment in *Covenant* of the human race as "a dying species grasping for resurrection" refers back to the aptly named earlier film. This paradigm shift within the universe is most explicitly thematized in the prequels, from Shaw's obsession with meeting her "makers" and the overall objective of the Prometheus to find the origins of humanity to David's genetic experiments. While procreation has been and still is readily understood as female-coded, emanating from "the logic that the female body is 'more appropriate' for reproduction,"[28] creation in the *Alien* universe appears to be a decidedly male domain. This is best illustrated by Peter Weyland (Guy Pearce): the genius behind Weyland Corporation, he is introduced as the creator of the android David in *Prometheus*, whom he considers "the closest thing to a son [he] will ever have." In the opening scenes of *Covenant*, this relationship is further elucidated. Here, creation emerges as an expression of a narcissistic drive to self-reproduce, ensuring the sustained viability of Weyland's ingenuity through David. We can read the relationship between Weyland and David as filial without responsibility—in other words, as a form of male-coded "motherhood" without mothering, quite in contrast to Ripley's displays of motherhood, which happen on both social and biological levels and which show her taking responsibility for these filial relations, even if this means killing one's offspring. In line with this, the idea of David being Weyland's son is rejected and David's ontological status is reduced to that of a creation rather than a relative. After all, Weyland's motivation for creating David in the first place, which is revealed when we learn that Weyland had been on board the Prometheus all along, is not to procreate but to create eternal life—for himself. Weyland's modus operandi, heedlessly creating facsimiles of himself, is mirrored in alien reproduction. The Queen, in "a projection of [. . .] overpopulation, specieism [sic], and parasitic imperialism,"[29] also reproduces indiscriminately by itself; hosts are merely a means to an end, stripped of any sense of agency, making both this and Weyland's form of pro/creation equally unsustainable.

In the opening scene of *Covenant*, David also develops a keen interest in creation, asking Weyland, "If you created me, who created you?" On the one hand, this can be read as a continuation of Weyland's legacy and as emphasizing his link to David. On the other hand, David scrutinizing the origin(s) of species—be it human or humanoid—and ultimately becoming a creator himself constitutes an extension of the Promethean theme that also permeates Shaw's convictions. However, in contrast to representatives of the patriarchy in the series (i.e., men as well as male-coded humanoids like David), Shaw is denied closure in the search for her maker since the engineer-head they retrieve in *Prometheus* implodes before she can gain further insight. She is also said to have died before David manages to land their ship in *Covenant*, leaving open the possibility of Shaw being used by David for genetic experiments. The prequels thus reinforce the separation of the sexes in accordance with gendered notions of agency: women simply cannot be(come) creators. While the dominance of male creationism in the two films serves to consolidate a discourse on disparate sexes and genders on the surface, this binary understanding results in instability if the films are not regarded as chronologically subsequent installments of the series but are approached as prequels.

It then shows that the female-coded procreation of aliens responsible for the cataclysmic alien infestations we see in the original series is, in fact, the result of male creation. Interestingly, upon closer inspection, *Covenant* more openly displays the Promethean theme than *Prometheus*, just like *Resurrection* more explicitly draws on the theme of procreation than *Alien*[3]. Similar to Prometheus—the titan who defied the Gods by stealing their fire and by creating humans from clay—David, who solely believes in creation by *man*, strives for perfection, which he claims to have found and created himself during his genetic experiments, further developing the alien species and eventually crafting the original Xenomorphs. His mocking of the gods is underscored by the music framing the film's opening and ending, Wagner's "The Entry of the Gods into Valhalla," and culminates in David planting facehugger fetuses in the Covenant's colony, a potential catalyst for the events of *Alien*. What the ending of *Covenant* unravels, therefore, is that aliens are a human creation of second degree, a painful realization that plays into the anxieties of, for example, cloning and artificial intelligence in a postmodern world. This is further explicated in the scene where David recites Shelley's poem "Ozymandias," which "argues effectively for the inevitability of mortality and transience":[30] in the context of the *Alien* series, where the creation, as well as the creation's creations, ultimately turn against their original creators, the sonnet's meaning takes on another dimension. Not only was Weyland's longing for immortality doomed to fail from the very beginning, but non-human entities—the statue of Ozymandias, the humanoid body, the alien—also become loci for the articulation of a critique of anthropocentrism, of man as creator both in the sense of *human* interference with the natural world and *male* supremacy. The interaction between David and Walter (Fassbender), an updated android model, unveils the underlying irony of this scene. By telling him that the poem was written by Shelley, as opposed to Byron, whom David credits with authorship, Walter shows that, in his quest for power, David has become "human" himself, and thus fallible. If we regard this movement from humanoid to human as parallel to Ripley's human-alien hybridization in *Resurrection*, what then follows from reading the film pairs as belonging to each other, as related iterations and as mutually influencing each other?

Creating the Mother: The Prequels and the Queering of the Serialized Form

Reading the films chronologically according to their release date, a shift from procreation to creation as the central theme can be discerned, which is related to an understanding of human evolution as a progression from body to mind, from instinct to reason—a shift that is also apparent in the initially described changes in cinematography in relation to female agency. Both the uninhibited procreation, as displayed by the aliens, and the indiscriminate creation, as shown by Weyland and David, are coded as negative in their respective representations and can accordingly be seen as parallels with a different focus. It is the relation between the two film pairs, however, that provides us with a more nuanced picture. The superficial feminist actualization in the prequels is met with the limiting temporal doctrine of narrative teleology that, following Jack Halberstam, signifies a shift toward "notions of the normal" within a linear (straight) "reproductive temporality."[31] Shaw's only function within the narrative, despite her display of agency, is to contribute to the reproduction of heteronormative subjectivity, and to uphold the subordination of "woman" to "man," which necessitates eradicating the alien threat. As prequels, *Prometheus* and *Covenant* alter the viewer's perception of the events in the original *Alien* series: the shift from procreation to creation becomes reversed. Moving instead from creation to procreation transfers the rejection of masculinist notions of creation into the emergence of procreation and motherhood as a substantiation of female agency, adding the notion of mothering, of responsibility for one's offspring. In this sense, the prequels invite a queering of the *Alien* series by working not only *with* but also *on* the original material: they leave "the temporal frames of bourgeois reproduction and family, longevity, risk/safety, and inheritance"[32] in favor of cross-temporal mergings that can be described as queer and non-assimilationist.

In this sense, the original *Alien* series becomes an emancipatory quest narrative,[33] in which women expand on the gender gap of the prequels' anthropocentric criticism, prying open and, to a degree, subverting male-dominated power structures. While the male imagination of creation so far followed the premise "sometimes to create, one must first destroy," as is explained in *Prometheus*, this imperative is inverted in the original series and reinstated in the character of Ripley, who, to destroy the aliens, must first—at least metaphorically—pro_create,[34] that is, establish either social or biological kinship relations. What we suggest here is that, in contrast to Shaw, who "can't create life," Ripley holds the capacity to defeat aliens based on her (social) role as a mother. As such, Newt's death between *Aliens* and *Alien*[3] becomes a vehicle that drives the plot forward, because Ripley's motivation to eliminate the aliens now derives from a feeling of vengeance evoked by the loss of her "daughter."

Coming back to our opening examples of *Alien*[3] and *Prometheus*, this difference can be accredited to the performativity of motherhood: Ripley becomes intelligible and is constituted as a meaningful subject within the *Alien* universe because for her, "outness," the open self-identification as and performance of motherhood is "an historically available and affordable option."[35] Shaw, in contrast, cannot become a mother in the normative understanding of gender that underlies the films. Yet, she is impregnated and forced to take on a maternal role; it is her *proximity*[36] to being a mother that makes her the other. This is further sustained by the necessarily heterosexual alignment of this gender matrix. Because Shaw's partner Charlie (Logan Marshall-Green) dies,[37] Shaw can become neither wife nor mother. She ultimately does not succeed in trying to make sense of her situation because, for her, this disorientation—not fitting the prescribed norms—results in a virtually *reproductive* crisis. As a violation of the rules upon which the *Alien* universe is built, Shaw is erased from the surface in the end, whereas Ripley self-determinedly leaves this world behind. In other words, her "new identity as 'the monster's mother' "[38] allows Ripley to outlive and vanquish aliens throughout the series.

Unmaking the Mother? Female Agency and Non-Female Motherhood

Procreation and motherhood may then be reframed in terms of their correlation with female agency: in line with Promethean thought—and as a subversion of creation as a male prerogative in *Prometheus*—Ripley (unwillingly) becomes a maker herself and is therefore able to "unmake" her creation/ offspring. Similarly, socially constructed kinship relations in the series tie in with the capability of defeating aliens, as the endings of the first two films show respectively. Ripley's agency, then, is constituted as female precisely because she *assumes* the role of mother. As Butler contends, "if there is *agency*, it is to be found, paradoxically, in the possibilities opened up in and by that constrained appropriation of the regulatory law."[39] Adequately framing mothers in the *Alien* series, therefore, means to delineate the sort of double consciousness that arises through their duality as *creators* and *creations*: Constituted as such in the context of a matrix of power that dictates and determines their intelligibility in relation to gender and heterosexuality, mothers performatively reproduce discourses of maternality in society. The identity of "mother" is thus claimed in "a space of negotiation rather than negation, where identity is continually reconfigured in relation to the past rather than eternally fixed by it."[40] Rather than identifying different qualities of female agency in the individual parts of the *Alien* series, the proposed relationship between the prequels and the original films demonstrates that agency is necessarily tied to the "regulatory norms" of the system in which it takes place: "'agency' or 'freedom' or 'possibility' is [. . .] produced by the gaps opened up in regulatory norms [and is] always negotiated within a matrix of power."[41] Already established understandings of motherhood underlie the representations in the *Alien* films and allow the performing subject to reconfigure precisely these notions rather than uncritically reproducing existing discourses. The representation of patriarchal power structures, for example, by the Weyland(-Yutani) Corporation, and along with it images of women as mothers, is a necessary part of the *Alien* films in that it allows for alternative understandings of womanhood and motherhood by creating spaces of negotiation that focus on motherhood as a social role, thus moving away from female-coded procreative biology, in turn questioning essentialist notions of gender.

Alienating motherhood from its biological connotations, the *Alien* series displays a range of maternally coded kinship relations that go beyond the possibilities afforded by the patriarchal system. As Stephanie Turner points out, "cloning scenarios," as well as non-female and non-human pregnancies, "offer popular culture consumers an opportunity to re-imagine the maternal and reproduction."[42] Making motherhood a central theme establishes connections to texts like Mary Shelley's *Frankenstein; or, The Modern*

Prometheus (1818), which meditate on the consequences of unnatural creation.[43] Expanding on this thought, we may argue that the queer temporal mergings the *Alien* series is confronted with through its prequels similarly open up possibilities for imagining alternative modes of mothering—if we follow the idea of serial relatives and the prequel becoming the mothership's mother—and models of motherhood, of pro/creation, since the prequels cast a new light on representations that simply were not available before. If maternality is conceived of as both a biological connection between mothers and their offspring as well as a social relation or emotional bond between these parties, the collocations of motherhood in the systemic use of language are exposed as tainted. Since there is simply no word for non-female mothers, our deliberations may well be read as a critique of the cis-normative bias of culture and may further discourses of motherhood in society beyond cis-femaleness. Ripley, in her oscillation between embracing and rejecting motherhood, transgresses gendered expectations and willingly claims her own otherness as her identity and as a form of female agency, which in turn allows her to face and overcome the alien threat, making the mother a true heroine. Neither male creators nor the alien can *un*make as this form of agency is reserved for the mother. This mother, however, is herself unmade: as the sole origin of species and series, she is displaced by the circular temporal relations introduced by the prequels. The *Alien* series as a whole (including sequels *and* prequels) constitutes a queer genealogy of mothers with its multiplicity of simultaneous origins: they are at once creators and creations just as they are both mother and daughter of one another. It is through this paradox, then, that motherhood can transcend the norms that bind it to a subordinate position within heteronormativity and become a site of female agency.

Acknowledgements: The authors would like to thank Alexandra Hauke, Christie Rinck, and Heidi Kramer for their feedback and thoughtful comments on earlier versions of this chapter.

Notes

1. See, for example, Frances A. Kamm's chapter " 'Must Be a Chick Thing': Ripley, the Alien Franchise and the Female Gothic," in this collection.
2. Barbara Creed, "*Alien* and the Monstrous-Feminine," in *Alien Zone: Cultural Theory and Contemporary Science Fiction Cinema*, ed. Annette Kuhn (London: Verso, 1990), 128.

3. Susan Yunis and Tammy Ostrander, "Tales Your Mother Never Told You: Aliens and the Horrors of Motherhood," *Journal of the Fantastic in the Arts* 14, no. 1 (2003), 68–76.

4. Catherine Constable, "Becoming the Mother's Mother: Morphologies of Identity in the *Alien* Series," in *Alien Zone II*, ed. Anette Kuhn (London: Verso, 1999), 173.

5. Constable, "Becoming the Mother's Mother," 174; see also Kamm in this collection.

6. Stephen Scobie, "What's the Story, Mother?: The Mourning of the Alien," *Science Fiction Studies*, 20, no. 1 (1993), 87.

7. Our analysis of the *Alien* series will only consider the films' theatrical releases, which exclude Ripley having a biological daughter, whose existence is revealed in a deleted scene of *Aliens* and who later becomes the protagonist of the videogame *Alien: Isolation* (2014).

8. Constable, "Becoming the Mother's Mother," 186.

9. Yunis and Ostrander, "Tales," 71.

10. Amy Taubin, "The 'Alien' Trilogy: From Feminism to Aids," in *Women and Film: A Sight and Sound Reader*, ed. Pam Cook and Philip Dodd (Philadelphia, PA: Temple University Press, 1993), 94, emphasis added.

11. Ronald A. L. Cruz, "Mutations and Metamorphoses: Body Horror Is Biological Horror," *Journal of Popular Film and Television* 40, no. 4 (2012), 161.

12. Barbara Creed, "Horror and the Carnivalesque: The Body-Monstrous," in *Fields of Vision*, ed. Leslie Devereaux (Berkeley: University of California Press, 1995), 133, 152.

13. Jason Mittell, *Complex TV: The Poetics of Contemporary Television Storytelling* (New York: New York University Press, 2015.

14. See also Kamm in this collection who reads the quotations within the franchise through the lens of the Female Gothic.

15. Scobie, "What's the Story," 80.

16. Ben Davies. "Prequel Ontology and Temporality: The Thresholds of John Updike's *Gertrude and Claudius*," in *Prequels, Conquels and Sequels in Contemporary Anglophone Fiction*, ed. Armelle Parey (London: Routledge, 2018), 27.

17. Matt Hills, "Transmedia Paratexts: Informational, Commercial, Diegetic, and Auratic Circulation," in *The Routledge Companion to Transmedia Studies*, ed. Matthew Freeman and Renira Rampazzo Gambarato (London: Routledge, 2019), 290.

18. Henry Jenkins, *Convergence Culture: Where Old and New Media Collide* (New York: New York University Press, 2006), 95.

19. Samuel Kimball, "Conceptions and Contraceptions of the Future: *Terminator 2, The Matrix*, and *Alien Resurrection*," *Camera Obscura* 17, no. 2 (2002), 95.

20. Sara Ahmed, *Queer Phenomenology: Orientations, Objects, Others* (Durham, NC: Duke University Press, 2006), 74.

21. Judith Butler, "Critically Queer," *GLQ: Journal of Lesbian & Gay Studies* 1 (1993), 22.

22. Judith Butler, *Bodies That Matter: On the Discursive Limits of "Sex*," (London: Routledge, 2011), 5.

23. Ahmed, *Queer Phenomenology*, 158.

24. Scobie, "What's the Story," 84.

25. Butler, *Bodies*, xxi.

26. Ibid., 71.

27. Louise Speed, "*Alien3*: A Postmodern Encounter with the Abject," *The Arizona Quarterly*, 54, no. 1 (1998)m 128.

28. Eva P. Bueno, "Writing the Mother, the Mother Writing: The Space of Motherhood and Feminine *Ecriture* in *Alien* and *The Matrix*," *Acta Scientiarum: Language and Culture* 32, no. 1 (January 2010), 77.

29. Yunis and Ostrander, "Tales," 70.

30. Hugo G. Walter, *Sanctuaries of Light in Nineteenth-Century European Literature* (New York et al.: Peter Lang, 2010), 22.

31. Judith Halberstam, *In a Queer Time and Place: Transgender Bodies, Subcultural Lives* (New York: New York University Press, 2005), 4.

32. Halberstam, *Queer Time*, 6.

33. See also Speed (1998), who reads Ripley in the original *Alien* series as breaking the conventions of the slasher horror genre and the trope of the Final Girl, an interpretation which is sustained (if not even amplified) through our readings of the prequels.

34. A brief note on the shift from pro/creation to pro_creation: while a chronological reading maintains pro/creation as a dualism in a way that contrasts the individual installments, at this point, the clear distinction between procreation and creation is complicated, and queered, through the films' serial relations. In this, we identify a space for reworking and rearticulating gender norms and their relation to agency, represented by the underscore, which imbues Ripley's relationship to creation and procreation with potential, opening it up for more than their perceived duality allows.

35. Butler, "Critically Queer," 19.

36. Ahmed, *Queer Phenomenology*, 128.

37. Other instances in the series attest to this as well, such as Daniels losing her husband in *Covenant* and Ripley's (sexual) relationship with Clemens in *Alien*[3].

38. Constable, "Becoming the Mother's Mother," 193.

39. Butler, *Bodies*, xxi.

40. Simon Bacon, "Life's a Mutha! Motherhood, Melancholia, and the Loss of Self in *Ann Veronica* by H. G. Wells and *Alien Resurrection* by Jean-Pierre Jeunet," *The Wellsian* 34 (2011), 84.

41. Butler, "Critically Queer," 22.

42. Stephanie S. Turner, "Clone Mothers and Others: Uncanny Families," in *Scifi in the Mind's Eye: Reading Science through Science Fiction*, ed. Margret Grebowicz (Chicago: Open Court, 2007), 112.

43. See also Kamm in this collection.

11

Melodrama of the Unknown
Woman Lost in Space

A Cavellian Reading of the *Alien* Franchise

Mario Slugan

In his two book-length genre studies on comedy of remarriage and melodrama of the unknown woman, Stanley Cavell argues that these are among
the rare film genres that provide female characters with a genuine voice.[1] In
his discussion of the latter, for which *Letter from an Unknown* (Max Ophüls,
1948) serves as a paradigmatic case, Cavell suggests that it is structured as an
answer to what a woman wants. And the answer provided by the melodrama
of the unknown woman, Cavell proposes, is to be known. The presence of
strong female leads is regularly recognized in work on the *Alien* franchise,
but it is usually discussed in terms of horror and science fiction genres. My
goal here is to add to these interpretations by reading not only the first installment of the franchise in a melodrama of the unknown woman key, but
by proposing that many of the genre's traits, as elaborated by Cavell, apply
to other instantiations of the franchise as well, including the video game
Alien: Isolation. I commence with how *Alien* (Ridley Scott, 1979) establishes
the female lead only mid-film, making her dramatic change in identity
even more pronounced, and then propose that the alien life form she faces
presents a specific form of horror clarified by the appeal to the melodrama of
the unknown woman—the horror of being known without being acknowledged. I then turn to the genre's other traits—the child/mother relationship,
the negation of communication, the struggle against the lack of recognition,
the choice of solitude, and the aforementioned radical change in identity—
to demonstrate how our understanding of both the *Alien* tetralogy and its
prequels is enriched by attending to these features. Crucially, if, according to
Cavell, the main characteristic of the melodrama of the unknown woman is
that it depicts the heroine undergoing a significant transformation through

Mario Slugan, *Melodrama of the Unknown Woman Lost in Space* In: *Alien Legacies*. Edited by:
Nathan Abrams and Gregory Frame, Oxford University Press. © Oxford University Press 2023.
DOI: 10.1093/oso/9780197556023.003.0011

emotional upheaval, then the emotion that underscores this transformation in the *Alien* franchise is horror. I conclude the chapter with the discussion of the acclaimed *Alien: Isolation* video game, suggesting that it provides a novel variation on the horror of being known without acknowledgment explored throughout the franchise. Whereas with films the viewers made-believe this horror for the protagonists, the players now make-believe fearing this fate for themselves.

Alien and the Horror of Being Known without Acknowledgment

Let me start off with the claim that what is at stake in the *Alien* film is our relation to our gendered body. This is vague enough, yet at the same time seems to strike a chord to be followed. But what is the whole tune? One of the questions that any analysis of *Alien* is bound to try to resolve is that of the role of the lead character. For a significant part of the film (approximately two-thirds), we presume that the main protagonist is the male captain, Dallas (Tom Skerritt)—Ripley (Sigourney Weaver) is third in command. Surely, this is supported by the fact that he appears to hold the lead actor's role, as Skerritt's name is the first to appear on screen and Weaver's the second. In addition, even after Mother, the ship's main computer, fails to advise Dallas on a course of action or to approximate his chances against the intruder, displaying nothing more than the onscreen line, "It does not compute," he nevertheless tackles the threat head on. It turns out, however, that Dallas cannot be the hero for he is taken out of the picture while trying to use the ventilation system to catapult the alien into space.[2]

With Ripley now set up as the heroine, the mode of confrontation with the alien shifts; it is no longer direct. Instead, the decision is made to blow up *Nostromo* and to escape in the shuttle. In his reading of *Alien*, heavily influenced by Stanley Cavell's ideas, Stephen Mulhall finds that this gender swap in the main protagonist's role is of utmost importance.[3] His reading focuses on the alien's lifecycle and the horror it creates. According to Cavell, horror is something inherent to humans, the fright of finding out that we are something else than we thought we were; therefore, first and foremost a question of human identity. For Mulhall, the horror spurs more specifically out of issues of gender identity: the alien represents the threat of feminizing the whole of humanity by the very biomechanics of its lifecycle. It is a parasitic form that after hatching needs to find a host to attach itself to; it inserts a part of itself into the host leaving it paralyzed and wraps its tail around the host's neck threatening suffocation if any removal is attempted. This act of penetration is compared by Mulhall to that of a sexual act by which a woman is made mute in the framework of the patriarchal heterosexual matrix:

> [t]he monster itself is the incarnation of masculinity, understood as penetrative sexual violence; but as such, it threatens the human race as a whole with the monstrous fate of feminization, forcing our species to occupy the sexual role (that of being violated, of playing host to a parasite, and of facing death in giving birth) that women are imagined to occupy in relation to men.[4]

This reading is somewhat problematic because it leaves out the fact that the first installment of the franchise does not account for the full cycle of the alien form. Admittedly, the sequels spell it out more clearly, but to use them to prop up this specific reading would be anachronistic. We do not know how the grown alien produces an egg (and if it even does at all): does it mate with another (are they discretely sexed creatures?); is it capable of laying eggs by itself; could the impregnator attach itself to a grown form showing no more mercy for one of its own kind than to Kane (John Hurt); could the alien cocoon itself and undergo a metamorphosis inside this egg-cocoon transforming into the impregnator; or is it perhaps that none of the above apply, that this specific instance is not capable of producing eggs at all, that its species is somehow similar to insects, insects with caste systems, ants perhaps, the queen being the only one capable of laying eggs?

It is at no point implied that this grown specimen could directly impregnate another life form. This suggests that we need to look at the grown life form separately from the impregnator with one key feature in common: their ability to violently penetrate bodies. Thus, Mulhall's quote breaks into two parts; the grown form could be read as masculine sexual violence and the impregnator as enforcing both the violence and the femininity of childbearing onto us. But it is the grown form that lurks in the shadows of *Nostromo*, the impregnator is disposed of relatively quickly, and it is not nearly as dreadful as its offspring. This suggests, I believe, that an even deeper horror underlies that of concerns with gender identity, one closer to Cavell's ideas.

First, an observation on the horror of Kane's unexpected demise. What is most harrowing here is the knowledge that our bodies can fail us; that this failure can be abrupt, violent, and agonizing, that our bodies themselves could be nurturing the very thing that is killing us, providing material and its regulatory pathways to the abuser. That this metastasizing lump of tissue and out-of-control virus spreading their way through the bloodstream are as much a part of us and our bodies as they are alien to us. This, however, is by no means gender specific and therefore we need to press further.

In sketching the history of skepticism, Cavell points out how by creating the private sphere, the period of Enlightenment (much of what is attributed to Rousseau's *Confessions* and Descartes' work) has made it possible for one to desire both to be known and to know the other.[5] Penetration becomes the mode of knowing: to make oneself known is to be penetrated, whereas to know another is to penetrate. This notion of knowing as an infringement on one's privacy is further eroticized, enacted in sexual life and, by the time Romanticism has met its demise, sadism and masochism (as expressions of extreme activity and passivity, absolute knowing of another and being known) become theatricalized.

We have seen how the alien's grown form comes hand in hand with Cavell's concepts of eroticized penetration and sadism—we will come to the question of its theatricalization soon enough—so it seems that we finally have our answer to the riddle of what is so horrendous about this creature. It can read us like an open book, it can stick its two mouths into our body, it can take us with its fangs and tail generating orifices on our surface at will, it can know everything there is to know about us, how feeble we are, how fragile our bodies are, how afraid and overrun by emotions we are. But what do we know about it? How can we penetrate it when it is shielding its body with silicon, bleeding acid when we somehow do manage to break the skin and its every action reminding us that we cannot talk to it, that no matter what we express it will not change its mind, that its form of life is one in which communication is absent? A lifeform incapable of, to use Cavell's key term, acknowledgment.

Admittedly, the (first) movie tells us nothing about how the alien might communicate with its own kind. But the very fact that it is alone and doing quite well suggests that it is self-sufficient and in no need of expressing itself to another (of its kind)—surely, a form of life that is unintelligible to us. And furthermore, if it does not express itself in any other way than what we perceive as sadism, is there anything to know about it at all? Could it just be a body without a soul, and if so: what is its body an image of? A body (without any life internal to it) enacting itself might be seen as theatrical in the very same way as a mechanical waving automaton, repeating over and over the same line, with that fake grin on that plastic exterior of theirs. Acknowledgment of them is not a possible mode of interaction; it would amount to nothing, we just could not get them out of their roles: the grown alien form will continue with its carnage and mutilation, whereas the automaton will wave and wave, and wave.

Mulhall finds Ripley's role as a heroine as giving a touch of irony to the movie: it is a woman who saves humans from their terrible fate of serving as child bearers to this horrendous breed. Moreover, by the very fact that she is a woman she is aware of the peril of serving no other purpose than procreation, and thus from the very beginning takes steps to protect her body from the intrusion (her insistence on quarantine for the crew coming aboard is disobeyed by the science officer Ash [Ian Holm]). As I said before, this is coherent only if we do not distinguish between the impregnator and the grown form, and does not really explain why the other female crew member, Lambert (Veronica Cartwright), does not take the same stance, but rather falls apart as a nervous wreck.

All that takes place on the *Nostromo* and *Narcissus* could be read as Ripley's nightmare. The scene in which the alien meets its end, being catapulted into space by jet propulsion, reminds one immediately in style of the scene near the beginning of the film with the crew waking up out of hibernation.[6] In both, the use of montage provides a dream-like effect, jumping briefly ahead in time but dissolving between the two close moments (with the jet engine exhausts providing an even more glittering effect in the closing sequence). Apparently, it is Ripley's nightmare then (one seldom dies in one's own dreams and this could account for Lambert not surviving nor stepping up as Ripley does; I am the hero of my own dream). But what is the nightmare exactly of? Ripley's nightmare should be understood as a fear of specific conditions under which being known might become horrifying. As I discussed earlier, first and foremost, it is the horror of there being nothing private that could be known to me alone and not to anybody else. In such a position, I am completely exposed to the other and the relation between the two of us is one of full asymmetry: there is nothing I know about the other and in finding the other unreadable, I start to doubt whether there is anything to know at all. But there is nothing gender specific about this, so it still fails to account for the heroine. What can be said to be gender specific (to an extent) is a particular mode in which being penetrated is to be known without being acknowledged: that of a rape. This is the reason Dallas goes directly at the grown form (not nurturing a fear of that sort) and Ripley essentially tries to run away (it is better to avoid the confrontation altogether). It also might account for Lambert being the one that is the most afraid when face to face with the grown form: implying that Lambert has internalized the idea that the fate of being raped might be worse than death. Ripley will not allow herself to be known by this penetrative force without being acknowledged.

Melodrama of the Unknown Woman Lost in Space

Hitherto, I have tried to articulate the specific horror *Alien* evokes with recourse to a key trait of the melodrama of the unknown woman theorized by Cavell—her desire to be known—and the way in which this desire can be transformed into horror. I am not claiming that *Alien* is of the melodrama of the unknown woman genre, but, as the analysis in this section will show, several of the genre's features do apply, not only in the first installment but throughout the franchise. Poaching from Cavell's account, these include emphasis on the relationship with a child and a mother figure, the negation of communication, the struggle against the lack of recognition, the choice of solitude, and the radical change in identity that takes place over the course of the film.[7] Here, as I already mentioned, it is *Letter from an Unknown Woman* that serves as a paradigmatic example for Cavell: the titular Lisa (Joan Fontaine), having spent a single night with Stefan (Louis Jourdan), the man she loves, chooses not to reveal the so-begotten child to the father, and lives her whole life, estranged from her mother because of the affair, only to divulge the story in a letter to him on her deathbed. Crucially, she realized that the man never loved her, that on the three different occasions they met he always failed to recognize and acknowledge her, and that he only knew her on that one fateful night.

Starting with the first trait, Ripley's relation to the cat is that of, as Mulhall puts it, displaced maternal care. On first inspection, Ripley's behavior toward the cat near the end of the film strains credulity. Having been so careful not to expose herself to the grown form since she took over command, putting oneself in harm's way now, letting precious opportunities to escape slip away to save the cat all appear to be completely out of character. Even more so, it is melodramatic in the ordinary sense of the word: there is drama where one is not necessary. From the perspective of the melodrama of an unknown woman (lost in space), however, it makes perfect sense. What would be more typical of the genre introduced by Cavell (and exemplified) by Laura than a selfless sacrifice for the child figure? Especially when all other life which offers at least some opportunity for communication has been extinguished?

But this is not the only mother-daughter relationship on board. The metaphor is literalized in the *Nostromo*'s main computer. Aptly named Mother, it behaves at first as a mother would (sheltering her little ones as they doze in their hibernation units and decoding the signal from the stranded ship to be a warning, not a distress call—admittedly, too late) only to deny her only surviving daughter salvation in her care when she fails to comply with her procedures (it is only a matter of seconds when Ripley fails to stop the self-destruct sequence). Ripley foams with impotent rage while Mother insists on abiding by rules and regulations—so much drama to be avoided if only a common language could be found. When the melodrama of the unknown woman takes place in space, Lisa's estrangement from her mother is radicalized into a question of life and death.

To continue with character relations in Cavell's list of the genre's key features, if we are to see Ripley and the alien's grown form as a couple, then their interaction is surely one of complete absence of communication, that is, utter absence of mutual acknowledgment, further radicalizing Lisa and Stefan's relationship. The image of Ripley's and the grown form's coupling presents itself most vividly in the scene before the finale in which Ripley takes her clothes off in preparation for sleep only to find her unwanted consort is already there next to her, sharing her quarters, mistaken for the escape shuttle's wires and ventilation ducts. It is impossible to fathom what the grown form is doing. Is it resting, is it preparing to strike, does it even notice its bride as she gags herself to stop herself from screaming?

And this is also where the woman's struggle against the recognition that does not take place (only this craving to be known which eventually leads Laura to her titular letter) comes to a climax insofar as Ripley is finally forced to tackle the grown form head on and rid herself of it once and for all, by ejecting it out of their shared chambers. It is a process that symbolically starts by getting dressed again—a renunciation of the horrific version of intimacy where no communication takes place. The companion's ejection is literal—it is shown the door by jettisoning the airlock and, when it refuses to leave, by gripping the airlock frame tight, there is a single moment when a weapon does break its skin and sends it across the doorstep. But not even this is enough: the grown form manages to scuttle behind the engine, and it is only the engine thrust which dissolves into dream-like glitter that puts an end to this horrific partner.

In the end, Ripley is alone, waiting to be rescued, to be woken up, or perhaps to wake up herself. It is much like the solitude that is the woman's choice in the melodrama of the unknown woman exemplified by Laura. The grown form, in this key, also left Ripley with an orphaned child to care for, alienated her from Mother, was unable to acknowledge her, and merely sought to penetrate her. In response, Ripley chose solitude in an escape pod and a letter of her own, a pre-hibernation message broadcast to whoever might be listening.

The overarching principle that Cavell's genre and *Alien* share, thus, is the radical change of identity that the female protagonist undergoes. Ripley is cast not only into the role of commander of the ship but also into the role of the main protagonist. Where the key difference lies is that whereas in the melodrama of the unknown woman, the process is defined by emotional upheaval, in *Alien* it is one filled with horror because it concerns identity.

Alien is, of course, not the only instance in the tetralogy or its prequels where these features identified by Cavell come to the fore and color the science-fiction horror genre with melodrama. Several *Alien* seque.. ~d prequels end in a variation on the theme of solitude. Although by the end of *Aliens* (James Cameron, 1986), Ripley is admittedly not alone (there are other survivors this time), they all enter hibernation, resting alone in the pods in the hope for a return to earth that, as *Alien*[3] (David Fincher, 1992) reveals, never comes, and for an awakening that awaits only Ripley. In the epilogue of *Prometheus* (Ridley Scott, 2012), the protagonist, Elizabeth Shaw (Noomi Rapace), is the sole survivor of another expedition embarking on a multi-light-year voyage to meet humanity's makers. And in the finale of the latest installment *Alien: Covenant* (Ridley Scott, 2017), Daniels (Katherine Waterston) retires to stasis only to find out that she is all alone insofar as she has nobody to rely on, that she has placed her trust in somebody, or, more precisely, something that turned out to be something else altogether, an android posing as another android, David (Michael Fassbender), bent on submitting her to the impregnator.

When it comes to maternal relations discussed by Cavell, if the relationship with Mother sours over the course of the first installment, *Aliens* ushers in a mother that precludes the establishment of any caring rapport with humans—the Queen. A figure of monstrous maternity, a notion discussed in more detail by Julia Kristeva, Barbara Creed, and, in relation to melodrama, Sarah Arnold,[8] she is a vehicle of breeding, the source of a humongous egg sack ovipositor that immobilizes her during the egg-production stage. This provides another glimpse at the alien's lifecycle—it is this mother who gives birth to the eggs out of which the impregnators hatch—but the mystery of where the Queen comes from (much like that of her sex) remains. Are different embryos nested in human chests, most of them producing the grown form of *Nostromo* with a rare few maturing into a Queen? Or perhaps a grown form can transform itself into the Queen making it—rather than she—a next stage in this hypothetical lifecycle? Is there an act of fertilization preceding the growing of the egg sack ovipositor, a male to a female, perhaps a King to a Queen, or at least an underling? Or is the Queen's egg production a spontaneous sexless act, not unlike pupation or even the division of amoeba? Put differently, what if the Queen is a sexless mother, nothing but a life-spewing machine? If the grown form and the impregnator pose the threat of masculine sexual violence and the menace of enforced femininity, respectively, then the Queen presents the horror of reproduction itself, coded as a mother figure, yet strictly speaking sexless and potentially self-perpetuating.

Much as she refused a male penetrative force coming to know her without acknowledgment in the first part, so does Ripley reject this type of motherhood as well. Admittedly, in *Aliens* the Queen, unlike the impregnator and the grown form, does introduce the possibility of communication—it not only seems to be directing other grown forms but is even able to establish a rapport with Ripley, who demonstrates her use of the flamethrower as a threat to destroy the eggs unless the Queen lets her go. At a safe distance, however, Ripley goes back on her word and unleashes a fiery fury on the breeding colony and the Queen's egg sack ovipositor alike. Crucially, it is the sight of an egg hatching—the clearest image of an automatic gush of life—that sickens and propels her to the shooting spree.

But for all her evasion and fighting, by the end of the third installment, Ripley finds herself impregnated so that, having killed herself to terminate the horrendous gestation, in the fourth installment we find a clone in her stead—Ripley 8. Importantly, Ripley 8's DNA is a hybrid of Ripley's and alien's genetic material and has also been used to produce a new breed of Queen—one that having laid eggs enters another cycle and develops a uterus. No longer a ravenous breeding machine, the new Queen bears a single hybrid offspring, and, just when it seems we are to witness the spectacle of alien care for a newborn, the hybrid fails to recognize the new Queen as its mother and instead tears her face off in a single swipe. A more familiar horror of matricide through birth or the perils of childbearing, but a horror nonetheless.

Where a cat served as a child surrogate in the first installment, Ripley comes to care for a girl Newt (Carrie Henn), the sole survivor of a colony outpost overrun by grown forms in *Aliens*. There the child serves a more classical function of focusing audience empathy and concern with a particularly vulnerable character. As later installments appear, however, the relationship to the child takes an ever more monstrous turn as it gets inextricably bound up with Ripley's own body and identity in Cavell's sense. By the end of *Alien³*, Ripley has realized that she has become the vessel for the alien life form and that the only way to stop the new cycle of horror is self-immolation. Near the end of *Alien Resurrection* (Jean-Pierre Jeunet, 1997), the newborn hybrid recognizes Ripley 8 rather than the Queen as its mother due to the genetic material the hybrid shares with Ripley 8. Their bond is played out in a horrific dance of caresses and drooling excretions, stopped short by Ripley 8's decision to again catapult her unwanted partner, this time as much mute penetrating force as it is a needy interspecies hybrid. Where the original consort presented a horror of intimacy without a shred of acknowledgment, here traces of acknowledgment degenerate the intimacy into incestuous embraces that bestow on the offspring a fate perhaps even more horrific than the one forced on human breeders. If the unwanted young explodes the chest of its feminized host killing him or her after a relatively brief agony, at the end of *Alien Resurrection* the hybrid offspring's insides are not only vacuumed out in a systematic and protracted fashion, but it is the mother (she used her own now acidic blood to create a hole in the window and cause the decompression) that both bears the responsibility for the deed and shares in the mental anguish arising from it.

But the most horrifying relation with the child in the series must be the one from its first prequel, *Prometheus*. If hitherto the series played on fears of humanity's transformation into passive breeders of an unknowable alien life and upped the ante by offering a glimpse into a potential relationship with it that is invariably incestuous, then *Prometheus* reveals that this alien life already always shared in human lineage. In a crucial part of a convoluted genealogy of this alien life, it is *Prometheus*'s protagonist Elizabeth Shaw who gives birth by way of Caesarean to a creature that will impregnate one of the Engineers and produce the first grown forms. In other words, the alien life was always a part-human hybrid—the horror always shared a part of our DNA, of our own genetic makeup. We might say that we have come full circle—if Kane's death preyed on our fears that our bodies can fail us when faced with an unacknowledging foreign invasion (be it parasitic or violently masculine), Elizabeth's near-death experience demonstrates that even consensual intercourse and an acknowledging partner may lead to a no less unwanted and murderous bodily failure, one that is now no longer due to our regulatory systems being hijacked, but is simultaneously partly identical to us and partly alien. In a Cavellian framework where horror rests on finding out that we are something other than what we thought we were, there is hardly anything that could be more shocking.

This is then the radical overarching change in protagonists' identity that all the *Alien* sequels and prequels share with the melodrama of the unknown woman. What for one woman starts as being cast into the lead and culminates in the discovery that, as a cloned version of herself, she has mothered the very alien that has threatened her human existence, finally climaxes in another woman being thrown into the role of biological Eve as she stands at the beginning of a new alien life form that will haunt not only Ripley but the whole of humanity with its threat of feminization (in *Alien: Covenant* Elizabeth's hibernated body is assailed even more as a vessel for the android David's further experimental alien life form designs).

It is, therefore, no mistake that in each of the six feature installments of the *Alien* franchise a woman comes to be or is the film's protagonist (in *Alien: Covenant* it is Daniels who survives where her colleagues have failed, only to meet the same fate by David's hand as Elizabeth). It is their lived experience as women, and the intimate recognition of the patriarchal role of childbearing, that first makes them wary of the alien threat but, in a further twist, they are abused (by male-coded androids or male scientists) to turn them into breeders par excellence, either to provide genetic material for new hybrid forms or to function as the origin of a whole new species.

Importantly, much like in the melodrama of the unknown woman, it is the males that are responsible for this "scientific" abuse, which in this context is nothing but the absence of communication or desire to know without acknowledgment by another name. While originally it was Stefan who consistently failed to acknowledge the woman with whom he fathered a child, the paradigmatic example of this behavior in the *Alien* franchise is surely Ash from its first installment. Throughout the movie there is a feeling that something is not quite right with Ash. He is the one making it possible for the quarantine procedure to be broken; when everybody is stunned and disgusted by what is happening to Kane on the dining table, the camera gives us cues that he might know what is amiss even prior to the grown form making its exit (or, better yet, an entrance). It turns out that something *is* terribly wrong with him and that he is nothing more than an android conducting itself on the behalf of the corporation, making it possible for the alien life form to be retrieved at all costs. At the moment in which Ash's humanity is most explicitly cast in doubt (when Ripley finds out the real nature of the mission), when we ask ourselves what kind of a human being can abide with such an inhumane corporate protocol (we still believe Ash *is* human), the camera starts to shake as we track Ripley backing out of the confrontation with Ash into the corridor (at this point Ripley seems to be at her most vulnerable, so distressed that her nose starts bleeding). Moments later, a white, thick, gooey single stream descends slowly down Ash's face revealing that he might *not* be human but something else. Only when he is finally broken in two do we recognize it as an android.[9] When jacked up it explicitly expresses admiration for the grown form and loathing of human sentiments such as consciousness and morality, and just before Ripley pulls the plug, she is met with its sympathies, with a grin on its face. Mulhall rightfully points out how Ash even tries to identify with the grown form in trying to suffocate Ripley with newspapers through an act of penetration. It is no surprise, therefore, that when Parker (Yaphet Kotto) finally demands Ripley turn Ash off because he has had enough of it, it is because of the knowledge Ash has, knowledge that is, to come to Cavell once again, without any acknowledgment of the other. The scene gives us a ghastly image of epistemology completely dissociated from ethics in which everything neck down is to be disregarded (Ash is mounted on his neck so its head does not fall while speaking) and in which only pure rationale is of importance.

The Video Game Horror

In lieu of conclusion I would like to devote a few remaining words to a part of the franchise that has received far less critical attention—the video game *Alien: Isolation* (Creative Assembly, 2014).[10] *Alien: Harvest* (Benjamin Howdshell, 2019), one of the five short films released as a part of the celebration of the fortieth anniversary of the franchise's beginning, revolves around the attempt to escape from an alien-contaminated ship using only a motion detector.[11] The device had appeared already in *Alien*, but there it was just a part of a toolkit, weaponry included, used to tackle the grown form, most notably in Dallas's failed attempt. *Alien: Harvest* reintroduces the movement scanner, but now essentially as the sole device at one's disposal, transforming the horror back into one of systemic evasion as opposed to that of confrontation, one of listening for signs of an unseen monster rather than staring in simultaneous revulsion and fascination at its horrendous sight. It is again Ripley's horror at its purest, the horror of being known without acknowledgment as Cavell puts it. And although *Alien: Harvest* only rehashes the trope, it is *Alien: Isolation* that essentially takes the same plot device as its organizational structure, that offers a genuinely novel experience in the franchise—the chance to face this horror not through sympathy or empathy with the protagonist but by make-believing being the protagonist.

In *Alien: Isolation* the player takes the role of Ripley's daughter, Amanda Ripley, who has learned that the flight recorder of *Nostromo* has been recovered fifteen years after the events of the original *Alien*, and that it is on board of orbital station Sevastopol. Amanda agrees to take part in the company's expedition to the station but on arrival is separated from the rest of the group and discovers that the outpost has descended into chaos after the grown form has been unleashed on its personnel. It is at this point that the gameplay commences, throughout which the player, as Amanda, needs to find out her mother's fate and escape the station using only limited resources such as the motion tracker. Crucially, the grown form can never be killed.

Linda Williams has famously described horror and melodrama (as well as porn) as "body genres," whose success rests on the ability to cause the viewers' bodies to spasm and convulse.[12] But it is one thing to shriek, cover one's eyes or jump out of the seats in the film and quite another to do so while playing a video game. Admittedly, the underlying horror in both is the one of being known without being acknowledged, but the immediate bodily reactions stem from elsewhere. For film protagonists in horror, it is the fear for their life, but in the melodrama of the unknown woman it is, as Cavell explains, the failure to be recognized. Yet for viewers and players it is something different altogether. For viewers, it cannot be what is usually termed identification with the character, if that means to feel what the character feels because of what the character feels, as though we could somehow fear the grown form because Ripley fears it, or as if we could in some way weep for being unacknowledged because Lisa is not recognized by her one-night lover. Ripley's fear does not cause the viewer's fear, and the object of Lisa's unrequited affections is not the viewer's object of affections. Put differently, the viewer's emotions are neither caused by the protagonist's emotions nor do the objects of those emotions coincide.[13]

The gameplay, however, does offer this coincidence or, more precisely, its make-believe or imagining. Unlike in cinema, in survival-horror video games we are invited to make-believe being the protagonist, to imagine having her motivations, to make-believe feeling her emotions, to imagine weeping her losses, and to make-believe fearing her fears. Imagining fearing for one's life is still different from fearing for one's life, but it is closer to it than make-believing that somebody else is fearing for one's life, as we do in fiction cinema.[14]

That traditionally understood character identification is a phenomenon that describes video-game-playing experience better than that of film viewership, however, should not stop us from repeating that the fundamental horror in *Alien: Isolation* as a part the *Alien* franchise is, from a Cavellian perspective, that of being known without acknowledgment. There are undeniably direct bodily convulsions and spasms, unmediated by any make-believe or imagining, in cinema and games alike. A jump scare works essentially the same in both media, an unexpected noise or an appearance will cause us to flinch, or even scream, and jump out of our seat. A gruesome appearance of the monster, similarly, often capitalizes on hardwired phobias, in the case of *Alien* resting on the combination of the creatures' insectoid- and snake-like features. Shrieking sounds will elicit immediate fear responses irrespective of the medium. But all these we could call technical scares. The horror of being known without being acknowledged is, unlike the logical possibility that something like the grown form might exist somewhere out there, a plausible threat for which it is not necessary to travel to outer space to face, but rather one which many are already living under.

Notes

1. Stanley Cavell, *Pursuits of Happiness: The Hollywood Comedy of Remarriage* (Cambridge: Harvard University Press, 1981); Stanley Cavell, *Contesting Tears: The Hollywood Melodrama of the Unknown Woman* (Chicago: University of Chicago Press, 1996).

2. Although it is interesting to note that unlike all of the other alien's victims, his body is never accounted for, nor is the very act of killing depicted. Rather, Scott cuts from a brief shot of the alien to another short shot of a tracking device losing signal. By doing so, we are left with a lingering feeling that Dallas might eventually show up somehow, that he might still be alive.

3. Stephen Mulhall, *On Film* (London: Routledge, 2002), 13–54.

4. Mulhall, *On Film*, 20.

5. For the full account see Cavell, *The Claim of Reason*, 468–496.

6. To emphasize the isolation of the crew and to pave the way to the state of incommunicability they will confront later on, there is not a sound of human voice for the first six minutes.

7. For an account of the genre's main features, see Cavell, *Melodrama of the Unknown Woman*, 4–46. There has, of course, been a lot of work on melodrama, including on its relationship with horror, such as Sarah Arnold, *Maternal Horror Film: Melodrama and Motherhood* (Basingstoke: Palgrave Macmillan, 2013). I am not claiming that Cavell's melodrama of the unknown woman (sub)genre is somehow paradigmatic of the melodrama genre overall but simply that it is a productive way of discussing *Alien*, that is, to point out that there are more generic elements to it than the horror and science fiction hybridization that is usually focused on.

8. Julia Kristeva, *Powers of Horror: An Essay on Abjection* (New York: Columbia University Press, 1982); Barbara Creed, *The Monstrous Feminine: Film, Feminism, Psychoanalysis* (London: Routledge, 1993); Arnold, *Melodrama and Motherhood*.

9. On closer examination we will see Kane's and Ash's gestures when they meet their end (hands fidgeting in tremor) to be similar; both of their bodily expressions failed to account for what was inside them. For further explorations of ideas of acknowledgment in another Scott film, see Mario Slugan, "Epistemology as Ethics: Skepticism in *Blade Runner*," *Film and Philosophy* 16 (2012), 84–100.

10. See, for example, Robin Sloan, "Homesick for the Unheimlich: Back to the Uncanny future in *Alien: Isolation*," *Journal of Gaming & Virtual Worlds* 8, no. 3 (2016), 211–230; Brendan Keogh and Darshana Jayemanne, "'Game Over, Man. Game Over': Looking at the Alien in Film and Videogames," *Arts* 7, no. 3 (2018), https://www.mdpi.com/2076-0752/7/3/43/pdf; Reuben Martens, "'Hissing in the Air Vents': Decoding the Narrative-Verse of *Alien: Isolation* (2014)" in this volume.

11. https://www.youtube.com/watch?v=Za0jUxBPQTw. The other four include *Alien: Ore* (Spear Sisters, 2019) (https://www.youtube.com/watch?v=Zv55of6Pb70), *Alien: Alone* (Noah Miller, 2019) (https://www.youtube.com/watch?v=XGWEihrIBvk), *Alien: Night Shift* (Aidan Brezonick, 2019) (https://www.youtube.com/watch?v=GYgoolcKszc), and *Alien: Specimen* (Kelsey Taylor, 2019) (https://www.youtube.com/watch?v=wKl-fU3WC7s)

12. Linda Williams, "Film Bodies: Gender, Genre, and Excess," *Film Quarterly* 44, no. 4 (1991), 2–13.

13. Noël Carroll, *The Philosophy of Motion Pictures* (Malden: Blackwell, 2008), 161–164

14. This is not simply due to the game's first-person nature, for if *Alien: Isolation* were a third-person game it would still invite make-believing being the protagonist. What changes is the type of simulated embodiment, not the imaginary relationship with the protagonist. Finally, in cinema, it is possible to also genuinely fear for oneself, but this is again not because we make-believe the protagonist fears for oneself or because we (make-believe) fearing for the protagonist but out of irrational, yet logical reasons (potential existence of monsters) that horror as a genre dramatizes: Mario Slugan, "The Moral Problem of Fiction: Rethinking the Emotional Effects of Fictional Characters," in *Does Fiction Change the World?*, ed. Alison James, Akihiro, Kubo, and Françoise Lavocat (Legenda: Oxford, 2023), 69–81.

12

Remediating Ripley

Negotiating the Patriarchal Gaze in the *Alien* Franchise Video Games

Bronwyn Miller

Since the release of *Alien* (Ridley Scott, 1979), Ellen Ripley (Sigourney Weaver) has frequently been the subject of academic analysis. Her character has often been read as a subversion of representational female norms, particularly in the science-fiction and horror genres of cinema, thereby offering an alternative to the male action hero. As a combination of the "survivor of slasher with the heroic astronaut of science fiction,"[1] the depiction of Ripley as one of the first "final girls"[2] has been credited with influencing the emergence of "new strong female roles in film, television, and video games."[3] However, while there is a large corpus of research on Ripley and her cinematic impact, no academic research exists about her avatar form and the effect of video game remediation on this character's representation. This research addresses this gap and proposes a new adaptation of "male gaze" film theory to video games.

The films of the *Alien Quadrilogy*[4] have inspired an enormous variety of entertainment modes, becoming an expansive franchise that continues to be adapted and remediated across numerous platforms including films, video games, novels, comics, and card games. Video games have been the most efficacious in terms of consumer numbers and video game remediations of the *Alien* films continue to be released across a variety of platforms. (See Appendix A.) In 1982, the first video game adaptation, *Alien*, was released by Fox for an Atari 2600. Since then twenty-two others have been released, the latest being a mobile game called *Alien: Blackout*, released in January 2019. There are also sixteen *Alien* and *Predator* crossover games.

However, the film's protagonist Ripley is present, in limited form, in only nine out of the twenty-three *Alien* franchise games. The presence of Ripley diminishes over time, with her last appearance as a protagonist avatar in

Bronwyn Miller, *Remediating Ripley* In: *Alien Legacies*. Edited by: Nathan Abrams and Gregory Frame, Oxford University Press. © Oxford University Press 2023. DOI: 10.1093/oso/9780197556023.003.0012

Alien Resurrection (Argonaut Games, 2000). The avatar body of Ripley is instead substituted with anonymous soldiers and monsters, eroding the possibility of spectatorial identification with Ripley's cinematic character, her objectives, and her female body. Ripley's erosion problematically implies that a woman, even a prolific action hero, is not welcome in video game environments. This has been common practice in the video game industry, which frequently presents women as a caged object of desire, such as a princess trapped in a tower. If this narrative motivation is avoided, video games tend to revert to either sexualizing the female avatar or excluding the female body altogether.[5]

In fact, the dominant culture of video games, both historically and currently, includes a distinctly masculine, and even misogynistic, component.[6] This is due to a self-perpetuating masculinist gender bias, which presupposes a male consumer, throughout the historical and economic construction of video games that produces "maleness as the default gender for computer gamers."[7] This bias also exists in both the production and content of video games. In 2017, only 21 percent of game developers identified as female, and less than 3 percent identified as transgender.[8] Likewise, an examination of 489 video game characters found 14 percent female characters compared to 86 percent, male, consistent with three other studies.[9]

This male-dominated production, and the tendency for developers to cater to a conservatively defined gaming audience, lead to formal processes of identification of a cinematic feminist character shifting once remediated in video games. My research asserts that a film character's representation and objectives, once remediated, are altered to mirror recurring gaming tropes that largely structure game form, repeatedly subjugating a player through positions and actions that comprise a patriarchal gaze in video games.

Ideological Gazes

This research is a qualitative, comparative, feminist investigation of Ripley's adaptation into video games. It analyzes the content of both the film and video game *Alien Resurrection* (1997/2000) to identify the formal and structural processes at work in the construction of character/avatar motivation and action, particularly those which attempt to subjugate the viewer in processes of identification. The primary form of investigation is textual analysis in order to examine "narrative structure, symbolic arrangements and the ideological potential of media content."[10] This research builds on feminist and post-Marxist theorizations of what it means to "look," with particular attention paid to how interpellation and ideology play important roles in understanding the impact of representation.

The following analysis is also reliant on the scholarship of Barbara Creed, and her semiotic considerations of the female body within horror films, and Donna Haraway's image of the cyborg.[11] These are used to deconstruct the character of Ripley in *Alien Resurrection* (Jean-Pierre Jeunet, 1997), who has been resurrected through a cloning process that genetically hybridizes her with a xenomorph. Ripley becomes an exemplar of Creed's "monstrous feminine"[12] as her existence compromises the boundary between human and nonhuman, hero and monster. This futuristic technological birth also codes Ripley as a cyborg, "a cybernetic organism, a hybrid of machine and organism."[13] Haraway and Creed's texts elucidate how Ripley's monstrous/cyborg reconstruction challenges the "deepened dualisms [. . .] in the social practices, symbolic formulations, and physical artifacts associated with high technology and scientific culture."[14]

In addition, I use Louis Althusser's notion of ideology and Laura Mulvey's "male gaze" to examine how institutional ideologies intervene in the visual experience of film and video games. Analyzing cinema and video games as institutions facilitates a critical examination of the role of ideology in representational systems and the manner it addresses, or manifests, normalized cinematic or video game subjects. That is, the visual construction of cinematic and gaming apparatuses is an ideological gaze—interpellating spectators as cinematic subjects and players as gaming subjects—that presents a reality to viewers in the form of a distinct institution.[15] The process of interpellation is structured by ideology, which functions by constituting individuals as subjects who are then able to recognize and identify with onscreen representations.

Understanding cinema and gaming industries as institutions sees them as a cultural Ideological State Apparatus through which "men represent their [believed] real conditions of existence to themselves in an imaginary form."[16] Film and video games are examples of these imaginary forms, and unawareness that media depictions are structured by ideological industries can result in a reinforcement of problematic divides, such as depictions of gender, which attach and reinforce expected social roles and stereotypes. What is actually being conveyed is "their relation to those conditions of existence which is represented to them."[17] That is, the conditions of existence that are represented to media viewers are of images and ideologies to which they have previously been subjected. Therefore, the depiction of a subjective reality is actually the representation of repeated ideologies. The means by which ideology disguises itself within the subjective reality of cinema and video games is through the normative alignment of the screen to an eye in order to encourage identification through the visual displacement of a spectator/ player's "look" into carefully controlled, ideologized images that manifest a gaze. Consequently, subjects of video game cinematic representations are unconsciously interpellated into a ruling ideology that, as it has the ability to shape depictions of reality, is consequently able to alter social norms.

The dominant ideology of video games was made particularly visible in 2014 when it was vehemently defended by a misogynistic section of the gaming community that began to feel threatened by feminist critique of video games, colloquially called Gamergate. Anita Sarkeesian was extensively ha- rassed by members of the gaming community who attempted to have her content—the deconstruction of stereotypes and tropes that surround the representation of women in games—taken down; doxed her;[18] and generated a significant amount of hate mail, including threats of rape and murder.[19] The backlash against Sarkeesian's work shows how the gaming industry's standardization of content created an ideology that is actively defended by interpellated subjects of the gaming community.

Mulvey's semiotic investigation, "Visual Pleasure and Narrative Cinema," established how film investigation is able to consider not only self-contained ontological considerations but also how ideologies, such as patriarchy and capitalism, structure film form.[20] Mulvey contends that the structural imple- mentation of established patriarchal norms regulates the viewing experience of cinema, controlling the female image and ensuring it is viewed through erotic ways of looking, and spectacle.[21] That is, the experience of cinematic "looking" is demarcated along lines of control and objectification. The effect of patriarchy on film is to produce what Mulvey terms a "male gaze," a priv- ileged, totalizing position that requires all women to look at depictions of themselves through a patriarchal, eroticized lens. This patriarchal gaze also constructs women as signifying the "male other," bound by a symbolic order, and therefore positions them as bearers rather than makers of meaning.[22]

The representational problems in both the film[23] and video-game[24] industries demonstrate the patriarchal control of images, which objectifies and interpellates subjects into a "male gaze."[25] Throughout this chapter, I refer to this as a "patriarchal gaze" to emphasize that representations of female bodies, or the lack of, are in large part due to the institutionalized repetition of formal elements that permeate and structure content within representational norms, rather than a film or videogame creator's assigned gender at birth. I argue that in video games this gaze manifests through shaping the objectives and agency of a protagonist avatar within patriarchal First Person Shooter (FPS) gaming tropes, where environments, characters, and narrative are experienced through weaponized action. This adaptation shifts consideration away from a "male gaze" being primarily attached to sexualized images of women, focusing instead on the systemic erasure of female bodies and action.

Patriarchal gaze theory is as applicable to video games as it is to cinema for many reasons. Beyond sharing gender inequality in production and content, film and video-game industries are becoming increasingly entwined. Single-player video games, such as *Alien Resurrection*, provide a larger focus on narrative than Massively Multiplayer Online games (MMOs) and, consequently, employ formal cinematic practices in order to encourage a player to identify with their avatar's world and motivations. Many video games have taken their audio and visual structural cues from film, as previously seen in genres such as full motion video games and contemporary tendencies to include special effects, celebrities, and a narrative basis.[26] The technologies of the two mediums have also become progressively mutual. For instance, computer-generated imagery has significantly blurred aesthetic divisions between cinema and video games. Moreover, parent companies of film studios are frequently invested in the development of video games.[27] For example, 20th Century Fox was a production company of *Alien* (Scott 1979) and Fox Video Games was the developer and publisher of the first franchise video game *Alien* (1982). Given the entwinement of these two industries, the application of a patriarchal gaze theory to video games enables a feminist examination of visual ideology, even in the absence of a visible body due to a first-person avatar position.

The following examination is divided into four sections: "Identifying Ripley" looks at the unified experience of playing Ripley's avatar compared with her hybrid cinematic characterization; "Cleansing the Maternal from the Technological" considers Ripley's various relationships to technology in each medium and how each grapples with the "monstrous feminine"; the third section, "The Resurrected Patriarchal Gaze," analyzes external factors that contribute Ripley's erasure from the *Alien* video game franchise; and the final section discusses the newer *Alien* franchise video game, *Alien: Isolation* (Creative Assembly 2014) as it demonstrates a method that avoids reproducing a unified patriarchal gaze conventional in First-Person Shooter (FPS) video games.

Looking Through Resurrected Ripley:
Film and Video Game Analysis

Alien Resurrection, directed by Jean-Pierre Jeunet and written by Joss Whedon, is a science-fiction horror film that first arrived in cinemas in November 1997, produced and distributed by Fox. The following analyzes the 109-minute theatrical release as Jeunet credits the 1997 original as being his director's cut and is the visual arrangement through which most spectators have viewed *Alien Resurrection*. The video game remediation, *Alien Resurrection*, is a single-player video game released in 2000 in North America for the PlayStation console. Published by Fox Interactive, it uses the basic narrative of the film within the first-person shooter, survival horror video game genre. Produced by Gary Sheinwald and lead programmer Simon Hargrave for Argonaut Games, *Alien Resurrection* is divided into ten levels, which are played through four avatar protagonists: Ripley for seven levels and one level each for Call, Distephano, and Christie.

Identifying Ripley

Ripley's hybrid identity and emotional complexity are central to the film's narrative. Ripley's appearance—with powerful, muscled arms that hold a massive flame-thrower—creates an image that supplants the male action hero with a leather-clad female cyborg, reminiscent of Haraway's ironic dream. The resurrected Ripley could not "recognize the Garden of Eden; [she is] not made of mud and cannot dream of returning to dust"[28]; now a hybrid cyborg, she exists in the "chaotic spaces between organic and artificial."[29] Ripley's cyborg characterization creates ambiguity around her allegiances, genetics, and sexuality, and offers a counternarrative to "the Western ideal of the unitary self."[30] Similar to Haraway's cyborg, Ripley has "no truck with bisexuality"[31] but will not tolerate male objectification. As demonstrated in the gym scene, Ripley's actions destabilize male authority through two means: her aggressive refusal of male objectification and the control over, or imperviousness to, masculine symbols such as the basketball and weight-lifting barbell.

Although Ripley becomes "the illegitimate offspring of militarism and patriarchal capitalism,"[32] as Haraway predicted, she is exceedingly unfaithful to her origins as her "fathers, after all, are inessential."[33] The hybridization of Ripley, from human and xenomorph, culminates in her embodiment of both aspects of hero and monster that puts the relationship between cinematic subject and object into crisis. Subsequently, "the driving question of the film becomes, 'Who are you?' "[34] and both Ripley and the viewer are required to piece together a new identity for Ellen Ripley.

Forming new identification processes with Ripley in *Alien Resurrection* is complex, as her post-human reconfiguration incorporates the "monstrous feminine": she embodies both the "castrating woman" and "the archaic mother [who possesses a] monstrous womb."[35] Ripley's embodiment of these antithetical identities problematizes "the viewing subject's sense of a unified self."[36] This is particularly the case when the film places viewers into threatening or horrific spaces that compromise the safety of the body. For instance, looking through Ripley's first-person perspective as she chokes a human, albeit the detestable, Wren, illustrates the problematic nature of spectatorial identification through a hybridized Ripley, as it asks audiences to not only look *at* what is monstrous but to look *through* it. As a result, Ripley's corporeality is simultaneously a space of threat and salvation; as she is both human and xenomorph "she can neither be destroyed like her offspring and her predecessors, nor can she straightforwardly be the heroine and the object of our identification."[37] Furthermore, Ripley's comfortable and sympathetic interaction with the monstrous signifies "recognition of their similar status as potent threats to a vulnerable male power"[38] and jeopardizes the authority of the traditional male subject position and its gaze.

Three years after the film's release, the video game adaption opens with a two-and-a-half-minute montage of different scenes from the film rendered into computer graphics, locating the player within the film's narrative. The film's dark, militarized, and violent aesthetics translate well into an FPS video game: set on a spaceship called the USM Auriga, the simple militaristic aesthetics of the environment, combined with the game's low lighting, mean that regardless of the video game's low computer graphic resolution and limited diversity of gameplay areas, the remediated environment (mostly monochrome walls, halls, and air ducts) remains aesthetically similar to the film.

Players are thrown directly into the first level of the game without a tutorial, waking in the first-person view as Ripley's avatar in her cell with green on-screen information. The first-person configuration has the advantage of avoiding stereotypically gendered signifiers for Ripley, as it does not represent the physicality of the avatars during play, such as exaggerated/eroticized body types that reinforce socially constructed binary forms of gender expression.[39] That being said, there are no character-based signifiers of Ripley during gameplay whatsoever: Ripley has no voice during cut scenes and the only audio indicators of a subjectivity are her steps and grunts when wounded. In the absence of a corporeal object for players to identify with, players are subjectivized into first-person games through their actions and the motivations behind them.

The limitation of possible action within gameplay—which includes aim, fire, weapon select, item select and use inventory item—and the lethal motivations behind them divorce Ripley's avatar subject position from her complex cinematic character and create a subject position unified with the avatars of established FPS franchises. The experience of *Alien Resurrection*'s game environment is largely moving through rooms or hallways/air ducts that limit what can be seen, creating a literal tunnel vision towards attackers that always approach directly at the center of screen. This removes the ability to avoid killing through hiding or maneuvering, which are possible actions with this level of video game technology. The consistent structure of these attacks, and the view through which players experience the game, closely resembles the structure of the 1992 game *Wolfenstein 3D*[40] that has been credited with establishing the FPS genre and is similarly divided into ten levels. The avatars of *Alien Resurrection* (Argonaut Games 2000) have increased mobility in regard to looking, walking, running, but otherwise a player's experience largely repeats the original shoot-and-run template.

To move past Level One, Ripley's avatar must find a pistol with which to kill attacking marines and a xenomorph. The lack of special treatment Ripley receives from (or gives) xenomorphs codes Ripley's avatar as human, rather than hybrid. Moreover, these kills greatly diverge from the cinematic character; Ripley goes to great lengths within the film to avoid killing humans, even those who have harmed her. The form of violence in the game *Alien Resurrection* is more akin to that in established militaristic FPS games, rather than a reflection of the original film, such as Ripley's signature choking, ripping out of "souvenirs," or strategic use of acid blood. That is, the game's violent content in itself is not divergent from the film, just its unoriginal reproduced form.

While the game subjectivizes the player by reproducing the dichotomy of a heavily coded FPS gaming trope, i.e., "self" and "other," the film breaks down the dichotomies it sets up: humane/antihuman, humanoid/xenomorph, objective-scientific/emotional-intuitive understanding, male/female and military/non-military. The divides between these themes are eroded throughout the film, destabilizing a viewer's ability to wholly identify with any single category, encouraging acceptance of heroic protagonists with contradictory and othered identities.

The single unique variation to avatar identification in *Alien Resurrection* is Christie's level where the avatar holds two pistols, creating a direct link back to his cinematic character the other avatars lack. Overall, the game replicates previous FPS structures, rather than identification with the film's characters, interpellating a subject's look into a gaze that unifies a player's perspective with a patriarchal gaming diegesis. Even though the first-person shooter avatar position may be considered a "blank slate," the environment and its engagement limitations is filled with codes and patterns that exclude different forms of problem-solving outside the essentialized armed, able-bodied male soldier.

Cleansing the Maternal from the Technological

The first image of Ripley in the film is as a growing clone, suspended in an enormous woman-sized test-tube, surrounded by four male scientists who "clinically gaze"[41] at her body's naked development. This scene is narrated by Ripley, who explains how her mother was mistaken in thinking that there are no real monsters. Directly after her voiceover confirms that there are in fact monsters, the pull-back shot reveals the gazing scientists, thereby aligning the male scientist with the monstrous (depicted in Figure 12.1). This is the beginning of a long series of inferences that underline a problematic connection between science and technology, and antihuman values, largely

Figure 12.1 Gazing at Ripley (*Alien Resurrection*, Jeunet 1997).

embodied in the masculine characters. Furthermore, this is the last time Ripley is oblivious to/passive in her subjection to the male gaze. After her "birth," the objectifying patriarchal gaze, or attempts to control her, are always met with Ripley's verbal or physical responses.

Directly following the caesarean of the xenomorph, Ripley is again contained in a cylindrical cell, this time lying in a white cloth sack at the bottom of a metal well, which military boots walk over above, reaffirming a presence of control through surveillance.

The film parallels the military and scientific medical personnel as both assuming a godlike position to create and control their subjects through a dominating, scientific "eye that knows and decides, the eye that governs."[42] Foucault contends that the concept of "gaze" is not faithful, nor subject, to truth without synonymously "asserting [...] a supreme mastery: the gaze that sees is a gaze that dominates."[43] Both the military and scientists attempt mastery over their respective subjects, the xenomorphs and Ripley, through institutionalized forms of scientific observation and training. This is seen in the military's training of the xenomorph—using torture—and the scientists' detached and condescending treatment of Ripley whom they attempt to discipline through scientific teaching methods. Both Ripley and the xenomorphs quickly escape their watch, signifying that scientific authority and military technologies are ultimately unable to control Ripley or the xenomorph.

Ripley's treatment by the scientists and disregard for guns in the film means that her video game objectives in Level One to find a gun and free a scientist are somewhat dubious. The film manifests tension between disembodied patriarchal technology and the embodied monstrous feminine, for example, the spaceship's computer system, "Father," and the weaponized military's failure to control the monstrous corporeality of Ripley, the android Call, and the xenomorphs. Ripley and the xenomorphs use their acidic blood to escape their computerized cells and Call internally connects her cyborg body to override Father and crash the ship. Conversely, in the game this tension is replaced with mission objectives that require players to sustain the ship and continually upgrade their weaponry. In Level Two, "Engineering Deck," the game is re-entered in Call's perspective whose principal objective is to save the ship which requires players to disable security systems, shut down a generator, and release pressure and power flow to the reactor to sustain the ship and the computer, "Father." The video game also gives the ability to control Father to Distephano's avatar, which, during the fifth level, must reset Father's core. Despite the cinematic "Father" being an ally of the inhumane scientists and easily overridden by a female cyborg, the video-game remediation makes the role of Father essential and requires players to regulate it as a male soldier.

Mary Ann Doane's essay "Technophilia: Technology, Representation, and the Feminine" asserts that "technology promises more strictly to control, supervise, regulate the maternal—to put limits upon it. But somehow the fear lingers—perhaps the maternal will contaminate the technological."[44] This is clearly seen in the film, where military scientists attempt to "train," control, supervise, and regulate Ripley and the xenomorph species. Through a different lens, this tendency of technology can also be applied to Ripley's gradual exclusion from the video game franchise—a male-dominated technology that fears being "contaminated" by maternal/feminine avatars and erases any signifiers of the female cyborg within its avatar position.

Cleansing the maternal from the technological can also be interpreted as one of the game's main objectives, finding and killing the seven failed

Figure 12.2 All four clones that must be hunted in *Alien Resurrection* (Argonaut Games, 2000).

clones of Ripley. This task structures the objectives of four out of ten levels. For example, Ripley's primary mission in Level Three, "Clone Research," is to find and destroy two clones; the player/Ripley must shoot a clone on a surgical table and a clone suspended in a human test tube. Level Four has very similar mission objectives, requiring Ripley to kill two clones— shooting one and boiling the other in the water of her tank (see Figure 12.2 below). This is a distinctly unmerciful act, which consequently only explodes the abject body but not the technology sustaining it (the tank in which it boils).

In the film, upon discovering the seven unsuccessful clones, Ripley goes to each of them and looks into their faces, gently touching their glass test tube casings, the camera frequently cutting to first person to represent the horror of her experience to the spectator (Figure 12.3). Hearing a sharp intake of breath off to the side, Ripley discovers a surviving clone, whose body's monstrous externalization of hybrid genetics is juxtaposed against a human head, which begs to be killed. Ripley, for the first time in the film, looks truly distressed and leans in to look at her alternate version and covers up her naked

Figure 12.3 Depicts Ripley's discovering her clones in *Alien Resurrection* (*Alien Resurrection*, Jeunet 1997).

body with a surgical cloth, perhaps attempting to counter the scientists' cruel, objectifying treatment. She begins to cry and accepts a flamethrower from Call (Figure 12.3). After the room is incinerated, Ripley walks vengefully towards Wren, flamethrower in hand, struggling to control herself but ultimately throws the weapon at his feet.

This scene paradoxically introduces emotionality and humane restraint into the characterization of Ripley directly after the revelation of her monstrous origins and internal genetics. It continues the film's contradictory construction of her identity, complicating spectatorial identification with Ripley. In the film, Ripley's destruction of the first seven clones is, in part, an act of mercy. However, in the video game clones are hunted and destroyed violently, not just by Ripley but also by Distephano. The annihilation of the seven clones in the video game serves as an act of cleansing, or purification of the abject feminine, which Creed identifies as "the central ideological project of the popular horror film"[45] and, as seen through its level objectives, the video game *Alien Resurrection*.

The Resurrected Patriarchal Gaze

To summarize, *Alien Resurrection*'s representation of Ripley is merely gestural. Replacing Ripley's cinematic characterization with FPS norms and privileging technology over her embodied strength ultimately forms a patriarchal gaze that excludes Ripley's character from the gameplay of *Alien Resurrection* regardless of being a protagonist avatar.

Overall, the ten levels of *Alien Resurrection* are uniform in the identification processes of all four avatar positions and their available actions and objectives. While Ripley has the largest number of levels, her avatar only exists in relation to the male definition of gaming and does not have a character of her own with which to identify, partly offering an explanation of why her character was not able to inhabit other video games, such as the *Alien vs Predator* franchise where her character does not exist. This is partly owing to the game's permanent shift into a subjective viewpoint, but more so to the alteration of character motivation and action. The plateaued nature of these avatar forms manifests a patriarchal-signified video game environment that duplicates previous game structures, rather than attempting to implement the versatile approaches of the film. These structures define and realize Ripley's subject position through a gun and in opposition to enemies that must be destroyed. Conversely, though identification with Ripley is consistently problematized in the film, through her genetics and sexuality, she is nevertheless the primary site of identification for viewers.

Figure 12.4 Top from left to right: *Wolfenstein 3D* (idSoftware 1992), *Doom* (idSoftware 1993), *Quake* (idSoftware 1996), *Alien Resurrection* (1997).

The duplication of objectives, actions, and gaming environments—from games such as *Doom*[46] or *Quake*[47]—embeds a patriarchal perspective in *Alien Resurrection* (Figure 12.4). As Elkington clarifies, this is partly due to transmedia games being largely "based on pre-existing franchises in an attempt to minimize risk."[48] That is, *Alien Resurrection* duplicates previous structures, which reach back to the 1992 game *Wolfenstein 3D*, in order to be able to appeal to an established male fanbase, predict sales and capitalize upon a structure of games previously "market tested."[49]

This is problematic because, as Sarkeesian highlights, in male-identified societies, men and male experience become associated and synonymous with human beings in general.[50] In other words, identification in video games "manifests as the tendency for all characters to be male by default unless there is some special reason or specific justification for women to be present in the story."[51] Although this justification exists, the game does not in any way distinguish Ripley's perspective or actions from previous avatars, such as *Doom*'s (1993) unnamed space marine or the marine Distephano.

This actively works against a feminist avatar position as it uses a female character to reinscribe a male viewing position through the tropes of the game. Consequently, the avatar of Ripley is forced into actions to which her cinematic character is resistant.

The tendency to duplicate previous structures is shared by the film institution; however, after many more decades of critique, it offers a broader array of subject positions that represent marginalized identities. Even though *Alien Resurrection* was made forty-nine years after the first video game and was based on the 1997 film that subverts understandings of monstrous and traditional action heroes, the game has no investment in reproducing the strong female presence that is present throughout all four of the *Alien* films. While the FPS perspective is able to circumvent stereotypical gendered signifiers of the female avatars, the reintroduction of determinate categories of "self" and "other" diminish the presence of the cinematic Ripley in favor of male perspectives and actions, thus reinforcing the patriarchal gaze conventional in video games.

Alien Isolation

In contrast with *Alien Resurrection*, the video game *Alien: Isolation* (Creative Assembly 2014) serves as an example of how gameplay mechanics can avoid reproducing a patriarchal gaze in first-person horror video game environments. That being said, Ellen Ripley is still not a playable avatar in her own game franchise except in *Alien: Isolation*'s bonus content,[52] where players experience the last scene of the first *Alien* film through Ripley's avatar. However, this level is not part of the game and must be purchased and downloaded separately. Nevertheless, *Alien: Isolation* demonstrates a strong relationship to the film, for example, the actor who played Ripley voiced her character for the game's cutscenes. Weaver, explaining why she agreed to work on the project, stated that it was different from other games she had been approached about as it created "an experience for the gamer that really puts you back on that [Ridley Scott's] ship."[53] As discussed by Martens in following chapter, *Alien: Isolation* is a complex amalgamation of adaptation, remake, and sequel, which closely mimics the first *Alien* film in terms of themes, storyline, and aesthetics.

Players are therefore reconnected with the feelings of the film, rather than the FPS video game genre.

Alien: Isolation is set fifteen years after the first film; the protagonist avatar is Ripley's daughter Amanda who is searching for her mother. Amanda's viewpoint may be better shortened to "first-person" as players have no single weapon that can kill the xenomorph that hunts them. In an interview, Alistair Hope, *Alien: Isolation*'s creative lead for creative assembly, discussed the game with GameSpot reviewer Dan Hindes. Crucial to the horror of *Alien: Isolation* is that "technology isn't the answer. It communicates that there's no locker somewhere with a massive gun that's going to be the answer to your problem."[54] This aspect of the game is dissimilar to nearly every other game based on the *Alien* franchise. Players must use creative problem solving to avoid the xenomorph, including hiding and using found objects to set up distractions. The driving force of this game is not to shoot but to improvise and survive being hunted by a xenomorph using the "mundane, basic and clunky"[55] technology of the 1970s.

The creators of *Alien: Isolation* assert that they did not "set out with any agenda" and credit the universality of the film to its high stakes: "what you're up against is an unknowable, mysterious creature. Whatever sex you are, it's merciless."[56] This highlights a problematic tendency in mainstream media, that the stakes have to be so unrealistically high for gender norms to be challenged, for strong women to be included, and for gender to become irrelevant to narrative action and gameplay. Nevertheless, *Alien: Isolation*'s diversified gameplay and artificial intelligence-driven xenomorph has encouraged player engagement, as seen in the game's positive reception, numerous accolades, novelization and other transmedial influences (discussed further by Martens in the next chapter). This development demonstrates that, even without an intended feminist agenda, stronger investment by video games in a woman-positive film is able to intervene in the repetitious structures that marginalize female roles in video games.

Conclusion

The remediation of *Alien Resurrection*'s Ripley within video game culture divorces her character from the radical exploration of gender roles, looking positions, and the underlying feminist impetus seen in the films. The cine-matic Ripley, while being created by men, undermines traditional patriar-chal structures and, although she may not entirely break free, "she is seen, she is heard, and she is remembered."[57]

The interpellation of subjects by both the film and game becomes problem-atic through differing means. The film continually compromises the viewer's sense of a unified self through the protagonist's monstrous embodiments. Conversely, the unified patriarchal FPS gaze simplifies a subject position into a movable gun, a phallic technology that can violently keep the monstrous at bay, detaching the player from the film's characterization of Ripley. The erosion of Ripley's character in favor of established masculinist perspectives and actions demonstrates the effects of the game industry and its culture upon processes of identification with women. The gaming industry's desire to cater to a specific consumer for predictable financial gains contributes to the entrenchment of these tropes that force subject identification through weaponized action.

This comparative approach to the interpellation of viewers and players demonstrates the entrenching effect of capital-based institutions reproducing processes that permeate subject identification. Critically applying intersec-tional feminist considerations to the respective versions of *Alien Resurrection* (1997/2000) enables a mapping of the alteration to the identification process that elicits understandings of the patterns and ideologies, which go beyond representational images and into game structure. In order for first-person video games to be inclusive of multiple forms of player identification, di-versity needs to be prioritized on production and content levels *and* in gameplay strategies. The inclusion of action, avatars, and games industry employees outside the dominating established patriarchal perspective will push for a more welcoming gaming culture for everyone, not just for girls and women.[58][59]

Appendix A Alien Franchise Video Games[60]

Title	Year	Console	Developer and Publisher	Is Ripley an Avatar?
Alien	1982	Atari 2600	D&P: Fox Video Games	No
Alien	1984	Commodore 64 Amstrad CPC (1985)	D: Amsoft, Concept Software, Argus Press Software P: Argus Press Software	Yes, text-based indicators
Aliens: The Computer Game	1986 1987	Commodore 64 and ZX Spectrum Apple IIe, Amstrad	D: Activision and Mr. Micro. P: Electric Dreams Software	Yes
Aliens: The Computer Game (*Scrolling Shooter*)	1987	Commodore 64, ZX Spectrum, MSX, Amstrad	D: Software Studios P: Electric Dreams Software and Ricochet	Yes
Aliens: Alien 2	1987	MSX	D&P: SquareSoft	Yes
Rebelstar II: Alien Encounter	1988	ZX Spectrum	D: Julian Gollop P: Silverbird Software	No
Aliens	1990	Arcade	D&P: Konami	Yes
Alien 3	1992	Amiga, Commodore 64, Sega Master System	D: Probe Entertainment and Eden Entertainment Software	Yes
	1993	Nintendo Entertainment System, Sega Genesis	P: Arena Entertainment, Acclaim Entertainment	
	1994	Sega Game Gear		

(continued)

Appendix A Continued

Title	Year	Console	Developer and Publisher	Is Ripley an Avatar?
Alien 3	1993	Gameboy	D: Bits Studios P: LJN	Yes
Alien 3: The Gun	1993	Arcade	D: Sega P: Sega	No
Aliens: A Comic Book Adventure	1995	PC	D: Cryo Interactive Entertainment P: Mindscape	No
Alien Trilogy	1996	PlayStation, Sega Saturn and PC	D: Probe Entertainment P: Acclaim Entertainment	Yes
Aliens Online	1998	PC	D: Mythic Entertainment P: Kesmai	No
Alien Resurrection	2000	PlayStation	D: Argonaut Games P: Fox Interactive	Yes
Aliens: Thanatos Encounter	2001	Gameboy Colour	D: Wicked Witch Software and Crawfish Interactive P: THQ	No
Aliens: Unleashed	2003	Mobile Phone	D&P: Sorrent	No
Aliens: Extermination	2006	Arcade	D: Global VR P: Play Mechanix	No
Aliens: Infestation	2011	Nintendo DS	D: WayForward and Gearbox Software P: Sega	No

	Year	Platform	Developer/Publisher	Playable female
Aliens: Colonial Marines	2013	PC, PlayStation 3, Xbox 360, and Nintendo DS	D: Gearbox Software and Nerve Software P: Sega and 20th Century Fox	No
Aliens: Armageddon	2014	Arcade	D: Play Mechanix P: Raw Thrills	No
Alien: Isolation	2014	PC, PlayStations 3 and 4, Xbox 360 and Xbox One	D: Creative Assembly P: Sega	No
Crew Expendable (DLC)				Yes
Last Survivor (DLC)				Yes
Aliens vs. Pinball	2016	Android, iOS, PS3, PS4, PS Vita, Steam, Wii U, Windows 10, Xbox 360, Xbox One	D: Zen Studios P: Zen Studios	No (Ripley is part of the pinball machine but not a playable avatar)
	2017	Nintendo Switch		
Alien: Blackout	2019	Mobile Phone	D: D3 Go! FoxNext, Rival Games P: D3 Go!	No

Notes

1. Ximena Gallardo and Jason Smith, *Alien Woman: The Making of Lt. Ellen Ripley* (New York: Continuum, 2004), 8.
2. Carol J. Clover, *Men, Women, and Chain Saws: Gender in the Modern Horror Film* (Princeton: Princeton University Press, 1993), 46.
3. Gladys L. Knight, *Female Action Heroes: A Guide to Women in Comics, Video Games, Film, and Television* (Santa Barbara: Greenwood, 2010), 108.
4. The "*Alien Quadrilogy*" refers to: *Alien* (Ridley Scott, 1979); *Aliens* (James Cameron, 1986); *ALIEN3*, (David Fincher, 1992); *Alien Resurrection* (Jean-Pierre Jeunet, 1997).
5. Anita Sarkeesian, "Ms. Male Character—Tropes vs Women" (November 18, 2013), video, 25:01, https://feministfrequency.com/video/ms-male-character-tropes-vs-women/ (accessed November 10, 2020).
6. Research on the sexist and misogynistic history of games includes: Mia Consalvo, "Confronting Toxic Gamer Culture: A Challenge for Feminist Game Studies Scholars," *Ada: A Journal of Gender, New Media, and Technology* 1 (2012), 1–6, http://adanewmedia.org/2012/11/issue1-consalvo/ (accessed November 10, 2020); Edward Downs and Stacy L Smith, "Keeping Abreast of Hypersexuality: A Video Game Character Content Analysis," *Sex Roles* 62 (2010), 721–733; Jennifer Johns, "Video Games Production Networks: Value Capture, Power Relations and Embeddedness," *Journal of Economic Geography* 6, no. 2 (2006), 151–180; Marie-Josée Legault, Victoria O'Meara, Johanna Weststar, *Developer Satisfaction Survey 2017 Summary Report*, International Game Developers Association (2018), https://igda.org/news-archive/igda-dss-2017-press-release/ (accessed November 10, 2020).
7. Diane Carr, "Contexts, Gaming Pleasures, and Gendered Preferences," *Simulation & Gaming* 36, no. 4 (2005), 467.
8. Legault, O'Meara, and Weststar, *Developer Satisfaction Survey 2017 Summary Report*, 11.
9. Downs and Smith, "Keeping Abreast of Hypersexuality," 729.
10. Elfriede Fürsich, "In Defense of Textual Analysis: Restoring a Challenged Method for Journalism and Media Studies," *Journalism Studies* 10, no. 2 (2009), 239.
11. Donna Haraway, "A Cyborg Manifesto: Science, Technology, and Socialist-Feminism in the Late 20th Century," in *The International Handbook of Virtual Learning Environments*, ed. Joel Weiss, Jason Nolan, Jeremy Hunsinger, and Peter Trifonas (Dordrecht: Springer, 2006), 117–158.
12. Barbara Creed, *The Monstrous-Feminine: Film, Feminism, Psychoanalysis*, (London: Routledge, 1993).
13. Ibid., 117.
14. Ibid., 121.
15. Lois Althusser, "Ideology and Ideological State Apparatuses (Notes Towards an Investigation)," in *The Anthropology of the State: A Reader*, ed. Aradhana Sharma and Akhil Gupta (Oxford: Blackwell Publishing, 2006), 92.
16. Ibid., 100.
17. Ibid., 101.

18. Doxing refers to publishing a person's identifying or private information online with malicious intent.

19. Sal Humphreys and Karen Orr Vered, "Reflecting on Gender and Digital Networked Media," *Television & New Media* 15, no. 1 (2014), 3.

20. Laura Mulvey, "Visual Pleasure and Narrative Cinema," in *Visual and Other Pleasures*, (Bloomington: Indiana University Press, 1989), 14.

21. Ibid., 14.

22. Ibid.

23. Martha M. Lauzen, *The Celluloid Ceiling: Behind-the-Scenes Employment of Women on the Top 100, 250, and 500 Films of 2018*, Center for the Study of Women in Television and Film, San Diego State University (2019), 1–7. http://womenintvfilm.sdsu.edu (accessed November 10, 2020); *The Celluloid Ceiling: Behind-the-Scenes Employment of Women on the Top 100, 250, and 500 Films of 2019*. Center for the Study of Women in Television and Film, San Diego State University (2020), 1–9. http://womenintvf ilm.sdsu.edu (accessed November 10, 2020).

24. Legault, O'Meara, and Weststar, *Developer Satisfaction Survey 2017 Summary Report*.

25. Mulvey, "Visual Pleasure and Narrative Cinema," 12.

26. Trevor Elkington, "Too Many Cooks: Media Convergence and Self-Defeating Adaptations," in *The Video Game Theory Reader 2*, ed. Bernard Perron and Mark J. P. Wolf (New York: Routledge, 2009), 213.

27. Elkington, "Too Many Cooks," 213.

28. Haraway, *A Cyborg Manifesto*, 119.

29. LeiLani Nishime, "The Mulatto Cyborg: Imagining a Multiracial Future," *Cinema Journal* 44, no. 2 (2005), 44.

30. Nishime, "The Mulatto Cyborg," 44.

31. Haraway, *A Cyborg Manifesto*, 118.

32. Ibid., 119.

33. Ibid.

34. Gallardo and Smith, *Alien Woman*, 130.

35. Creed, *The Monstrous-Feminine*, 118.

36. Ibid., 29.

37. Jackie Stacey, "She Is Not Herself: The Deviant Relations of *Alien Resurrection*," *Screen* 4, no. 3 (2003), 262.

38. Linda Williams, "When the Woman Looks," in *Re-Vision: Essays in Feminist Film Criticism*, ed. Mary Ann Doane, Patricia Mellencamp, and Linda Williams (Frederick, MD: University Publications of America, 1984), 65.

39. Sarkeesian, "Ms. Male Character—Tropes vs Women."

40. idSoftware, *Wolfenstein 3D* [DOS], Digital game directed by Tom Hall, published by Apogee Software (1992).

41. Michel Foucault, *The Birth of the Clinic* (London: Routledge, 2003).

42. Ibid., 108.

43. Ibid., 45.

44. Mary Ann Doane "Technophilia: Technology, Representation, and the Feminine," in *Liquid Metal: The Science Fiction Film Reader*, ed. Sean Redmond (London: Wallflower Press, 2004), 186.

45. Creed, *The Monstrous-Feminine*, 14.

46. idSoftware, *Doom* [MS-DOS]. Self-published digital game (1993).

47. idSoftware, *Quake,* digital game directed by John Romero, published by GT Interactive (1996).

48. Elkington, "Too Many Cooks," 231–232.

49. Ibid., 232.

50. Sarkeesian, "Ms. Male Character—Tropes vs Women."

51. Ibid.

52. The DLC expansions, *Crew Expendable* and *Last Survivor,* were made available at for download the same time as *Alien: Isolation* (2014).

53. YOGSCAST Kim, "Sigourney Weaver and Alien Isolation," YouTube, July 24, 2014, https://www.youtube.com/watch?v=azzZzetXUWo (accessed November 10, 2020).

54. Dan Hindes, "How Alien Isolation Is Going All In On Authentic Sci-Fi Horror," YouTube, August 13, 2014, video, 3:58, https://www.youtube.com/watch?v=LmQe h6bGpdo&ab_channel=GameSpot (accessed November 10, 2020).

55. Hindes, "How Alien Isolation Is Going All In On Authentic Sci-Fi Horror."

56. Ibid.

57. Gallardo and Smith, *Alien Woman,* 9.

58. Consalvo, "Confronting Toxic Gamer Culture," 3.

59. This paper is based on work originally submitted in 2014 in fulfillment of an honors thesis with the Digital Cultures department of the University of Sydney, Australia.

60. This list does not include the VR experience *Alien: Convenant in Utero* (2017) nor games that were playable at temporary exhibitions.

13

Hissing in the Air Vents

Decoding the Narrative-Verse of *Alien: Isolation* (2014)

Reuben Martens

Alien: Isolation[1] is a videogame released in 2014 for PlayStation 3, PlayStation 4, Xbox 360, Xbox One, and Windows (and macOS, Linux, and Nintendo Switch at later stages). It was licensed by 20th Century Fox, published by SEGA, and developed by Creative Assembly. The game received overall positive accolades, being praised for its visual aesthetic and feeling that closely adheres to that of the original *Alien* (1979) film and the artificial intelligence of the Alien. Counting as an official sequel to *Alien*, *A:I*'s story takes place in 2137, between the events of *Alien* and *Aliens* (1986) and revolves around Amanda Ripley (based on the likeness of Kezia Burrows, voiced by Andrea Deck), daughter of Ellen Ripley. Fifteen years after her mother disappeared with the Nostromo, Amanda is informed by the Weyland-Yutani Corporation that the Nostromo's flight recorder has been recovered and brought back to the Sevastopol space station. Amanda is invited to travel with three others—Samuels, Taylor, and Verlaine—to Sevastopol to retrieve the flight recorder and its vital contents that should explain why the Nostromo was lost fifteen years earlier. Once onboard, Amanda is met with a mostly abandoned, derelict space station, hosting only a few human survivors who appear very hostile and extremely scared, and some remaining Working Joes (synthetics like Ash from *Alien*). Amanda soon discovers that a Xenomorph "Drone"—a lifeform that she has never encountered before—has infested the space station and is hunting down the remaining survivors. Those aware of the original storyline from *Aliens* can quickly deduce it probably got on board when the Nostromo was salvaged.

At first, Amanda can separate and jettison the Alien in a remote section of the station. However, after said action, the ship's Working Joes suddenly turn hostile and attack the remaining human survivors. As it turns out,

Reuben Martens, *Hissing in the Air Vents* In: *Alien Legacies*. Edited by: Nathan Abrams and Gregory Frame, Oxford University Press. © Oxford University Press 2023. DOI: 10.1093/oso/9780197556023.003.0013

Sevastopol, previously owned by Seegson, was quickly decommissioned following the Alien infestation, and subsequently bought up by the Weyland-
Yutani Corporation just a week before Ripley's arrival. They then instructed
the onboard artificial intelligence APOLLO to protect the Alien, by all
means, necessary through Special Order 939 (similar to Ash's order 937
on the Nostromo). When Ripley questions APOLLO on this order, stating
that the Xenomorph has been thrown off the ship and so the order should
be invalid, the AI directs her towards the ship's core, where Ripley discovers
a Xenomorph nest, teeming with eggs, notorious Facehuggers, and grown-
up Alien creatures. Amanda proceeds to destroy the nest, but some can flee.
After finally obtaining the Nostromo flight recorder, Ripley realizes the only
way to escape and kill the creatures is to destroy the whole space station, so
she ventures to do just that—were it not that a Xenomorph slipped on board
her escape vessel (again, much like in *Alien*). In the final act, Ripley throws
herself and the Alien out of an airlock, and drifts off before being woken by a
searchlight, which is where the story "ends."

This chapter will explore how the *Alien: Isolation* game fits within the larger
narrative universe of *Alien*, and how the transmedial narratives that relate
to *Alien: Isolation* help bring a renewed understanding of the game's story
and our knowledge of the series while complicating and disrupting conventional notions of adaptation (and remake) within the context of transmedial
franchises. However, although one does not need to play *Alien: Isolation* or
read its associated paratexts to enjoy or understand the films, I will argue
that doing so does enhance and deepen the pleasures offered by popular
cultural texts and the experience of the *Alien* franchise in particular. This
chapter will also explore whether players who have never interacted with
the *Alien* franchise before playing *Alien: Isolation* would be able to achieve a
successful horror gaming experience—which in this context means that the
reader-player's knowledge and understanding of the *Alien* series are essential in getting the enjoyment out of the game that was intended—arguing for
the importance and recognition of transmedia storytelling as a key factor for
such success.

Alien: Isolation Isolated between Intertextuality and Transmedial Storytelling

As Alex Hort-Francis has suggested, *A:I* is "an example of the intentional
remediation of *Alien* through a new medium and an official transmedia

co-created addition to the existing *Alien* franchise. *A:I* is also a clear example of 'convergence culture': the collision of old and new media."[2]—an instance that already starts to blur the lines of the concept of "adaptation." *A:I* has been created through a multitude of narrative practices that come together, which undoubtedly makes it a deeply narrative-focused survival horror game that relies on its transmedial context to tell a story that is consistent with its over-arching franchise, in themes, aesthetics, and narrative. The game has seen quite a large transmedial extension of its narrative, in the form of comic books, a novelization, and a web series—an *Isolation* "narrative-verse" within the franchise, to borrow a phrase from Herlander Elias and Flávio Almeida.[3] Said narrative-verse consists of the original *Alien* film; the *A:I* game; its official eponymous novelization (2019);[4] a 20th Century Fox-licensed 7-part web series (2019);[5] the novel *Alien: Prototype* (2019);[6] the mobile game *Alien: Blackout* (2019), and four comic books: *Alien: Isolation* (2014),[7] *Aliens: Defiance* (2017),[8] *Aliens: Resistance* (2019),[9] and *Aliens: Rescue* (2020).[10] The complexity of this narrative-verse is not to be underestimated and spans several separate, yet interrelated, storylines (with inconsistencies here and there), which rely on a larger understanding and knowledge of the franchise as a whole—although these media can all be enjoyed as separate entities, the reader would struggle to keep up with the transmedial storylines without at least basic knowledge of the first *Alien* film and the experience of the video game.

Carlos Alberto Scolari has noted that such diversification of media objects complicates the idea of a single central "story" within transmedial franchises:

> the story that the comics tell is not the same as that is told on television or in cinema; the different media and languages participate and contribute to the construction of the transmedia narrative world. This textual dispersion is one of the most important sources of complexity in contemporary popular culture.[11]

The piecing together of all these different strands into one "coherent" *Alien: Isolation* alpha-narrative should thus perhaps be framed in what Luc Herman and Bart Vervaeck have called "cybernarratology":[12] the reader-player[13] becomes an active, central figure in the meaning-making process of all hypertexts and their palimpsests, in an attempt to gain a deeper understanding of what Herlander Elias and Flávio Almeida call the "narrative-verse." A franchise, which is essentially a narrative-verse or a collection of multiple ones, performs as spaces of flow, where narratives interconnect by referring to a single semiotic ground and displaying bridges to many mediums in which the narrative-verse is connected to. As the background is the same semiotic universe, but the bridges outnumber the universe in inputs and outputs we witness many perspectives and a sort of multiplicity in space, as each and every person interacts with the narrative-verse differently by relying on the media that previously has chosen what we have to consume and understand.[14]

In this particular case, this single semiotic ground for the *Alien* franchise to which everything else relates is the original *Alien* film, or perhaps more accurately the Xenomorph from that film. It is the core meaning-making unit for the narrative-verse, to which all other events, characters, and settings relate. Elias and Almeida also point to the more insidious nature of the franchise narrative-verse, which continues to expand and feed the reader-player new books, comics, games, and TV shows, creating more and more bridges that further complicate the complete mastery of the narrative-verse, yet serves curiosity and is instrumental in trying to create a meaningful interpretation of the franchise for the reader-player[15]—the one who is most curious and thus consumes more of the franchise media products, is the one with the potentially most nuanced understanding of the narrative-verse. Or; the more *Alien* media one consumes, the more enjoyable one's experience of the franchise becomes. In a certain way, it reveals a somewhat exclusionary narrative system, where only those with the most accumulated knowledge have the best chance of grasping the complexities of the franchise.[16]

Let us illustrate this with the *Alien: Isolation* narrative-verse: take the comic book series *Aliens: Defiance* (2017), for example. Set between the events of *Alien* and *Aliens*, its storyline revolves around Colonial Marine Private Zula Hendricks who gets attacked by Xenomorphs while she is salvaging a derelict Seegson mass hauler, The Europa. She is rescued by a "Davis 01" synthetic (a Weyland-Yutani corporate security drone), who has defied his basic programming and is on a mission to destroy all the locations where W-Y suspects Xenomorph lifeforms. Zula initially resists, but then quickly joins his efforts to do so. Technically its storyline does not directly tie in with the events of the game as such, but it does rely on intertextual elements from the game: it features the only other visual appearance of the game's Seegson Security Access Tuner in any other *Alien* media, and mentions and depicts Amanda Ripley and events on Luna (which the game tells us nothing about), but which are in part described in the *A:I* novelization. While perhaps insignificant on the surface, these are semiotic traces and clues for readers that this comic series is somehow related to *A:I*, opening up new possibilities of meaning-making that were not present if one only considers the game's narrative. Reading *Aliens: Defiance* thus allows the reader-player to better understand the events of the comic book series *Aliens: Resistance* (a direct sequel to the *Defiance* series) and *Aliens: Rescue*, and the *Alien: Prototype* novel, which all feature Zula Hendricks and Davis. While this comic book series can thus be read as a standalone narrative, the reader's appreciation and enjoyment of the story may deepen if they are aware that the comic bridges events between the first and second *Alien* films, and so expand one's understanding of the franchise's larger transmedial storytelling.

However, *A:I*'s narrative in itself does not teach us much about the *Alien* franchise. The reader-player is introduced to Amanda Ripley, whom we learn is the daughter of Ellen, still searching for her mother fifteen years on from when the USCSS Nostromo went missing. Interestingly, the reader-player—assuming they are somehow invested in the franchise and have seen *Alien*—knows more than the player-character Amanda, as in they know what happened to the Nostromo. From playing the game, one learns mainly what has happened on the Sevastopol Station, and how a Xenomorph got on board. The game features an extensive analeptic scene roughly halfway through, where the player-character changes from Amanda to Henry Marlow, captain of the USCSS Anesidora. He recounts a story of how he and his crew landed on LV-426—the planet where Ellen Ripley landed and found the Derelict, which is revealed to be located within the same sector in space as the Sevastopol Station, Zeta Riticula—to inspect a distress signal, where they were attacked by a Facehugger. They then flew to Sevastopol for help but did not obey quarantine rules, and therefore the Alien was set loose on the station.

A:I closely adheres to the narrative premise of the first *Alien* film and mimics it closely in terms of thematics, storyline, and aesthetics. This makes it something of a special case in terms of adaptation, as "it is not only a sequel or an adaptation, but an amalgamation of both," while it "is also a 'type of remake' of the original."[17] In a way, we could compare it to *Star Wars: The Force Awakens* (dir. J. J. Abrams, 2015), a chronological sequel to *Star Wars* (dir. George Lucas, 1977), but also almost identical in terms of narrative setup and thematics. Film adaptation scholar Thomas Leitch devised his own terminology to speak about different forms of adaptation which avoids the original versus imitation bias of many approaches to (film) adaptations. Leitch names four forms of adaptation that he believes to occur frequently: the "celebration," an adaptation which aims to replicate as many elements of the source text as possible; the "adjustment," the most common form which modifies the source text whilst aiming to preserve the original enunciation; the "superimposition," where a work is adapted into another genre or for another purpose; and the "revision," which still hypertextually relates to the original source, but reimagines and deviates from it in significant ways.[18] In Leitch's terms, A:I could very much be regarded in terms of a celebration and adjustment adaptation of Alien. But in this context of adaptation, the novelization also requires consideration as it is mostly a celebration adaptation (and significant narrative expansion) of the game—this has implications not only for the game's narrative in itself but also for the effects it has on reader-players and the construction of the Isolation narrative-verse.

A:I is in large part a celebration adaptation of Alien, in the sense that it has a very close adherence to the source text: the chronotope is set in a singular, isolated spacecraft with a strong female protagonist who is trapped with a Xenomorph, a timespan of not much more than a day, but with an implied second temporality that is much longer and includes the lifecycle of the Xenomorph, an absence of proper materials to fight the creature that eventually needs to be confronted but will prove impossible to kill. Furthermore, as Brendan Keogh and Darshana Jayemanne have discussed, A:I closely mirrors the affective, aesthetic and socio-political dimensions of the original film, and reproduces more of the techno-pessimist, feminist and arguably even anti-capitalist themes from Ridley Scott's original, rather than the heavy military focus of James Cameron's Aliens.[19] Yet, A:I could also be seen as an adjustment adaptation, where the original sense and feel of Alien is very much kept in place,[20] but the source text is modified enough so that one can recognize the original in the adaptation, without it feeling exactly the same (not as in a remake).[21] While there is indeed significant overlap, the narrative of A:I is different enough—except for the analeptic narrative (playable) sequence, which is an almost identical shot-for-shot remake of the opening sequence of Alien—to consider it a successful adaptation, rather than a remake.

However, the transmediality of the Isolation narrative-verse further complicates the notion of A:I as an adaptation of Alien, especially concerning its novelization—the adaptation of a game into a novel is, by all accounts, a rather uncommon process. Stobbart describes how such processes of adapting games into other media forms changes the ways we engage with adaptations and intertextual narratives.[22] In the case of *A:I*, the concept of adaptation becomes complicated as the novel offers a completely new perspective on the game, by choosing to represent not only the events of the game itself but adding internal focalization to the character of Amanda Ripley, which then allows for exploration of her inner thoughts and emotions, rather than the "objective" view of her actions from the game (or *Alien*, where such internal perspective is also largely absent). Both film and game as media are capable of doing this, but it is the novelization that combines literary and filmic narrative structures to enrich the game's story. The novelization goes even further, as it offers the reader substantial exposition about Amanda's childhood—and thus also information about Ellen Ripley's life that is not available elsewhere[23]—about her time on Luna, and how she met Private Zula Hendricks. This, in turn, can enhance the gaming experience after reading the book, giving the reader-player a much keener sense of what Amanda is thinking and feeling throughout the gameplay, and exposing how certain actions and events relate to Amanda's life and the larger *Isolation* narrative-verse. In doing so, the novelization bridges hyper/intertextual semiotic connections between the game, *Alien*, the related comic book series, and also the web series, which opens with a word-for-word adaptation of the novel's ending.

Fear the Xenomorph: Manifesting Horror Gameplay Affects in Transmedial Narratives

Yet, while more or less fully adapting the game's storyline (intercut with flashbacks from Amanda's life), the novelization differs in some significant ways from *A:I*'s events, which I will not go into detail describing here. This makes the classification of the novelization in terms of adaptation even harder than that of *A:I*, as it sort of hovers between a celebration, adjustment, and revision, showing how transmedial narratives complicate the notion of adaptations. More often than not, it is difficult to retrace source material: "the intertextual in which every text is held, itself being the text-between of another text, is not to be confused with some origin of the text: to try to find the 'sources,' the 'influences' of a work, is to fall in with the myth of filiation,"[24] and the further we get away from *Alien*, the more complicated that retracing becomes.

We also need to account for the fact that the game (and its novelization) is not just an adaptation, but also a narrative sequel to the events of *Alien* (with elements that can be considered part remake)—after all, the reader-player needs to recognize that the game's story is part of the *Alien* franchise. "Fidelity to the world of the film franchise," Stobbart writes in her comprehensive study on horror in video games, "provide[s] players with an experience that is both nostalgic and uncanny."[25] Robin Sloan argues that the game specifically invests in fan nostalgia "for the memory of watching the film: of witnessing the Xenomorph for the first time, of watching and re-watching the film on VHS, and of consuming sequels and related media and merchandise."[26] Such affects, generated through the proximity to the source material, can already be seen in the game's opening sequences which establish that the protagonist is Amanda Ripley, daughter of Ellen Ripley, who will search for the Nostromo's flight recorder, aboard Sevastopol space station.

The first playable scene puts Amanda on a spaceship, the Torrens (an almost exact recreation of the Nostromo), and from thereon other characters in the game only refer to her as Ripley, blurring the sense that one is playing as Amanda, and not Ellen. Once aboard Sevastopol, which is significantly larger than the Nostromo used to be, the same 1970s sci-fi aesthetic of *Alien* is consistently used, complete with gadgetry from the original film, extending the sense of nostalgia and the uncanny; such design is important, as it can function as part of environmental storytelling—the design aesthetics of the Sevastopol game environment, for example, are eerily reminiscent of those of the Nostromo, suggesting nostalgia for the look and feel of *Alien*, while the Xenomorph is the visualization and embodiment of uncanniness, which comes to be part of the environment and thus its storytelling capacities. Both those elements are important factors for the game experience and indicate a narrative bridge between the game and the original film, illustrating how having a sense of the larger franchise's transmedial narrative can enrich the experience of its other media. Equally, Stobbart notes that because *A:I* so heavily relies on *Alien* for its narrative premise, "it is the horror, rather than the science fiction that is brought to the fore of both the film and the game."[27]

Survival horror then, Ewan Kirkland argues, is a genre label that implies elements of narrative and story, and bears, perhaps more than any other genre of games, a huge debt to a large tradition of other narratives (the nostalgia and the uncanny) to function as a scary game.[28] Learning the rules of the game, which will lead to survival, is mainly based on picking up environmental and narrative clues from within the game world. In *A:I* this is mainly achieved by "reading" a variety of such cues: the motion scanner, security hacking tool, computer terminals (with many archive logs and vital information such as passwords), audiotapes, rewiring boxes, identity cards, waymarkers, graffiti, and so on, most of which contain crucial information to survive the game, but also all function as semiotic clues in the larger whole of the *Isolation* narrative-verse. According to Kirkland, "the most productive gameplay strategy involves correctly reading these grammatical and visual cues, completing the actions being foreshadowed, and producing an audio-visual experience which ideally approximates that of narrative cinema."[29]

A:I very much intends for such an experience, and to do so, has to exhibit a significant narrative capacity—which challenges some long-held ludological notions about the relations between game and narrative (and adaptation). Caracciolo notes that "it is doubtful that something can be experienced as a story without an explicit or implicit understanding that it has been constructed or pre-structured *in order to* tell a story."[30] Interaction with narrative is driven by three 'master interests': suspense, curiosity, and surprise. These interests have experiential effects and are key to an affective response to the text—and arguably, all key elements of the horror (game) genre and effective methods of invoking fear. These master interests guide the game's narrative dimensions through a complex network of inter-/transtextual relations, as discussed above, and allows for *A:I* to support and extend the survival (horror) game experience within the larger franchise.

Because of *A:I*'s overt transmedial nature, it is not too difficult for the reader-player to read the game's environmental clues as informing the narrative master interests: for example, seeing a dead body with a hole in its chest immediately forms semiotic bridges to the infamous chestburster scene from *Alien*, enhancing the affects of suspense, curiosity, and possibly a very unwelcome surprise to a higher level. Dark, small industrial-looking hallways and air vents then can be read as dangerous lurking places for the Xenomorph, whilst rattling chains and dripping acid from high ceilings spell out death to the reader-player, whilst also serving transmedial clues once again to *Alien*. Such "narrative architectures," to use Kirkland's term, "are central to the genre's management of the interactive experience to fit a determined narrative pattern."[31] After all, the *Alien* franchise is a narrative, not a ludological franchise.

This does, however, raise questions as to whether *A:I* would be an enjoyable survival horror experience for those that are unfamiliar with the franchise, given that the entirety of the game, from its narrative premise to its design, is fully informed by said franchise, with the specific purpose of unlocking and serving a certain sense of nostalgia for fans of *Alien*. Sloan argues that "indeed, *Alien: Isolation* would arguably lose much of its appeal if it were a survival horror game set within an entirely unfamiliar world" and notes how nostalgia and the uncanny are fundamental elements of the player experience.[32] A "successful" experience of this game, therefore, is heavily intertwined with one's knowledge of the transmedial narrative-verse of *Alien*—equally, the game is perhaps also only successful as an adaptation when one recognizes the extent of transmedial narrative bridging. Horror scholar Adam Daniel describes in his book on affective intensities and horror forms how he responded viscerally to playing *A:I*, and links this experience to the game mechanics: "I noticed my real-world breathlessness and racing heart, an experience that was to me more akin to the experience of shock while viewing a film than any previous gaming experience."[33]

While I would agree that game and narrative mechanics—such as the intelligent AI of the Xenomorph that stalks the player throughout the game, and the architectural design which offers only very precarious and scarce hiding places—influence the intense horror experience described by Daniel, what he does not take into account is his own familiarity with the horror of the stalking Xenomorph. In other words, though Daniel is correct that "any savvy, game-literate player would comprehend that an interaction with the alien is inevitable,"[34] the question remains: would someone unfamiliar with the *Alien* franchise (and the fact that *A:I* is a complex adaptation of the original film), blissfully unaware of how utterly indestructible the Alien is, have the same sensorial experience of encountering the creature as someone who understands the extent of the Alien's scariness? The question then becomes whether *A:I* can be a successful survival horror game regardless of its transmedial narrative contexts, and whether the gaming experience and the affect it creates in and of itself, namely a sense of horror and terror, can function on its own terms.

Stobbart characterizes terror as the psychological feeling of dread and fear, whereas horror is the realization of said fear, the actual representation of fear.[35] In *A:I*, for example, I would argue that the horror-terror experience has much to do with narrative agency, with *A:I* being somewhat a special case where the game is experienced through a first-person perspective (despite not being a shooter), whereas most other survival horror games are experienced through a third-person perspective. The narrative distance between player and player-character is minimized through the use of the first-person perspective, which amplifies the identification between the player and the player-character, and also the experientiality of the game space. This is where the game offers quite a significantly different mediation of the visceral fear that the Xenomorph evokes in the film; the narrative distance between viewer and the film's Alien is much larger than the one between the game's Alien and the reader-player. It effectively makes the fear of the Alien one of embodiment in the reader-player—the first-person perspective puts the player in Ripley's shoes, where being attacked by the Xenomorph means dying a (virtual) death, raising the stakes much higher than the film ever could—once again, complicating simplistic notions of the adaptation form, especially across different media.

Yet, other *Alien* games, like *Aliens: Colonial Marines* (2013), which is a first-person shooter featuring hordes of aliens, are arguably nowhere near as scary as *A:I* despite having similar first-person narrative frameworks, and can be enjoyed without any or much knowledge about the franchise. Is the missing element then, a familiarity with the mechanics of horror games, be it game or narrative, and is that a prerequisite for having a successful horror gaming experience? Many game reviewers noted that *A:I* is an excellent stealth survival horror game, often remarking on the importance of game mechanics such as the Alien AI, sound design, lighting, environmental design, and so on. However, it would seem that all the critics are aware of the larger transmedial *Alien* franchise, as many refer to *A:I*'s superiority over other franchise games, with claims such as "this is the game the *Alien* series has always deserved."[36]

I would argue that the transmedial narrative context, and at least a basic understanding of the Xenomorph and the larger *Alien* franchise, is instrumental for a successful horror gaming experience when playing *A:I*. An illustration: watching an *A:I* playthrough by popular YouTuber PewDiePie, one may observe that he has very little knowledge about the *Alien* franchise. He confuses Amanda Ripley with Ellen Ripley, for example, which translates in his approach to the game and his playing style: he attempts to shoot the Xenomorph when attacked by it (which any *Alien* fan would know to be useless), carelessly runs around the station, instead of sneaking, and does not seem to grasp the usefulness of hiding in the lockers to prevent being seen by the creature. As a result, while *acting* scared when encountering the Alien, he does not seem truly terrified (or even enjoying) playing the game. Arguably, this has nothing to do then with the game mechanics, which are similar to other survival horror games, but with his lack of understanding of the semiotic codes that are embedded in the game (and the series), barring him from experiencing the full horror and terror affects. As such, the horror experience must be located within not just the genre's conventions and mechanics of survival horror, as the presence of the Xenomorph is not the prerequisite, but within the specific nostalgia and uncanniness that is created through and within the larger transmedial narrative-verse that surrounds the game, affirming the centrality of narrative and understanding the *Alien* franchise in playing *A:I* (which then further extends the reader-player's comprehension of this narrative-verse).

Given this insight, I want to propose that *gaming is an act of (inter-)active reading*—at the very least, in a transmedial franchise-setting that is. From interpreting signs to reading in-game prompts, picking up books, listening to audiotapes, to "reading" an environment, inferring intertextual relations bridging different transmedial narratives, gameplay is an interactive mode of (transmedial and inter-/hypertextual) reading: while arguably the player-character's actions in the game are simulations, they are also very much active narrative descriptions. Roland Barthes once noted that "the text is experienced only in an activity of production";[37] well, let the reader-player's (inter-)activity be an act of production, one that allows for an experience of an inherently transmedial text that would otherwise be impossible. In that regard, perhaps we also need a new or renewed understanding of the plurality of the reader-player; I propose to classify the reading position of the reader-player into Barthes' distinction of two kinds of readers:[38] not as that of the "consumer" (a passive reader, who reads for stable meaning), but that of the active "reader," a productive writer of text and meaning, where reading becomes performance (quite literally through the interactive dimensions of the videogame medium and the transmedial interactions this evokes).

While transmediality is thus obviously not limited to the literary sphere, narrative seems to be the foundation upon which the experience and understanding of a franchise are built. This is not a challenge of the intricacies of the "cybertext" (videogames in this particular instance) or its medium-specific mechanisms for conveying meaning, affect, and experientiality, but note that the operative word is *text*. Lastly, in continuing with borrowing from Barthes, it would appear that notions of "authorial intent" hardly matter in the active meaning-making of the transmedial text; whatever interpretation the reader-player distils from playing *A:I* is valid, regardless of whether it is in line with whatever its creators envisioned. The point is that the *active reading* practice of the reader-player "writes" the meaning of the text, not the game itself or its scriptwriters. Meaning is generated in the delicate interactions of intertextuality, transmediality, genre conventions, various narrative mechanisms, and the medium-specific design of the videogame.

Conclusion: Read-Playing the Alien Across Transmedial Borders

In 1982, long before the onset of videogame studies, celebrated British novelist Martin Amis wrote a non-fiction book about arcade games—perhaps as one of the first to do so, with an introduction by none other than Steven Spielberg—in which he critically examined the dynamics of the arcade games to which he became addicted. He wrote: "the things that impel you [about games] is the straightforward desire to know *what happens next*. Yes, oh dear me yes, the video game tells a story. [...] The better you get, the longer the story lasts,"[39] before going into the details of what he considers the story of *Space Invaders*. Amis was perhaps one of the first to recognize the narrative potential of games, how they can extend beyond their life on the screen, and impact the life of the reader-player. Ludologists used to stake some wild claims about the videogame medium and its narrative potential (the infamous "ludology vs. narratology" debate), perhaps best illustrated by Grant Tavinor when, in his chapter on 'Fiction' in *The Routledge Companion to Video Games Studies*, he sketches out some still widely held assumptions about narrative, fiction and games:

> [I]t is plausible that video games contain elements of fiction. [...] accounts of video games as fictions have often been associated with so-called 'narratology' [...]. within games studies, there has also been some resistance to the idea that video games are fictions, or at least doubts that these fictional elements, even if they exist, are all that important to the game. [...] Other writers, though agreeing that games do involve fictions, have been tempted to downplay the centrality of this fictional aspect, seeing fiction as of secondary importance relative to game mechanics and gameplay.[40]

While Tavinor himself debunks these claims, it illustrates that many ludologists continue to assume the incompatibility of games and narratives.

This chapter has shown that such opposition is pointless, especially in the age of transmedial franchises; moreover, I have argued that without the reader-players intertextual understanding of the *Alien* franchise, playing and understanding the events of *Alien: Isolation* may result in a failed survival horror gameplay experience. Furthermore, the game's story is instrumental in the creation and understanding of semiotic bridges within the *Alien* narrative-verse. Readers of the comic book series mentioned in this chapter, who have not played the game, will have a reduced understanding of those storylines, and will probably find themselves engaging with the game (or its novelization or web series) if they want to gain a better insight into those other media products and the overarching storyline that makes up the *Isolation*-verse.

In line with a longstanding critical tradition, most famous through Roland Barthes' idea of the "death of the author,"[41] a game (like a novel or a film) cannot produce meaning by and of itself: it needs a "reader," a player, to do so. However, without the presence of a narrative to be interpreted and made sense of, meaning cannot exist. Elias and Almeida put it best when they write that

> when we deal with the narrative-verses, we behave like players, we accumulate points, we move from one level of understanding to another, we go from amateurs to professionals. We become *connoisseurs*. We are surrounded by new movies, games, apps and books, episodes of fiction that connect to something bigger. Our role here is to become "connectors" of something greater.[42]

This chapter has engaged in a discussion of trying to accurately position *Alien: Isolation* within the larger *Alien* franchise. It seems that it is neither a remake, an adaptation, nor a true sequel and that it challenges those definitions in a transmedial context. As such, it reveals a certain degree of inadequacy of the existing terminology used to describe transmedia objects: what do we do with a game like *A:I*, that is so clearly inspired by (the origins of) the franchise in which it functions and should be understood, whilst also playing host to a smaller (sub)narrative-verse that then further influences other media objects within said larger franchise? *Alien: Isolation* forms a narrative bridge between *Alien* and *Aliens*, and while on the face of it the game does not perhaps reveal much new information about the franchise in itself, its extended narrative-verse carries an incredible amount of semiotic elements that can foster a larger understanding of the franchise as a whole: the novelization, for instance, offers many details about the early life of Ellen Ripley that is not available anywhere else.

The comic books, then, explain how Zula and Amanda know each other, and how they ended up on a mission together to destroy Xenomorphs near Zeta Reticuli. But the novel also expands the narrative potential of the game upon which it is based, by giving us insight into the thoughts of Amanda as she navigates all the horrors onboard Sevastopol, thoughts which are absent in the game's narration. The game mainly functions to bridge the story of *Alien* and its own, as it repurposes themes, music, environmental designs, storylines, and so on, from the original film so that the reader-player is confronted with a sense of "uncanny" nostalgia.

As noted, it appears that a rather unusually high degree of "reading," in the Barthesian sense of active meaning-making rather than passive consumption, is central to obtaining a satisfactory experience of playing *A:I*; the intensity of reading required may well be a unique factor of transnarrative storytelling, and the more of the meaning-making process the reader-player can accomplish by relying on their larger knowledge of the franchise, the more pleasure may be derived from interacting with the game's storyworld. Specifically here, it is the combination of nostalgia and the uncanny, and an understanding of the specific semiotic codes of the *Alien* franchise narrative verse on part of the reader-player that are responsible for creating a successful horror game experience of *A:I*. The centrality of the reader-player is thus vital, as it is them who, in engaging with the multitude of complex forms of adaptation and transmedial narratives in the *Isolation* narrative-verse, can create renewed meaning and a more nuanced understanding of the *Alien* franchise for themselves.

Notes

1. Creative Assembly, *Alien: Isolation (Nostromo Edition)*, PlayStation 4 ed. (London: SEGA of Europe, 2014). Video game. Hereafter abbreviated to *A:I*.
2. Alex Hort-Francis, "Adaptation, Remediation; Isolation: Identifying Critical Theory at Work within *Alien: Isolation* (2014)" (accessed February 12, 2021), web.archive.org/web/20180823005617/http://hortfrancis.com/adaptation-remediation-isolation/.

3. Herlander Elias and Flávio Almeida, "Narrative-Verse: On Transmedia, Narrative and Digital Media Audiences," *Estudos em Comunicação* 27, no. 2 (2018), 3–16.

4. Keith R.A DeCandido, *Alien: Isolation* (London: Titan Books, 2019).

5. Fabien Dubois, dir. *Alien: Isolation—The Digital Series*, "Episode 1–7." 2019, on IGN. www.ign.com/videos/2019/02/28/alien-isolation-digital-series-episode-1.

6. Tim Waggoner, *Alien: Prototype* (London: Titan Books, 2019).

7. Dan Abnett and Dion Lay, *Alien: Isolation (San Diego Comic-Con Exclusive)* (Milwaukie, OR: Dark Horse Comics, 2014).

8. Brian Wood, *Aliens: Defiance*, vols. 1–2 (Milwaukie, OR: Dark Horse Comics, 2017), comic book.

9. Brian Wood, *Aliens: Resistance* (Milwaukie, OR: Dark Horse Comics, 2019).

10. Brian Wood, *Aliens: Rescue* (Milwaukie, OR: Dark Horse Comics, 2020).

11. Carlos Alberto Scolari, "Transmedia Storytelling: Implicit Consumers, Narrative Worlds, and Branding in Contemporary Media Production," *International Journal of Communication* 3 (2009), 587.

12. Luc Herman and Bart Vervaeck, *Handbook of Narrative Analysis (Second Edition)* (Lincoln: University of Nebraska Press, 2019), 120.

13. I will also adopt the term "reader-player" from Herman and Vervaeck here throughout, as it seems more than apt in this situation, where I take *A:I* as the core narrative from which one pieces together the rest of the *Isolation* narrative-verse (the amalgam of transmedial narratives that directly relate to the events of the game).

14. Elias and Almeida, "Narrative Verse," 4.

15. Ibid.

16. This has to a large extent also to do with the commercial aspect of the transmedial Alien franchise, which is now owned by Disney (as part of their Fox takeover), where content keeps being generated in order to keep the franchise profitable. For instance, *Alien* comic books have always been printed by Dark Horse Comics, but earlier in 2021, Marvel, as a part of the Disney conglomerate, also started publishing an *Alien* comics series, which now opens another, new revenue stream but also a new line of *Alien* transmedial narrative content.

17. Dawn Stobbart, *Videogames and Horror: From Amnesia to Zombies, Run!* (Cardiff: University of Wales Press, 2019), 77–78.

18. Thomas Leitch, *Film Adaptation and Its Discontents: From Gone with the Wind to The Passion of the Christ* (Baltimore: The Johns Hopkins University Press, 2007), 93–126.

19. Brendan Keogh and Darshana Jayemanne, "'Game Over, Man. Game Over': Looking at the Alien in Film and Videogames," *Arts* 7, no. 43 (2018), 1. Most of the previously developed video games and comics have relied heavily on the style and tone of Cameron's *Aliens*. It is intriguing that *A:I*, as an almost solitary exception, returned to Scott's *Alien* as its frame of reference, especially as Scott has begun to reassert authorial control over the (film) franchise with *Prometheus* and *Covenant*. The new upcoming *Aliens: Fireteam* game, scheduled for Summer 2021, will again revert to Cameron's style for its gameplay and narrative conceits.

20. Andy Kelly has reported that Creative Assembly, the game developer, was supplied by 20th Century Fox (the first film's production company) with three terabytes of original production material, including "design blueprints, continuity polaroids, costume photography, concept art, and thousands of photos of the sets," which was used extensively to give the game the same feel as the film, to ensure continuity. See Andy Kelly, "The Making of *Alien: Isolation*," *PC Gamer* (accessed February 13, 2021), www.pcgamer.com/the-making-of-alien-isolation/.

21. Eduard Cuelenaere makes a similar point about remakes, noting that the original versus remake bias is too simplified a construct, and has suggested a new model of systemic (textual) analysis of remakes in order to circumvent such (and many other) issues and to discuss remakes in all their complexity. See his "The Film Remake as Prism: Towards a Model of Systemic Textual Analysis," in *European Film Remakes*, ed. Eduard Cuelenaere, Gertjan Willems, and Stijn Joye (Edinburgh: Edinburgh University Press, 2021), 19–32.

22. Dawn Stobbart, "Adaptation and New Media: Establishing the Video Game as an Adaptive Medium," in *The Routledge Companion to Adaptation*, eds. Dennis Cutchins, Katja Krebs, and Eckart Voigts (London and New York: Routledge, 2018), 382–389.

23. Xenopedia, the "official" wiki for all things *Alien* (and *Predator*), states "much of the backstory for Ellen Ripley revealed in the novel in fact ties up with the original behind the scenes notes for the character written by Ridley Scott during the production of *Alien*." No source is provided for this information, https://avp.fandom.com/wiki/Alien:_Isolation_(novel).

24. Roland Barthes, *Image—Music—Text* (New York: The Noonday Press, 1977), 160.

25. Stobbart, *Videogames*, 78.

26. Robin Sloan, "Homesick for the Unheimlich: Back to the Uncanny Future in Alien: Isolation," *Journal of Gaming & Virtual Worlds* 8, no. 3 (2016), 217.

27. Stobbart, *Videogames*, 78.

28. Ewan Kirkland, "Storytelling in Survival Horror Video Games," in *Horror Video Games: Essays on the Fusion of Fear and Play*, ed. Bernard Perron (Jefferson, NC: McFarland, 2009), 62–78.

29. Ibid., 69.

30. Marco Caracciolo, "Playing *Home*: Videogame Experiences between Narrative and Ludic Interests," *Narrative* 23, no. 3 (2015), 234.

31. Kirkland, "Storytelling," 68.

32. Sloan, "Homesick," 217.

33. Adam Daniel, *Affective Intensities and Evolving Horror Forms* (Edinburgh: Edinburgh University Press, 2020), 167.

34. Ibid., 165.

35. Stobbart, *Videogames*, 3.

36. Kelly, "The Making of *Alien: Isolation*."

37. Barthes, *Image—Music—Text*, 157.

38. Roland Barthes, *The Pleasure of the Text*. [Le plaisir du texte] (New York: Farrar, Straus and Giroux, 1975).

39. Martin Amis, *Invasion of the Spave Invaders: An Addict's Guide to Battle Tactics, Big Scores and the Best Machines* (London: Jonathan Cape, 2018), 19.

40. Grant Tavinor, "Fiction," in *The Routledge Companion to Video Game Studies*, ed. Mark J. P. Wolf and Bernard Perron (New York and London: Routledge, 2014), 434.

41. Roland Barthes, "Death of the Author," *Aspen*, no. 5 + 6 (1967).

42. Elias and Almeida, "Narrative Verse," 6.

Index